Feminist Praxis against U.S. Militarism

Postcolonial and Decolonial Studies in Religion and Theology

Series Editor: Sheryl Kujawa-Holbrook, Claremont School of Theology

This series responds to the growing interest in postcolonial studies and reexamines the hegemonic, European-dominated religious systems of the old and new empires. It critically addresses the colonial biases of religions, the academy, and local faith communities, in an effort to make these institutions more polyvocal, receptive, and empowering to global cultures and epistemologies. The series will engage with a variety of hybrid, overlapping, and intersecting definitions of postcolonialism—as a critical discursive practice, as a political and ideological stance concerned with exposing patterns of dominance and hegemony, and as contexts shaped by ongoing colonization and decolonization. Books in the series will also explore the relationship between postcolonial values and religious practice, and the transformation of religious symbols and institutions in postcolonial contexts beyond the academy. The series aims to make high-quality and original research available to the scholarly community. The series welcomes monographs and edited volumes which forge new directions in contextual research across disciplines and explore key contemporary issues. Established scholars as well as new authors will be considered for publication, including scholars "on the margins" whose voices are underrepresented in the academy and in religious discourse. Authors working in subdisciplines of religious studies and/or theology are encouraged to submit proposals.

Recent titles in the series:

Colonialism and the Bible: Contemporary Reflections from the Global South, edited by
     Tat-siong Benny Liew and Fernando F. Segovia
Ecologies of Participation: Agents, Shamans, Mystics, and Diviners, by Zayin Cabot
Feminist Praxis against U.S. Militarism, edited by Nami Kim and Wonhee Anne Joh

Feminist Praxis against U.S. Militarism

Edited by Nami Kim
and Wonhee Anne Joh

LEXINGTON BOOKS
Lanham • Boulder • New York • London

Published by Lexington Books
An imprint of The Rowman & Littlefield Publishing Group, Inc.
4501 Forbes Boulevard, Suite 200, Lanham, Maryland 20706
www.rowman.com

6 Tinworth Street, London SE11 5AL

British Library Cataloguing in Publication Information Available

Library of Congress Cataloging-in-Publication Data

Names: Kim, Nami, editor. | Joh, Wonhee Anne, editor.
Title: Feminist praxis against U.S. militarism / edited by Nami Kim and Wonhee Anne Joh.
Description: Lanham : Lexington Books, [2019] | Series: Postcolonial and decolonial studies in
    religion and theology | Includes bibliographical references and index. | Summary: "Feminist
    Praxis against U.S. Militarism provides critical feminist and womanist analyses of U.S. militar-
    ism that challenge the ongoing U.S. neoliberal military-industrial complex and its multivalent
    violence that destroys people's lives, especially women and other vulnerable populations"--
    Provided by publisher.
Identifiers: LCCN 2019045711 (print) | LCCN 2019045712 (ebook) | ISBN 9781498579216 (cloth) |
    ISBN 9781498579223 (epub)
Subjects: LCSH: War and society. | United States--Military policy. | Military-industrial complex--
    United States. | Feminist theory. | Womanism.
Classification: LCC HM554 .F46 2019 (print) | LCC HM554 (ebook) | DDC 303.6/6--dc23
LC record available at https://lccn.loc.gov/2019045711 LC ebook record available at https://
    lccn.loc.gov/2019045712

Contents

Introduction

Feminist Praxis Against U.S. Militarism

Nami Kim and Wonhee Anne Joh

> Our strategy should be not only to confront empire, but to lay siege to
> it. To deprive it of oxygen. To shame it. To mock it. With our art, our
> music, our literature, our stubbornness, our joy, our brilliance, our
> sheer relentlessness—and our ability to tell our own stories. Stories that
> are different from the ones we're being brainwashed to believe.... An-
> other world is not only possible, she is on her way. Maybe many of us
> won't be here to greet her, but on a quiet day, if I listen very carefully, I
> can hear her breathing.[1]

How do we make sense of the past and present wars of the United States,
including the current war on terror "abroad" in relation to the United
States as a warfare, counterterrorist, carceral state where people of color
are constantly subjected to state violence? How do we talk about what is
happening in Ferguson, Chicago, Detroit, Standing Rock, and in occupied
Palestine, Yemen, Syria, and numerous other global sites in relation to the
ever-proliferating reach of U.S. militarism? The analytic of militarized
violence is not the only starting point for this volume. We believe militarism and colonialism have always been entangled with projects of genocide and conquest.[2] The founding principle of the United States is an-
chored to the logic of domination and elimination, or as Nick Estes
writes, settler colonialism's organizing principle is "Indigenous elimination, in all its orientations."[3] Estes notes that the continuation of this logic
has never come to an end and was clearly evidenced as well during the
siege against #NoDAPL camps north of Standing Rock Reservation.[4] This
militarist logic formed many other extensions across diverse populations
in the history of the United States. From settler colonial genocide in the
founding of the United States to the U.S. war against Mexico, from colonial annexation of Puerto Rico to the westward expansionism across the
Pacific, the grounding U.S. militarism's condition of possibility for the
multivalent U.S. global military interventions is founded on the destruction and dispossession of other people, lands, and resources. The United
States constitutes a continuous history of armed interventions all over the
world. A core rhetoric that operationalizes this U.S. military doctrine of

1

preemption is rooted in the notion of imminent probable threat as the very reason for unrelenting growth of militarism. Discussing the relationship between "nuclear terror" during the Cold War and the post-9/11 "counterterror" security state formations, Joseph Masco argues in *The Theater of Operations*, that "evoking existential threat became the core vehicle for building a military-industrial state," and the propagation of Cold War nuclear threat is actually a "model for contemporary counterterror politics."[5] He claims that both the launch of the national security state during the Cold War era and the United States's official declaration of a "new" counterterror state in the aftermath of 9/11 involved "the designation of new insecurities, new institutions to fight them, a public mobilization campaign grounded in fear, and above all, official claims that a new kind of war (a Cold War or a war on terror) was a multigenerational commitment, constituting a new mode of everyday life rather than a brief intensity of conflict."[6]

Similar to the Cold War's transnational political violence, while not experienced on the same terms all over the world, the logic of the war on terror continues to have enduring consequences on a global scale.[7] Just as the Cold War had no clear distinctions on the ground between declared and undeclared wars, so does the war on terror evade clear distinction as to whom this war on terror is waged against.[8] The vague ever-shifting and changing "enemy/other" is intentionally in place. It is not that there is a moving target but instead the open-ended shape of the other/enemy/target allows for facility of movement for the U.S. military. The United States's hyper-militarized global presence, including the ever proliferation of interrogation and detention centers, also known as "black sites," have been deployed within the United States, particularly in the militarization of domestic police forces as well as in efforts to securitize borders. The war on terror gave rise to an already present and burgeoning security state of the Cold War era that continues the work of perpetual war not only outside the United States but also increasingly in the intensification of yet another form of gendered and racialized state violence. The state of emergency has now become the rule that is undergirding the anxiety of future terrors that are considered still to come. The securitization of the state then is unending and the rationale for further militarization is justified, even as any distinction between war and peace continues to collapse. Moreover, the production of anxiety and paranoia intensifies the securitization logic of the state that bleeds into other logics like environmental security, bio-security, and food security to the extent that "capital and the state live off the production of insecurity, they must also ensure that security is never really achieved."[9] A core means of attending to this securitization of the state is to continue circulating people's fears and anxiety of probable and possible unknown and unforeseeable "terror." This provides the means for the military-industrial complex and the security state to expand and deepen forces of militarism.

As Masco argues, "terror" has a particular "American logic and domestic history," and the U.S. war on terror has been "enormously productive in the sense of building a new global war machine, a second defense department (the Department of Homeland Security), new biosecurity and cybersecurity programs."[10] However, its view has not included "crises in the domains of health, finance, and the environment to be a security matter."[11] The recent passing of a $716-billion defense bill by Republican Senators, joined by thirty-eight Democrats, can be just one telling example. The bill increases military spending by over $80 billion and authorizes another $21.6 billion for nuclear weapons programs. It was an 85–10 vote. There should be no doubt the primacy of U.S. investment and commitment to militarism. If the Pentagon's budget simply remained the same as it was in 2017, media analyst Adam Johnson notes that Congress "could have funded public college for every student in the United States and had $12 billion left over."[12]

U.S. militarism is contingent on escalation of conflict and not on de-escalation. In this regard, demilitarization seems impossible. For this reason alone, the belief of uncertain threat always already representing both imagined and real danger to the United States is an epistemological condition necessary to maintain, bolster, and ever-expand military power.[13] Within the U.S. political economy, and regardless of which party holds power in the capitol, U.S. commitment to militarism has never waned but steadily increased at an ever-accelerating and intensifying rate. The commitment to militarism by the security state is always adapting and forging new alliances and developing new technologies ranging from militarized private intelligence and security start-ups to forms of manifest destiny in relation to the new frontier. There is no end to militarism in the near future as full spectrum dominance and hegemony continue to spread wherever probable threat is presumed by the United States. This is further exacerbated by the persistent idea of the United States as the arbiter of international rule of law under the notion of its version of democracy. With the latter, a ruse of justification for U.S. military intervention is often invoked as necessary humanitarian interventions and even outright military involvement. However, the so-called humanitarian intervention proffered by the United States often comes as nothing less than military intervention. One of the most justifiable rationales for any form of U.S. intervention in various global regions is to trot out colonial logic that the other nations are incapable of self-determination and self-governance rooted in the Western style of democracy. This line of civilizational discourse at the heart of coloniality still gets invoked through the language in praise of democracy often in the language of "international human rights" as well.[14] It usually follows too that these places, often non-Western, are considered to not only lack the resources for self-determination and self-governance but also that these peoples and nations violate what the West has deemed as human rights. Mark Neocleous makes a critical link between the rise of "civilization" discourse in the political lexicon in Europe with the simultaneous use of "police." The lexical use of the term "to police" interchangeably with "to civilize" is of importance since "civilization and police were often used synonymously in the same way to designate a certain kind of order."[15] The United States holds itself as the arbiter of justice, enforcers of human rights and freedom, and the world's greatest democracy. As Sylvester Johnson notes, however, such democracy is *"implicated in racial formation and the colonial relation of power"* (emphasis original)."[16] Without going much further here, we still note the problems with this kind of logic in its very own violation of sovereignty of other nations.

Feminist Praxis against U.S. Militarism seeks to provide critical feminist and womanist theo-ethical analyses of U.S. militarism that challenge the ongoing U.S. neoliberal military-industrial complex and its multivalent violence that destroys people's lives. This volume situates the U.S. neoliberal military-industrial complex within the broader context of the U.S. military superpower that exploded since the beginning of the Cold War. While avoiding what Chickasaw scholar Jodi A. Byrd calls the "pervasive idea," that is, "the United States could be construed as imperialistic only at the moment it became interested in militarily violating the borders of other nation-states or acquiring overseas territories at the turn of the twentieth century,"[17] this volume continues to engage in a critique of U.S. militarism. As such, acknowledging the danger of a U.S. exceptionalism that posits U.S. militarist imperialism only in relation to "other" countries, this volume also pays close attention to the Cold War account of the "good war" or the rhetoric of the "war against evil" that continues to justify U.S. military involvement in various parts of the world.[18] As we have argued in *Critical Theology against U.S. Militarism*, there is a direct link between the expansion of the U.S. military-industrial complex and intensification of U.S. militarism around the world with continuation of the logic of the Cold War but under the new banner of the war on terror.[19]

Feminist Praxis against U.S. Militarism highlights the intentional critique of U.S. militarism from feminist and womanist perspectives that seek to show the ways in which gender, race, ethnicity, sexuality, and violence intersect to threaten women's lives, especially women of color's lives, and the broader environment upon which women's lives are dependent. We seek to challenge our readers to understand the United States as the warfare, counterterror, carceral state and its devastating effects on the everyday lives of women, especially women of color, locally, nationally, and globally. Militarized violence and violations function as a full spectrum spectacle of power and might of sovereign nations as well as its lack of. Militarism has become political theatrics deployed with calculation for incalculable outcomes. For example, walls and borders function as spectacles of terror inducing technologies tracking every move to the spectacular use of drones with precision. Militarism is no longer simply the deployment of military personnel.[20] As Stephen Graham notes, "the crossover between the military and the civilian applications of advanced technology—between the surveillance and control of everyday life in Western cities and the prosecution of aggressive colonial resource wars—is at the heart of a much broader set of trends that characterize the new military urbanism."[21]

This volume also seeks to help the reader understand racialized and gendered impacts of U.S. militarism in conjunction with the ongoing global economies of dispossession and militarized violence across the borders of nation-states. Interrogating U.S. military interventions in "other" countries can show how the U.S. war on terror directly affects U.S. "domestic" affairs and daily lives in the United States, and it is well documented in the exchange of information between the United States and Israel. When it comes to militarized violence against Palestinian civilians as well as in persistent dispossession of peoples from their lands through remapping of borders, information on strategies and tactics are shared between security states. Whether the entrenchment of an ever-militarized carceral state in the United States or in the systematic production of the biggest open-air prison that is Gaza, the economy of U.S. militarism is just as dependent on racial capitalism. Militarism and colonialism continue to produce global racial formations that can no longer be severed from economies of militarism and racial capitalism.

If we examine U.S. militarism exclusively as what goes on outside the borders of the United States, we can lose sight of U.S. militarist imperialism built on the genocide of Indigenous people, the enslavement of people of African descent, and the Orientalist exploitation of people of Asian descent inside its borders, as well as dispossession of lands and resources in tandem with militarized securitization along the U.S./Mexico border. The militarization of the U.S. border, according to Timothy Dunn, involves at least four general implications. Firstly, such militarization reinforces the myth of separate economic zones of investment and exploitation and thus the stratification of political and economic power between states. Secondly, this militarization serves to discipline and punish the "illegal" versus "citizen" status of workers who are necessary and needed for economic profiteering by reinforcing the subordinate status of workers as "disposable." Thirdly, it serves as an extension of aggressive U.S. foreign policy toward Central American refugees and immigrants. Fourthly, militarization of U.S./Mexico border functions to secure a potential economic region. What's relevant in terms of the militarization of borders and its connection to the urban context and the paramilitarization of the domestic police force is clearly evident in the Los Angeles Riots of 1992. The mobility of militarized Border Patrol agents and the porosity of the border was clearly demonstrated at that time. While not going into the details of those days, suffice to note here that in addition to over one thousand federal law enforcement agents sent in to LA during this time, Dunn notes there were an additional four hundred Border Patrol agents who were part of the contingent sent in, especially into Latinx communities near the riots. Over one thousand undocumented immigrants were arrested even though many were not even involved with the riot. This tactic is familiar and easily replicable elsewhere.[22]

The presence of militarism along the U.S./Mexico border was established by military force in the Texas Revolution of 1836 and the Mexican War of 1846–1848. The Treaty of Guadalupe of 1848 was the result of the U.S. conquest of Mexico, a forced surrender of its national territory and annexation. The notion of "border control" has become an evermore salient topic in the United States, most often replete with Orientalism, xenophobia, sensationalist tropes of undocumented immigrants, drug traffickers, and visions of a porous border through which terrorists flow freely. All these racial stereotypes are easily spurred and stirred up by institutions invested in solutions that will further militarization along the borders in the name of national security.[23] The U.S./Mexico border has become what Dunn refers to as a "low intensity conflict" zone for "war for all seasons"[24] or what Jason De León refers to as a zone of "structural violence" in which warfare technology combined with specific utilization of the natural environment along the border are used to enforce border control with violence and impunity.[25] It is no coincidence that after September 11, 2001, and the so-called war on terror and the U.S./Mexico border, as evidenced in the creation of the Office of Homeland Security, it became one of the first regions of intensified militarism. Creation and maintenance of borders and militarized security is also about economics.[26] Many military contractors like Lockheed Martin, Raytheon, and Northrop Grumman have become key partners in border construction, policing, and maintenance along the U.S./Mexico border. Partnerships involve high-tech military surveillance equipment like various drones used for military operations in high intensity conflict regions but also as partners in exchange of information regarding strategies for physical barriers as well as on-the-ground personnel.[27]

The same companies used to construct walls along the U.S./Mexico border are some of the same companies used to construct the walls along Israel and occupied Palestinian territories. Just as the U.S./Mexico border and militarism have come under much interrogation and analysis from activists to scholars, so too has the cozy relationship between the United States and Israel. U.S. financial assistance to Israel has been steadily increasing even as militarization in the occupied territories has intensified. Recent critical research released to the public examines the exchange of information when it comes to technology and surveillance, racial profiling, and strategies of population control, especially the control and management of protesting crowds, as well as the use of force between the Israeli military and police forces and U.S. law enforcement officials.[28] The relationship between Israel and U.S. law enforcement and military involves exchange programs of personnel trainings in either country that facilitate the sharing of practices as well as technologies for intelligence gathering, expanding surveillance, border security, checkpoints, strategies on how to suppress public protests through the use of militarized force, and even coordination with media. One of the most significant parallels in the use of militarized tactics deployed in the contemporary siege warfare against urban civilians is the deliberate destruction of modern infrastructure. Such deliberate targeting aims for a long-term, slow violence against specific communities with an ultimate goal of the slow disintegration of people without calling undue attention to their demise.[29]

U.S. feminist and womanist perspectives can assist us in challenging U.S. militarism by drawing our attention to the ways in which military violence is interlocked with other forms of violence both abroad and within the United States, and to feminist praxis of transformation that stems from transnational connections and networks of empowerment and resistance. It also helps us to see the unavoidability of making connections among ostensibly discrete forms of violence across the national borders. Perhaps it is more than unavoidability but rather a critical necessity to make connections across seemingly disparate places, movements, and struggles. For instance, a feminist perspective allows us to see the war on terror, to borrow Nadine Naber's words, "in terms of multiple violences with interconnected consequences that extend transnationally in similar spatio-temporal contexts."[30] Interrogating U.S. military interventions in "other" countries, then, should enable us to acknowledge how the U.S. war on terror also directly affects U.S. "domestic" affairs and daily lives in the United States. As Naber argues, ending military violence "abroad" and "the multiple, interconnected reverberations of empire within (heteropatriarchy, settler colonialism, gendered and sexualized racism, the criminalization of communities of colour, and so on)"[31] are not a separate matter.

Feminist Praxis against U.S. Militarism is a plea for engaged feminist praxis with the goal toward political solidarities to resist and provide alternatives to the ever-expanding U.S. military-industrial complex and its own unique and ever-pervasive militarized worldling. Although we are not naïve to think that militarism will become obsolete in any foreseeable future, we want to continue to engage and conjure alternative imagination in world-making that is not only absent of war but also without "imperialist desire" that requires, and is in fact grounded in, violence to others. We are interested in questions of how im/possible and necessary are the works of feminist praxis of building solidarity and resistance across shared experiences of U.S. gendered racial militarism all the while acknowledging nonequivalence. With this latter hope we examine how diverse formations are constitutive of our different relations with the U.S.

imperialist agenda. This book is also an effort to explore what our duties and responsibilities are as *relatively* privileged U.S.-based feminist and womanist scholar-teacher-activists in light of ever-escalating police violence, the quickly consolidating racial and militarized state, racialized surveillance, anti-Black racism, the prison-industrial complex, Islamophobia, misogyny, environmental destruction, and the intensification and acceleration of dispossession for those already precarious in the context of white supremacy and productions of the empire's reach. Critiques we offer here acknowledge the increasingly extensive ways militarism is constitutive of gendered, racial, and sexual violence.

This book is an assemblage of essays by a group of feminist and womanist scholars from a variety of institutional locations within the United States who critically engage U.S. militarism in doing critical studies of Christianity—theological, ethical, and interdisciplinary studies of Christianity. The contributors represent a diverse range of social and disciplinary locations. We have specifically gathered voices of U.S.-based Christian studies scholars with the understanding that implicit, if not explicit, Christian supremacy and its misguided interpretations of Christianity as an imperialist project coupled with American exceptionalism and, most critically, notions of violence tethered to ideas of redemption, have undergirded the logic of terror and perpetual war by the United States. Most of all, we engage U.S. militarism from feminist and womanist perspectives by acknowledging that militarized violence cannot be understood in isolation from various patterns of violence against women and other marginalized people, as well as from global ideas of race and colonial histories.

The volume highlights significant contributions made by feminist and womanist scholars covering a wide range of topics. Contributions include Andrea Smith's interpretation of the crucifixion as an example of military and sexual violence, Lisa Dellinger's interpretation of the Doctrine of Discovery as Christianized genocide in the lives of Indigenous women and their communities, and Keun-Joo Christine Pae's engagement with the collective body of Korean prostitutes during the U.S. military occupation in South Korea (1945–1948) and the Korean War (1950–1953). Additionally, Mai-Anh Le Tran interrogates militarized Orientalism and racism along the itineraries of U.S. military interventions abroad, specifically in Vietnam, whereas Pamela Lightsey offers analysis of militarized police forces in Black communities and offers insights into the transnational entanglements of militarism. Nami Kim's chapter examines the deployment of the notion of violence against women as a justification of the Muslim Ban, while Kate Ott and Kristen J. Leslie draw from a case study on the education of military chaplains and feminist strategies for working as outsider-insiders in the U.S. military. B. Yuki Schwartz reflects on the language of "Asian shame" and "shame culture" in Cold War-era shame discourse and the use of shame discourse to support the logic of militarized imperialism. To be sure, this project is not an attempt at comparative work through time, space, and lived experiences, nor is this volume an attempt to draw simple and false equivalences. We provide an introductory way of framing a conversation that is direly necessary today. We are interested in what Lisa Lowe is asking: "Instead of reading, teaching, and writing about our own histories separately, how would our theo-ethical discourse change if we try to see how 'intimately' our histories and experiences are interconnected?"[32] This volume seeks to make already existing relations of dispossession and militarized violence constitutive of these seemingly disparate sites and communities even more legible, specifically within critical Christian studies.

One of the hallmarks of this book is each author's autobiographical aspect in relation to U.S. militarism. We offer a challenge—to consider U.S. militarism as not simply an object of analysis, but as a reality within and through which we make our lives and our analytics grounded in the social and political realities of our lives. The autobiographical provision will help readers to move away from the dangers of theoretical abstraction when interrogating spectacular frames of war, militarism, and militarized violence. The autobiographical component also allows us to recognize how war and militarized violence as a global spectacle is always already in intimate proximity to the quotidian and everyday lives of individuals.

To be sure, we also acknowledge the limits and shortcomings of this volume. One of the limitations is that it is a U.S.-based and inadvertently U.S.-centered project. We acknowledge that we are not immune from some of the issues that are associated with U.S. global dominance, such as our reliance on the English language, the United States as a primary object of inquiry, and U.S.-based scholars. In order for us to continue our feminist and womanist praxis against U.S. militarism, it will require our future endeavors to be "conscious of incorporating scholars speaking from different histories, locations, and nations," and any approach that purports to be diasporic, transnational, international, or global.[33]

While there are groundbreaking texts addressing these issues emerging out of other disciplines, a critical interrogation of these issues in Christian studies from feminist and womanist, intersectional, and transnational perspectives is still not significantly noticeable nor readily available. If there is a sense of Christian theological discourse rooted in a trenchant critique of U.S. militarism, it is still not yet part of the dominant theological discourse. We note the current paucity of work in this area and have brought together feminist and womanist scholars in Christian studies to analytically engage the global reality of U.S. militarism, its destructive impact on women's lives, as well as women's ongoing resistance, both individual and collective.

For transformative and liberative relevance today, critical Christian studies must weigh in on the state of emergency that is current global reality. Political theorist Wendy Brown and numerous others have offered ways in which our political, secular notions are deeply entrenched in Christian theological ideas of sovereignty and power that continue to be deployed to theologically rationalize U.S. global military violence. For instance, the notion of Christian exceptionalism undergirds the logic of American exceptionalism that makes exclusive claims on "God and salvation" as (White) America's burden of global rescue mission. It is critical for Christian theological projects to delink Christian theological underpinnings to the still-ongoing logics of colonial and global military violence and the colonialist narratives that legitimize "civilizing" missions. Theo-ethical voices in this volume offer analyses of both the limits and problems of hegemonic Christian theology as well as the perils persistent in even more intensified global militarized violence today. Feminist and womanist theo-ethical analyses are needed in the necessary rupture to delink Christian theology from militarized violence. Feminist and womanist Christian theologians have been forging alliances and working in solidarity at these intersections. These scholars recognize the coterminous conditions of possibility for each of our communities. This means there is no succinct analysis of one experience without its formation shaped by experiences from elsewhere. Feminist and womanist scholars in this volume offer voices that make even more visible a particularly critical way of reading the world that is in direct contrast with a particular kind of liberalism pervasive in most of Eurocentric knowledge production—the "archive of liberalism."[34] As Lisa Lowe argues, the "others" of Europe were the very constitutive conditions to the very becoming of European subject and history. The United States as a military and militarized empire was and is only possible, then, through the destruction of peoples, particularly of non-European background, within and outside the borders of the United States. Feminist and womanist Christian scholars are recognizing the critical need to articulate how our community formations are never independent from each other. If Europe's formation is constitutive of other non-European subjects, so too of the possibility that U.S. formation was and is contingent upon others who are considered by some as neither U.S. citizens nor American as was the case in the incarceration of Japanese American citizens.

Editors of this volume acknowledge that our experiences of war and militarism are limited, but we also realize that the memories of the Korean War passed down to the generations that did not experience it have left an indelible impression in our lives and prompts us to see the connections between U.S. militarism "abroad" and its militarized violence against people of color in the United States and elsewhere in the past as well as in our current state of war in countless global sites. We are acutely aware of our relative privileges as U.S.-based academics with tenure, and, simultaneously, of how fragile any sense of security can be as women of color academics living in this turbulent political climate.

While our life experiences have more moments of convergence than of divergence, it is perhaps not so much about our "shared" histories and experiences that have brought us to pursue our work together, but more so based on our indignation at multivalent forms of violence here in the United States and "over there" as well as our vantage point from which we approach U.S. militarism that continues to generate unmeasurable havoc on the lives of an uncountable number of people, non-human living beings, and the environment. We hope multiplicity of movements by women across the world in the work of ending militarized violence will continue to be a force to reckon with. It is our hope that these global conversations continue to bring forth emergent transformative politics as well as, in the case of this volume, particularly Christian theologies invested in the work of counter world-making—that is, a world without war, another world that is on her way, as Arundhati Roy has poignantly said. We offer this volume as a point of entry for further conversations along shared theo-political ethics, projects, and movements of transnational liberation that focus on ending militarized violence and violations.

BIBLIOGRAPHY

Andreas, Peter. *Border Games: Policing the US.-Mexico Divide*. Ithaca: Cornell University Press, 2000.

Balko, Radley. *Rise of the Warrior Cop: The Militarization of America's Police Forces*. New York: Public Affairs, 2014.

Byrd, Jody A. *The Transit of Empire: Indigenous Critiques of Colonialism*. Minneapolis: University of Minnesota Press, 2011.

Brown, Wendy. *Walled States, Waning Sovereignty*. New York: Zone Books, 2010.

De León, Jason. *The Land of Open Grace: Living and Dying on the Migrant Trail*. Oakland: University of California Press, 2015.

Deadly Exchange: The Dangerous Consequences of American Law Enforcement Training in Israel, a report by Researching the American-Israeli Alliance in Partnership with Jewish Voice for Peace (September 2018).

Dunn, Timothy J. *The Militarization of the U.S.-Mexico Border: 1978–1992*. Austin: University of Texas Press, 1996.

Estes, Nick. *Our History is the Future*. New York: Verso, 2019.

Graham, Stephen. *Cities Under Siege: The New Military Urbanism*. New York: Verso Books, 2010.

Hoskins, Janet, and Viet Thanh Nguyen, eds. *Transpacific Studies: Framing an Emerging Field*. Honolulu: University of Hawai'i Press, 2014. Kindle.

Johnson, Sylvester A. "Black Religion, the Security State, and the Racialization of Islam." In *African American Religions, 1500–2000: Colonialism, Democracy, and Freedom*. Cambridge: Cambridge University Press, 2015.

Kim, Nami, and Wonhee Anne Joh, eds. *Critical Theology against U.S. Militarism: Decolonization and Deimperialization*. New York: Palgrave Macmillan, 2016.

Kwon, Heonik. *The Other Cold War*. New York: Columbia University Press, 2010.

———. "Sites of the Postcolonial Cold War." In *Ethnographies of U.S. Empire*, edited by Carole McGranahan and John F. Collins. Durham: Duke University Press, 2018.

Lowe, Lisa. *The Intimacies of Four Continents*. Durham: Duke University Press, 2015.

Masco, Joseph. *The Theater of Operations: National Security Affect from the Cold War to the war on terror*. Durham: Duke University Press. 2014. Kindle.

Massumi, Brian. *Ontopower: War, Politics, and the State of Perception*. Durham: Duke University Press, 2015.

"Millions Lack Food, Housing, and Healthcare, But 38 Democrats Just Joined GOP to Spend $716 Billion on Endless War and Empire." *Common Dreams*. June 19, 2018. www.commondreams.org/news/2018/06/19/millions-lack-food-housing-and-healthcare-38-democrats-just-joined-gop-spend-716. Accessed June 23, 2018.

Naber, Nadine. "Diasporas of Empire: Arab Americans and the Reverberations of War." In *At the Limits of Justice: Women of Colour on Terror*, edited by Suvendrini Perera and Sherene Razack. Toronto: University of Toronto Press, 2014.

Neoclelous, Mark. *Critique of Security*. Montreal: McGill-Queen's University Press, 2008.

———. *War Power, Police Power*. Edinburgh: University of Edinburgh Press, 2014.

Slotkin, Richard. *Gunfighter Nation: The Myth of the Frontier in the Twentieth-Century America*. New York: Harper Perennial, 1992.

———. *Regeneration through Violence: The Mythology of the American Frontier, 1600–1860.* . Norman: University of Oklahoma Press, 1973.

Yoneyama, Lisa. *Cold War Ruins: Transpacific Critique of American Justice and Japanese War Crimes*. Durham: Duke University Press, 2016. Kindle.

NOTES

1. Arundhati Roy, *War Talk*, (Boston, MA: South End Press, 2003).

2. Richard Slotkin, *Regeneration Through Violence: The Mythology of the American Frontier 1600–1860* (Norman: University of Oklahoma Press, 1973); Richard Slotkin, *Gunfighter Nation: The Myth of the Frontier in Twentieth-Century America* (New York: Harper Perennial, 1992).

3. Nick Estes, *Our History is The Future* (New York: Verso, 2019), 89.

4. Estes, *Our History is The Future*, 89–90.

5. Joseph Masco, *The Theater of Operations: National Security Affect from the Cold War to the war on terror* (Durham: Duke University Press, 2014), 6–7, Kindle.

6. Masco, *The Theater of Operations*, 5.

7. We acknowledge that the Cold War does not have a "single and globally identical phenomenon." See Heonik Kwon, *The Other Cold War* (New York: Columbia University Press, 2010), 25–26. We also talk about this in "Introduction," to *Critical Theology against U.S. Militarism: Decolonization and Deimperialization*, ed. Nami Kim and Wonhee Anne Joh (New York: Palgrave Macmillan, 2016), xii.

8. Heonik Kwon, "Sites of the Postcolonial Cold War," in *Ethnographies of U.S. Empire*, ed. Carole McGranahan and John F. Collins (Durham: Duke University Press, 2018), 221.

9. Mark Neoclelous, *Critique of Security* (Montreal: McGill-Queen's University Press, 2008), 156.

10. Neoclelous, *Critique of Security*, 7, 28.

11. Neoclelous, *Critique of Security*, 28.

12. "Millions Lack Food, Housing, and Healthcare, But 38 Democrats Just Joined GOP to Spend $716 Billion on Endless War and Empire." *Common Dreams*, June 19, 2018. www.commondreams.org/news/2018/06/19/millions-lack-food-housing-and-healthcare-38-democrats-just-joined-gop-spend-716 (accessed June 23, 2018).

13. Brian Massumi, *Ontopower: War, Politics, and the State of Perception* (Durham: Duke University Press, 2015), 5–7.

14. Mark Neocleous, *War Power, Police Power* (Edinburgh: University of Edinburgh Press, 2014), 123.

15. Neocleous, *War Power, Police Power*, 133.

16. Sylvester A. Johnson, "Black Religion, the Security State, and the Racialization of Islam," in *African American Religions, 1500–2000: Colonialism, Democracy, and Freedom* (Cambridge: Cambridge University Press, 2015), 399.

17. Jodi A. Byrd, *The Transit of Empire: Indigenous Critique of Colonialism* (Minneapolis: University of Minnesota Press, 2011), 4.

18. Lisa Yoneyama. *Cold War Ruins: Transpacific Critique of American Justice and Japanese War Crimes* (Durham: Duke University Press, 2016), 662–664, Kindle.

19. See Kim and Joh, eds., *Critical Theology against U.S. Militarism*.

20. For further analysis of the ways that building of walls and borders are more than simply about keeping "outsides" from coming in, cf., Wendy Brown, *Walled States, Waning Sovereignty* (New York: Zone Books, 2010).

21. Stephen Graham, *Cities under Siege: The New Military Urbanism* (New York: Verso Books, 2010), xiii. Cf., Radley Balko, *Rise of the Warrior Cop: The Militarization of America's Police Forces* (New York: Public Affairs, 2014).

22. Timothy J. Dunn, *The Militarization of the U.S./Mexico Border: 1978–1992* (Austin: University of Texas Press, 1996), 168. Cf., Timothy J. Dunn, *Blockading the Border and Human Rights: The El Paso Operation That Remade Immigration Enforcement* (Austin: University of Texas Press, 2009).

23. Dunn, *The Militarization of the U.S./Mexico Border*.

24. Dunn, *The Militarization of the U.S./Mexico Border*, 19.

25. Jason De León, *The Land of Open Grace: Living and Dying on the Migrant Trail* (Oakland: University of California Press, 2015), 16.

26. Wendy Brown, *Walled State: Waning Sovereignty* (New York: Zone Books, 2010), 35–42.

27. Peter Andreas, *Border Games: Policing the U.S.-Mexico Divide* (Ithaca: Cornell University Press, 2000), 158.

28. *Deadly Exchange: The Dangerous Consequences of American Law Enforcement Training in Israel*, A report by Researching the American-Israeli Alliance in Partnership with Jewish Voice for Peace (September 2018).

29. Graham, *Cities Under Siege*, 285. Graham offers a clear analysis of militarized urban warfare and examines Gaza as one particularly clear case, especially beginning with Operation Defensive Shield of 2002.

30. Nadine Naber, "Diasporas of Empire: Arab Americans and the Reverberations of War," in *At the Limits of Justice: Women of Colour on Terror* (Toronto: University of Toronto Press, 2014), 210.

31. Naber, "Diasporas of Empire."

32. Lisa Lowe, *The Intimacies of Four Continents* (Durham: Duke University Press, 2015), 18.

33. Janet Hoskins and Viet Thanh Nguyen, eds., *Transpacific Studies: Framing an Emerging Field* (Honolulu: University of Hawai'i Press, 2014), 593–595, Kindle.

34. Lowe, *The Intimacies of Four Continents*, 4.

ONE

The Militarism of Racialization, Colonization, and Heteropatriarchy

Andrea Smith

American Indians are fully aware of terrorist attacks. We also remember our ancestors who perished at Wounded Knee and Sand Creek. We remember those who perished during the "Trail of Tears" and the Potawatomi "Trail of Death." All of these tragedies occurred on American soil.[1]

The United States is not at war; the United States is war.[2]

Organizing campaigns against U.S. militarism generally focus on U.S. military efforts in other countries. However, as this quote from the Native News Network suggests, militarism constructs the United States itself. Hence, a feminist theological praxis against militarism must attend to not only specific U.S. military ventures around the world, but how the logics of militarism fundamentally structure the United States. An intersectional theological analysis of militarism then sheds new light on what may be a feminist praxis that can combat not only specific military actions, but dismantle the logics of militarism.

The concept of intersectionality as coined by Kimberle Crenshaw is foundational within feminist theory and praxis, even as there is no common understanding of what that term means. Crenshaw articulated this term to intervene in what she termed "additive" approaches to gender and race.[3] That is, all that is needed is to either add women to a racial justice analysis or praxis—without women or trans people in mind—or conversely, to add people of color to a white feminist agenda. Instead, "intersectionality" suggests that when a racial analysis is intersected with feminism, what is presumed to be "feminism" will fundamentally

15

change. Similarly, when a gender analysis is intersected with racial justice, what is presumed to be "racial justice" will also fundamentally
change.

Intersectionality, as critiqued by some theorists,[4] is often presumed to
be located through identity. Intersectionality focuses on the distinct experiences of those, generally women or trans people of color, who live at the
intersections of multiple oppressions. However, intersectionality can also
be an analysis that, while not dismissing the importance of identity, can
be used to examine how logics of domination intersect with each other to
structure the world, not just for those who directly face gender, racial, or
other forms of oppression, but for everyone. Thus, intersectionality can
be used not just to explore the intersections of race and gender but all
forms of domination to assess how they are mutually enabling. In that
spirit, this essay will trace out an intersectional theological analysis of
militarism through a re-narration of the crucifixion as a site of military,
racial, and sexual violence.

THE CRUCIFIXION AND RACIALITY

Many feminist and womanist scholars have critiqued western Christianity's emphasis on the atonement as a theology that enables abuse by
suggesting that those who are dominated should sacrifice themselves for
the betterment of all. Joanne Carlson Brown, Rebecca Parker, and Delores
Williams have noted that marginalized people, such as battered women,
are more likely to suffer and sacrifice than others. It is rarely those in
privileged positions who want to take up the cross. Brown and Parker
argue, "The imitator of Christ, which every faithful person is exhorted to
be, can find herself choosing to endure suffering . . . This glorification of
suffering as salvific, held before us daily in the image of Jesus hanging
from the cross, encourages women who are being abused to be more
concerned about their victimizer than about themselves."[5] According to
Anthony Pinn, the cross as a symbol of suffering is without value. He
states, "Suffering is evil and it must end; contact with it and endurance of
it do not promote anything beneficial. To think otherwise is to deny the
value of human life by embracing a demonic force that effectively mu-
tates and destroys the quality of life. *Suffering Has No Redemptive Qualities*."[6]

Some critical-race evangelical scholars, by contrast, have argued that
the problem with triumphalist Christianity is that it actually does not
dwell on the crucifixion and likes to go straight to the resurrection.[7] They
suggest that the crucifixion should be the site of lament for white evangelical complicity in patriarchy and white supremacy.

Meanwhile, while not focusing on Christian theology per se, many
Black studies scholars have contended that the pathway toward libera-

tion may not lie in demands that are legible and cognizable in the current world order, but it may exist in the places of complete degradation where other possibilities of the "human" can be glimpsed.[8] Scholars such as Sylvia Wynter, Denise Da Silva, and Alexander Weheliye have argued that raciality is not simply a result of unfortunate stereotypes from peoples of different cultural backgrounds, but the fundamental logic by which certain peoples are categorized outside the category of the human.[9] Or to quote Ruth Wilson Gilmore: "Racism, specifically, is the state-sanctioned or extralegal production and exploitation of group-differentiated vulnerability to premature death."[10] These understandings move us away from thinking about race as a noun in terms of set people groups, such as African Americans, Latinos, Native peoples, Asian Americans, etc., to racialization as a verb that can impact peoples differentially through time and space. Racialization is a process by which the marker between human and nonhuman is biologized even though who is being racialized and the markers of racialization may change. Thus, the anti-racist project of aspiring for humanity against "dehumanization" fails to account for how the "human" is already constructed through whiteness. Frank Wilderson and Weheliye suggest that it is the space of abjection rather than humanization that is the space to imagine a different kind of humanity not constructed through the logics of raciality generally and anti-Blackness specifically. States Wilderson: "In allowing the notion of freedom to attain the ethical purity of its ontological status, one would have to lose one's Human coordinates and become Black. Which is to say one would have to die."[11] Essentially, liberation may be seen not so much in the resurrection, but in the crucifixion.

> The slave had been recently at home in the African continent, but when one tribe fought against the other the losing side or some portion of it was sold into slavery just as Joseph was by his brethren. The Arab slave trader often brought him to a port and loaded him on a ship to be brought to the new America, first to the Indies and then to the plantations of the South. When he would debark from the ship he knew not what next. Nobody could tell him and he could tell nobody. He could neither read nor write. No one knew his name and it was yet some generations before he had a family or surname. To be freed from his recent captors and from the foul condition of the ship was for a moment a relief no doubt to this poor fellow when he was inducted into the wide open space of a Southern plantation with open air, food and kindness.[12]

Wilderson distinguishes between political antagonism and political conflict. Conflict can be solved through the transfer of land and resources. Antagonism cannot be resolved as such because it entails a fundamental ontological status. He contends that anti-Blackness is the category of political antagonism in which the coherence of whiteness is dependent upon anti-Blackness, but militarism involves conflict that could be re-solved through the exchange of resources.

A reading of the law as above, however, suggests this distinction be-tween antagonism and conflict may not be so clear because "war" pro-vides the ideological justification for racial antagonism. That is, militar-ism is never simply about an external conflict between two nation-states, but is the means by which racialization is consolidated with a state.

As seen in *Borders v Rippey*, the justification for slavery is that Black peoples exist in a natural state of war. Whiteness does not render Black people as property because Black peoples have already rendered them-selves property. The court in *Neil v. Farmer* explains: "This principle of the Law of Nations originated in the rights which war was originally held to confer. One of these rights was, that the victor might enslave the van-quished. This idea has been exploded by the States of Christendom, but obtains still, among many of the nations of the earth."[13] Essentially, slav-ery can be justified if war is the natural state of being that provides the foundation for enslavement. The court further holds that while a particu-lar state can abolish slavery, the natural law among states, unless other-wise qualified by a particular state, is consistent with the legality of slav-ery. International law provides for the freedom to enslave rather than the freedom to be free from slavery. However, the court goes on further to argue:

> Thus it is that we trace property in negroes to Africa. It is immaterial
> how slavery originated there; whether as a penalty for offences against
> the State, or by captivity in war, or by an immemorial and impenetra-
> ble slavery cast in some of the tribes of that dark land. It was there, as
> Lord *Coke* represents it, pure, unmitigated slavery, and so our ancestors
> received, and so it remained until legislation, prompted by christianity,
> softened its severities. The curse of the Patriarch rests still upon the
> descendants of Ham. The negro and his master are but fulfilling a
> divine appointment. Christ came not to remove the curse; but recogniz-
> ing the relation of master and servant, he prescribed the rules which
> govern, and the obligations which grow out of it, and thus ordained it
> an *institution of christianity*.[14]

While war generally provides a justification for slavery, Black peoples become ontologized as slaves because of the particular war-like nature that justifies "unmitigated" slavery. Christianity, then, is described as lessening the conditions of war and slavery that naturally exist in Africa. Christianity's role in instituting and perpetuating chattel slavery disap-pears from view.

> That mere wandering tribes of savages, or such as have a stated place
> of residence, should claim a vast extent of forest, as hunting grounds,
> for the nurture of wild animals, and exclude the cultivation of the
> earth, is unreasonable and unjust. The earth belongs to all men in gen-
> eral, destined by the Creator to be their common habitation; and all

derived from nature the right of drawing from it their subsistence and those things suitable to their wants. This it would be incapable of affording was it uncultivated. Every nation is, then, obliged by the law of nature to cultivate the ground that has fallen to its share . . .

And foes to each other, and foes to all men, our ancestors found the North American savages, the main business of their lives being war, and that a war of extermination (the foe taking no prisoners, save for the exercise of a refined cruelty—to burn him at the stake); a people that had no government, and with whom the right of the strongest alone was respected.

True, their lands might have been acquired by conquest. For although one nation cannot justly or lawfully make war upon another for the mere purpose of subduing it to the dominion of the invader, yet it is settled (8 Wheat. 543) that "conquest gives a title which the courts of the conqueror cannot deny, whatever the private and speculative opinions of individuals may be respecting the original justice of the claim which has been successfully asserted."

Where a just and necessary war is provoked, those who provoke it may lawfully be subdued to the dominion of the other nation, should it conquer, and be dispossessed of the soil at the pleasure of the conqueror.[15]

In *State v. Foreman*, the court justifies the conquest of Native peoples on the basis that they, like Black peoples, naturally exist in a state of war. In particular, Native peoples exist in a state of nature where the strong kill the weak as a matter of course. Hence, a white person killing a Native person is like a lion killing a zebra. This kind of reasoning presupposes a radical distinction between humans and nature in which Native peoples are in the category of nature. The death of nature is not mournable, and hence, Indigenous genocide is not grievable.

However, Native peoples, unlike Black peoples, can attain humanity if they shed their ontological status of nature by no longer being at war with whiteness:

That his Honor erred in charging the jury, that there were but two classes of free inhabitants of this State, recognized by the law, to wit: *white citizens* and *free persons of color;* and that there was no intermediate or third class, denominated *free Indians,* or persons of *Indian descent,* possessed of civil privileges, superior to those of other free persons of color; but that the exception in the Acts of Assembly in relation to free persons of color, of "Indians in amity with this government," is confined to Indians belonging to tribes, who possess an acknowledged national existence, and are in amity with this State, and who may be transiently within our jurisdiction. Whereas, it is respectfully submitted, that the privilege secured by the exception referred to by his Honor, to Indians belonging to tribes in amity with this State, is not extinguished by such Indians becoming residents within our territory, but continues in them and in their descendants, whose blood is not mixed with that of the African or negro race; and that proof of the continued

freedom of themselves, and their progenitors, of persons of Indian descent, unmixed with African or negro blood, without any of them ever
having been subjected to the condition of slaves, is conclusive evidence
that all such persons are the descendants of "Indians in amity with this
State," and therefore entitled to the civil privileges of their ancestors. [16]

In *State v. Belmont*, Native peoples can be free if: 1) they are "in amity
with this State," and 2) they are "not mixed with that of the African or
negro race." Of course, by coming in amity with the State, they then cease
to be Native. Thus, Native peoples have the option to either disappear
into whiteness or disappear into Blackness. If they disappear into Blackness, they remain in a state of war such that their death cannot be
mourned. If they disappear into whiteness, they escape their ontological
status of war that justifies their genocide, but in doing so, they are now
"in amity" and hence in agreement with their colonization.

> The adoption by Government, in the crisis of war and of threatened
> invasion, of measures for the public safety, based upon the recognition
> of facts and circumstances which indicate that a group of one national
> extraction may menace that safety more than others, is not wholly be-
> yond the limits of the Constitution and is not to be condemned merely
> because in other and in most circumstances racial distinctions are irrel-
> evant. [17]

Just as war provides the foundation for racialization, as seen in *Hirabayashi v. U.S.*, war always provides the justification for racism. What U.S.
jurisprudence correctly perceives is that war requires racism, and hence,
equal protection must always give way to military interests. As Sora Han
argues, the debates around whether courts should still apply strict scrutiny tests[18] for discrimination cases during times of national emergency are
largely irrelevant because courts will always find that national security
interests meet strict scrutiny. "Is national defense ever anything other
than compelling, necessary, urgent?" If war is the intent to destroy a
people, then racialization determines which peoples should be destroyed.
Or to quote Han: "The United States is not at war; the United States is
war." Rather than position war (and its attendant militarism) as an example of political conflict rather than political antagonism, war can be seen
as the foundation that makes the antagonisms of anti-Blackness and Indigenous genocide legible.

> Now at the festival he used to release a prisoner for them, anyone for
> whom they asked. Now a man called Barabbas was in prison with the
> rebels who had committed murder during the insurrection. So the
> crowd came and began to ask Pilate to do for them according to his
> custom. Then he answered them, "Do you want me to release for you
> the King of the Jews?" For he realized that it was out of jealousy that
> the chief priests had handed him over. But the chief priests stirred up
> the crowd to have him release Barabbas for them instead. Pilate spoke

to them again, "Then what do you wish me to do with the man you call the King of the Jews?" They shouted back, "Crucify him!" Pilate asked them, "Why, what evil has he done?" But they shouted all the more, "Crucify him!" So Pilate, wishing to satisfy the crowd, released Barabbas for them; and after flogging Jesus, he handed him over to be crucified. [19]

This dynamic between racialization and war is evidenced in the book of Mark's narrative of Jesus's crucifixion. As previously discussed, legal jurisprudence essentially erases white Christian responsibility for slavery and genocide by framing Black and Native peoples as always already in a state of war. Similarly, the narrative of Jesus's crucifixion erases the complicity of the Roman Empire in his death by depicting Jewish peoples in a state of war. Pilate is reasonable and rational and understands that Jesus has committed no crime. However, Jewish crowds are stirred up, and Pilate has no choice but to kill Jesus in order to appease the crowd. Because Jews are "foes to each other," their nation may be "lawfully subdued" by empire.

Thus, an intersectional analysis of militarism and race demonstrates that militarism is always an internal and external project that enables and is enabled by racialization. However, the dual nature of militarism is also enabled through sexual violence as a strategy of racialization and colonization.

THE CRUCIFIXION AS SEXUAL COLONIZATION

While U.S. Christian triumphalist theology generally places Jesus on the side of U.S. empire, liberation theologians point out that Jesus was in fact the victim of empire. He was from a colonized peoples living under Roman military occupation. But how does our understanding of the military violence to which Jesus was subject shift if we also understand that he was a victim of sexual violence? An intersectional reading of the crucifixion sheds further light on the fact that militarism and empire are fundamentally gendered projects. But it also sheds light on how sexual violence is fundamentally a racial project.

> Two of the best looking of the squaws were lying in such a position, and from the appearance of the genital organs and of their wounds, there can be no doubt that they were first ravished and then shot dead. Nearly all of the dead were mutilated. [20]

As I have discussed in greater detail in other works, colonization, and by extension, militarism, is structured by a logic of sexual violence. For instance, the history of Native colonization in the United States cannot be told outside the story of sexual violence. Indian massacres were also accompanied by rape and sexual mutilation. Sexual violence is always a necessary excess of militarism. The goal was not just to kill Native peoples but to kill their sense of even being a people. Native peoples were rendered inherently rapeable, and by extension their lands inherently invadable and their resources inherently extractable. Sexual violence also functioned to naturalize patriarchy within Native communities as well as to stabilize patriarchy within European societies by destroying alternative non-patriarchal socialities that Native communities represented.

In this respect, sexual violence is also always already a racial project. Sexual violence is a strategy for placing someone in the category of the nonhuman by rendering this person as an inherently violable being. If war is the project of destroying a people, racialization is the logic of determining which peoples are to be destroyed, and sexual violence is the tool of implementing this destruction. Henry Theriault makes the connection of how sexual violence is integral to militarism by asking the question: how does our analysis of rape committed in the course of war change if we calculate not just the number of people who are assaulted but the number of sexual assaults that are committed? He estimates that six hundred million acts of rape were committed against Korean comfort women in World War II and two billion acts of rape were committed in the course of WWII as a whole.[21] Essentially, rather than thinking of rape as something that happens in war, he suggests we should think of war *as* sexual violence. From this framework, I now turn to a theological engagement with the crucifixion as a site of militarized sexual violence.

> When Pilate heard this, he asked whether the man was a Galilean. And when he learned that he was under Herod's jurisdiction, he sent him off to Herod, who was himself in Jerusalem at that time. When Herod saw Jesus, he was very glad, for he had been wanting to see him for a long time, because he had heard about him and was hoping to see him perform some sign. He questioned him at some length, but Jesus[c] gave him no answer. The chief priests and the scribes stood by, vehemently accusing him. Even Herod with his soldiers treated him with contempt and mocked him; then he put an elegant robe on him, and sent him back to Pilate. *That same day Herod and Pilate became friends with each other; before this they had been enemies* (italics added).[22]

Jesus's crucifixion narratively begins by being betrayed by a kiss from Judas.[23] What was the point in this story of Judas betraying Jesus in this way? It was not sufficient for Judas to just simply point out who Jesus was. Rather the kiss is, as sexual violence generally is, a fleshly surplus of violence. This intimate act by a friend signifies not just a betrayal but an act of control and domination. A kiss involves a loosening of physical boundaries to establish both a physical and psychic connection, even if that connection is not sexual, specifically speaking. Judas's nonconsensual kiss then attempts to establish both his physical and psychic control of Jesus.

Jesus's death by crucifixion also can be read as an act of sexual colonization. Again, if the point was only to kill Jesus, there are certainly many more efficient ways to do so. But instead, through sexual violence, Jesus had to be rendered a nonperson, subject to empire. John 19:23–24 describes how Jesus is undressed by soldiers and put on display to make his violability public. The soldiers then divide his clothes and draw lots to see who can keep Jesus's undergarment. Essentially, the soldiers retain trophies to mark Jesus's sexual violation. In the symbol of the crucifixion, there is what Carol Adams terms an "absent referent." Adams explains this term by noting that the phrase "battered woman" ontologizes women as victims of battering. The person who is battering her is absent from this phrase.[24] Similarly, in the symbol of Christ, Jesus is ontologized as one who is crucified. The individuals who put him on the cross are erased as the perpetrators and are never depicted in pictorial representations of the cross. But because those responsible for Jesus's death are the absent referent in the crucifix, their responsibility for the crucifixion is erased. Those in power can thus glorify the ability to crucify others without culpability. It is simply the nature of Christ, and those who share his powerless role in society, to be crucified. Thus, the crucifixion functions to not only kill Jesus, but to render him as someone who is inherently killable, whose death must be mocked rather than mourned.

Colonization is not simply about the theft of land and resources, but about the ability to name reality for others. For instance, the colonization of Indigenous peoples in the United States is not just about the fact that Native peoples were killed and Indigenous lands were seized, but that colonists could name this genocide as "democracy" and render genocide invisible. Sexual violence follows a similar logic. It's not just that one is assaulted, but that the victim becomes the one who deserved it and who was "asking for it." Similarly, Luke 23:38 describes how soldiers placed an inscription on Jesus's cross stating, "This is the King of the Jews." Jesus can no longer name; he can only be named by others.

Luke 23:8 further describes how Herod and his soldiers ridiculed and mocked him. He is further mocked by soldiers while he is on the cross and given sour wine to drink in Luke 23:36. This narration echoes the recent testimony of Dr. Christine Blasey Ford during the Supreme Court hearings for Brett Kavanaugh when she stated that what she most remembered about the assault she suffered was the laughter. "Indelible in the hippocampus is the laughter, the laugh—the uproarious laughter between the two, and their having fun at my expense."[25] Essentially, sexual violence enables those deemed human to attain coherence through the rendering of someone outside the category of human.

But in addition, sexual violence becomes a strategy for consolidating the colonizers with colonial elites. As cited above, Luke 23:12 describes how Jesus's crucifixion becomes the occasion by which Herod (representing the colonized elite) and Pilate (representing the colonist) become friends. Sexual violence is a strategy to get colonized communities to internalize violence so that they become self-colonizing. Thus, militarized sexual violence as represented by the crucifixion represents a double-set of violences: internal violence within the militarized and colonized community and external violence from colonial powers. Jesus is both sexually violated by the state and betrayed by his own community. Unfortunately, as Rosemary Radford Ruther has noted, Christianity has often displaced this betrayal onto Judaism. However, as Jesus was betrayed by members of his own community, this betrayal is not evidence of particular problems with Judaism but is an example of the internal violences that happen within any community, including colonized communities. Essentially, Jesus would be able to say #churchtoo.

THEOLOGICAL RESOURCES FOR COMBATING SEXUAL COLONIZATION

In all of the churches I began to attend after I became a Christian, I witnessed or experienced sexual harassment and violence. Disillusioned, I joined the anti-violence movement and began working at a rape crisis center. There, a client came in for services who had been sexually assaulted by the executive director of one of the city's largest anti-violence agencies.

I attended a workshop for Native Christians in which one elder said that the number one issue Native peoples face is violence against women and children. "As long as we are destroying ourselves on the inside, we don't have to worry about enemies on the outside." His words inspired me to begin anti-violence organizing. But a few years later, I found out that he had also been arrested for child sexual abuse.

An intersectional analysis of the crucifixion as simultaneously an example of military and sexual violence sheds light on strategies needed to end both as well as inform liberation theologies. In particular, ending violence is always an internal and external process. It requires ending the structures of domination and empire that are naturalized by sexual violence and enabling it. But at the same time, it requires the radical transformation of subjectivities that have been shaped by violence.

This necessity is reflected in the biblical concept of being born again: "Very truly I tell you, no one can see the kingdom of God unless they are born again." [26] Jesus does not say, if you have the correct doctrinal beliefs, you will see the Kingdom. Rather, your humanity as you know it must come to an end, and you must become a new being all together. If racialization is the logic that defines the human over and against those who are not human, then ending racism is not simply about changing personal beliefs or even making structural change, but creating a new sense of humanity all together. "Therefore, if anyone is in Christ, the new creation has come: The old has gone, the new is here!"[27]

Thus, churches are not the places for the theologically or politically correct, as is evidenced by the very theologically suspicious peoples with whom Jesus associated. Rather, they should be places where we can create new practices that enable us to become different people. Even progressive organizations tend to organize around the "right" people who have the proper politics. But the reality is, if global oppression ended tomorrow, we would all be very confused, because our subjectivities are so fundamentally shaped by white supremacy, settler colonialism, capitalism, heteropatriarchy, and empire. Creating "church" is not about expelling people who represent these logics of oppression (since that would be all of us) but creating spaces that enable us to dismantle the logics of domination, both internally and externally, that structure all of us. While we may need organizing spaces that are specific for different people at different times, ultimately, it's not about white people, it's about white supremacy; it's not about settlers, it's about settler colonialism; it's not about cis men, it's about heteropatriarchy.

> The Pharisees and their scribes were complaining to his disciples, saying, "Why do you eat and drink with tax collectors and sinners?" Jesus answered, "Those who are well have no need of a physician, but those who are sick; I have come to call not the righteous but sinners to repentance."[28]

Jesus's articulation of a worship community as a place for sinners rather than the "righteous" is actually also a critique of liberation movements. That is, liberation theologies have often positioned God as really being on the side of the "oppressed" rather than the "oppressor." But these words suggest that God stands against oppression, no matter who commits it. There is no pure community before God—we are all sinners, and hence, we need to develop church communities that engage in continual and humble self-critique and interrogation to ascertain when, even with good intentions, we may be hurting others. We do not have to be "good" to be loved by Christ—Christ loves us in the midst of sin. And God works through us as sinners to help us become different people. It is never enough to organize around how we are oppressed. We must always simultaneously organize around our complicity in oppression.

Rather than see churches as "safe spaces" that are gatherings of saints, we should see them as dangerous places where sinners struggle together to create a world without oppression while transforming themselves in the process. Churches then do not have to be burdened with looking perfect to the rest of the world, but instead could be models of communities that are open about their failings and struggles, from which others can learn.

Jesus's crucifixion also suggests a different model of organizing beyond the politics of respectability. While the previously described critiques of the crucifixion as valorizing suffering are important, it may also be the case that the crucifixion suggests a different vantage point for imagining liberation. That is, rather than organizing movements around those who are the most respectable and acceptable to the mainstream society, perhaps movements could be centered around the assaulted, the raped, the denigrated, and the crucified. In these spaces of abjection, perhaps it is possible to imagine a different kind of humanity that is not structured through the logics of white supremacy, militarism, and colonialism—a humanity for which we as of yet have no words. It is not so much that being oppressed makes one a better person. Rather, when we organize not around gaining credibility and legibility in a society structured by violence, we may begin to imagine some possibilities beyond the current order. Such a project adds new weight to Jesus's words in Matthew 20:16: "So the last will be first, and the first will be last." By giving up an investment in humanity that coheres through racialization, it is possible to invest in a different kind of human for which we have no words. We can begin to create a future of new possibilities—a future in which we take the risk of going on a journey where we have no idea where we are going.

BIBLIOGRAPHY

Adams, Carol. *Neither Man nor Beast: Feminism and the Defense of Animals*. New York: Continuum, 1994.
Brock, Rita Nakashima, and Rebecca Parker. *Saving Paradise: How Christianity Traded Love of This World for Crucifixion and Empire*. Boston: Beacon Press, 2008.
Brown, Joanne Carlson, and Rebecca Parker. "For God So Loved the World." In *Christianity, Patriarchy and Abuse: A Feminist Critique*, edited by Joanne Carlson Brown and Carol Bohn, 1–30. New York: Pilgrim, 1989.
Crenshaw, Kimberle. "Mapping the Margins: Intersectionality, Identity Politics, and Violence against Women of Color." In *Critical Race Theory: The Key Writings that Formed the Movement*, edited by Kimberle Crenshaw, Neil Gotanda, Gary Peller, and Kendall Thomas, 357–383. New York: New Press, 1996.
Gilmore, Ruth Wilson. *Golden Gulag: Prisons, Surplus, Crisis, and Opposition in Globalizing California*. Berkeley: University of California Press, 2007.
Han, Sora. "Strict Scrutiny: The Tragedy of Constitututional Law." In *Beyond Biopolitics: Essays on the Governance of Life and Death*, edited by Patricia Clough and Craig Willse, 106–138. Durham: Duke University Press, 2011.
Pinn, Anthony. *Why, Lord? Suffering and Evil in Black Theology*. New York: Continuum, 1995.
Puar, Jasbir. *Terrorist Assemblages: Homonationalism in Queer Times*. Durham: Duke University Press, 2007.
Rah, Soong-Chan. Plenary Address, NAIITS Conference, Wheaton, IL, June 9, 2012.
Rickert, Levi. *Remembering 9/11*. Native News Network, September 11, 2012. www.nativenewsnetwork.com/remembering-9-11-2012.html
Sexton, Jared. "The Vel of Slavery: Tracking the Figure of the Unsovereign." *Critical Sociology* 42, no. 4–5 (2016): 583–597.

Silva, Denise Ferreira da. *Toward a Global Idea of Race*. Minneapolis: University of Minnesota Press, 2007.

Stanley-Becker, Isaac. "Christine Blasey Ford and the Dark Side of Laughter." *Washington Post*. September 28, 2018. www.washingtonpost.com/news/morning-mix/wp/2018/09/28/christine-blasey-ford-and-the-dark-side-of-laughter.

Theriault, Henry. "Against the Grain: Critical Reflections on the State and Future of Genocide Scholarship." *Genocide Studies and Prevention: An International Journal 7*, no. 1 (2012): 123–144.

Weheliye, Alexander G. *Habeas Viscus: Racializing Assemblages, Biopolitics, and Black Feminist Theories of the Human*. Durham: Duke University Press, 2014.

Wilderson, Frank. *Red, White & Black: Cinema and the Structure of U.S. Antagonisms*. Durham: Duke University Press, 2010.

Williams, Delores. *Sisters in the Wilderness: The Challenge of Womanist God-Talk*. Maryknoll: Orbis, 1994.

Wrone, David, and Russel Nelson, eds. *Who's the Savage? The Documentary History of the Mistreatment of the Native North Americans* Malabar: Robert Krieger Publishing, 1982.

Wynter, Sylvia. "Columbus, the Ocean Blue, and Fables That Stir the Mind: To Reinvent the Study of Letters." In *Poetics of the Americas*, edited by Bainard Cowan and Jefferson Humphries, 141–164. Baton Rouge: Louisiana State University Press, 1997.

NOTES

1. Levi Rickert, *Remembering 9/11*. Native News Network, September 11, 2012. www.nativenewsnetwork.com/remembering-9-11-2012.html

2. Sora Han, "Strict Scrutiny: The Tragedy of Constitutional Law," in *Beyond Biopolitics: Essays on the Governance of Life and Death*, ed. Patricia Clough and Craig Willse (Durham: Duke University Press, 2011).

3. Kimberle Crenshaw, "Mapping the Margins: Intersectionality, Identity Politics, and Violence against Women of Color," in *Critical Race Theory*, ed. Kimberle Crenshaw, et al. (New York: New Press, 1996).

4. Jasbir Puar, *Terrorist Assemblages* (Durham: Duke University Press, 2007).

5. Joanne Carlson Brown and Rebecca Parker, "For God So Loved the World," in *Christianity, Patriarchy and Abuse*, ed. Joanne Carlson Brown and Carol Bohn (New York: Pilgrim, 1989), 8. See also Delores Williams, *Sisters in the Wilderness* (Maryknoll: Orbis, 1994); Rita Nakashima Brock and Rebecca Parker, *Saving Paradise* (Boston: Beacon Press, 2008).

6. Anthony Pinn, *Why, Lord?* (New York: Continuum, 1995), 157.

7. Soong-Chan Rah, Plenary Address, NAIITS Conference, Wheaton, IL, June 9, 2012.

8. Alexander G. Weheliye, *Habeas Viscus* (Durham: Duke University Press, 2014); Jared Sexton, "The Vel of Slavery: Tracking the Figure of the Unsovereign," *Critical Sociology* 42, no. 4–5 (2016); Frank Wilderson, *Red, White and Black* (Durham: Duke University Press, 2010).

9. Weheliye, *Habeas Viscus*; Denise Ferreira da Silva, *Toward a Global Idea of Race* (Minneapolis: University of Minnesota Press, 2007); Sylvia Wynter, "Columbus, the Ocean Blue, and Fables That Stir the Mind: To Reinvent the Study of Letters," in *Poetics of the Americas*, ed. Bainard Cowan and Jefferson Humphries (Baton Rouge: Louisiana State University Press, 1997).

10. Ruth Wilson Gilmore, *Golden Gulag* (Berkeley: University of California Press, 2007), 28.

11. Wilderson, *Red, White and Black*, 23.

12. *Borders v. Rippey* (N.D. Tex. 1960) 184 F.Supp. 402, 405–407.

13. *Neal v. Farmer* (1851) 9 Ga. 555, 568–569.

14. *Neal v. Farmer* (1851) 9 Ga. 555, 581–582.

15. *State v. Foreman* (1835) 16 Tenn. 256, 266–344.

16. *State v. Belmont* (S.C. App. L. 1848) 35 S.C.L. 445, 447–448.

17. *Hirabayashi v. U.S.* (1943) 320 U.S. 81, 101.

18. Strict scrutiny is the most stringent standard the government must past before engaging in discrimination—the policy must be necessary to serve a compelling government interest. Strict scrutiny standards apply for racial and national origin discrimination, intermediate scrutiny applies for gender discrimination, and rational basis (the least stringent standard) applies for all other forms of discrimination.

19. Mark 15:6–15.

20. David Wrone and Russel Nelson, eds., *Who's the Savage?* (Malabar: Robert Krieger Publishing, 1982), 123.

21. Henry Theriault, "Against the Grain: Critical Reflections on the State and Future of Genocide Scholarship," *Genocide Studies and Prevention: An International Journal 7*, no. 1 (2012): 144.

22. Luke 23:6–12.

23. Luke 22:48

24. Carol Adams, *Neither Man Nor Beast* (New York: Continuum, 1994), 101

25. Isaac Stanley-Becker, "Christine Blasey Ford and the Dark Side of Laughter," *Washington Post*, September 28, 2018. www.washingtonpost.com/news/morning-mix/wp/2018/09/28/christine-blasey-ford-and-the-dark-side-of-laughter.

26. John 3:3.

27. 2 Cor 5:17.

28. Luke 5:30–32.

TWO

Manifesting Evil

*The Doctrine of Discovery as Christianized Genocide in
the Lives of Indigenous Women and Their Communities*

Lisa Dellinger

NOTHING NEW UNDER THE SUN

Images of yellow and brittle parchment lying among antique maps and
charts come to mind when hearing the phrase "The Doctrine of Discovery."[1] This Doctrine carries with it a history often portrayed as a nostalgic
and careful crafting of the origin story of U.S. democracy. The nation is
often falsely depicted through a sepia-tinted lens shaded with romantic
longings for adventure and wealth, backlit by the glow of settler colonial
pursuits for freedom, creating America ex nihilo.[2] The U.S. story is fully
developed through the labor of Christian men and women who, with
God's blessing, discovered then conquered this land to make the home of
the free and the brave. Pioneers, indivisibly forging our nation under
God with liberty and justice for all, are praised and memorialized.[3] The
discourse of the doctrine underscores these foundational claims of Euro-
American, Christian nation-building in ways that vilify and dismantle
Indigenous communities. Discovery implies God-given superiority over
non-Christians in such a way that biblically requires the genocide of
heathen pagans through military action. The purpose of this chapter is to
illustrate how the Doctrine of Discovery and its Christianized discourse,
especially the theological doctrine of sin, became the foundation of the
U.S. settler-colonial empire's genocidal action against Indigenous women
and their communities. The current sitting president, Donald Trump, em-

bodies a prime example of the influence of this long-standing practice of aggression and disrespect. Trump made anti-Native American statements well before and after his inauguration. Trump engaged in rhetoric about Native Americans to initiate his own antagonistic crusade on the growing Native American gaming business during the 1990s, which he regarded as a danger to his gambling interests. Trump covertly invested one million dollars of his own money to run ads that insinuated that Native Americans provided a haven for organized crime, that reservations were filled with criminals, and that dark-skinned Natives were fake Indians.[4] Most infamously, during a ceremony to honor three Navajo/Diné code talkers for their service in WWII, Trump used the occasion as an opportunity to make a slur against Democratic Massachusetts Senator Elizabeth Warren by mocking her claims of Cherokee ancestry. In this setting, Trump not only added insult to injury by praising the soldiers in front of a picture of President Andrew Jackson, who enforced the Trail of Tears, but he also used the name of Pocahontas to insult the woman who openly challenged his policies.[5] Trump's actions to ridicule Sen. Warren also served in demeaning all Native American women. His choice of Pocahontas as a pejorative term is in itself telling of the deep misogyny and fetishization of Native women throughout the United States's settler-colonial narrative and history. The story of Pocahontas is not one of a princess in love with a white man. It is a real life disaster of "a young Native girl who was kidnapped, sexually assaulted, and allegedly murdered by those [English men] who were supposed to keep her safe."[6] The desire to undercut the economic resources, define the cultural identity, and deny the integrity of Indigenous bodies continues through contemporary settler-colonial U.S. policy and practice.

The study that follows explicates how the language of the Doctrine of Discovery wed to ideas about the Christian doctrine of sin formed U.S. law to create a reality that reinforced this white, patriarchal supremacy and violence against Indigenous peoples, especially Native American female bodies.[7] My exploration is not strictly historical in nature but engages with how the foundational rhetoric of Christian conquest manifests in contemporary U.S. military actions taken against Indigenous women and their communities, both domestically and globally.

Context is important for understanding any writer's experience and motivation for investigating any subject. I begin by sharing some of the context that has shaped my work on the role of Christian Discovery in the lives of Indigenous women. Next, special attention is given to the biblical letter of the law in regards to the development of the Doctrine of Discovery, with its reliance on heathen language, which shapes the mentality and behavior of settler-colonial "management" of land and the Indigenous peoples encountered in this new world. Thirdly, I look at how the construction of the Christian identity of the settler-colonial system deploys a theological doctrine of sin to deem Indigenous bodies to be worthy of destruction within the legal code. Finally, I show how militarized violence against Native women is so normalized as a part of this U.S. identity that borders are violated or seen as irrelevant as others around the globe are Indigenized and marked for civilizing or extinction.

Contextualizing the Influence of the Doctrine of Discovery in Everyday Life

My understanding of my role in this celebrated history is complicated because of who I am and where I grew up. Less than four miles from Tinker Air Force Base in Oklahoma, I lived near streets named Mid America Boulevard, Air Depot, Boeing Drive, Soldier Creek, Choctaw Road, Indian Drive, and Sooner Road. All these names reflect a curious mash-up of military pride, American patriotism, and the veneration of the displacement of the Native peoples already removed from their ancestral homes.[8] Very aware of my Chickasaw, Mexican American, and Euro-American heritage, I was only vaguely cognizant of the paradox of my hometown's occupation and founding. This nascent awareness of the disconnection between the stories of military glory and the absence of Indigenous presence manifested as an uncomfortable awkwardness inside my physical being. I found myself occasionally, inexplicably recoiling from the norms of life in a city built to enable the U.S. military-industrial complex.[9] For example, my education took place where the institutional mascots representing our school spirit were the Eastside Jets, the Jarman Junior High Rockets, and the Midwest City High School Bombers. Though a child, I felt a nameless sense of anxiety seeing this embodiment of school pride that required the acceptance of tools of violence as essential to my own identity within my community. To this day, confusion and alarm fill me at the idea of children being asked to normalize aerial weapons of empire through processes of self-identification and valorization. In my quest to understand my feelings of displacement, as an adult I began to investigate the theological implications of the patriotic language of God and country. This pursuit led me back to the text of the Doctrine of Discovery. I gradually realized the Doctrine does not live in some distant past. The language of Christian Discovery continues to shape our Indigenous and settler-colonial community at the most rudimentary levels.[10] The Doctrine of Discovery is not just paper and ink. The Doctrine lives on in the skin and the blood of modern American society. The document compels each of us to function as ongoing mechanisms of imperial denial, cultural genocide, and/or as the victims of a predestined history. Christian settlers become the inheritors of an inevitable and glorious destiny, and the "heathen" American Indians become the living ghosts of a long-gone era.[11] The needed binary is never easily defined in flesh and blood contexts where these divisions are never cleanly or completely isolated.[12] The mythos of an arcane Discovery serves to erase the ever-expanding influence of this living document on U.S. imperialism, both domestically and at work globally. In order to understand how the Doctrine of Discovery continues to influence historic, cognitive, and gendered ideologies that materially impact the lives of Indigenous women and their communities beyond U.S. borders, an exploration must begin with the document's origins in a narrative of Christian empire and its induction into U.S. law.

From Biblical Words to the Doctrine of Discovery

Words hold a special power, especially in the Christian faith, where the Word is synonymous with Jesus, the One who speaks for God, and is the fulfillment of the Law. Jesus, in his capacity as the One, also issues the Great Commandment: Go and make disciples of all the nations.[13] These words of mission continue to ring out in the contemporary churches. When I hear them, I often remember when my grandfather once scolded me for saying God in a fit of exasperation. A Chickasaw and a Christian, he told me to never speak God's name in anger, glibly, or without serious consideration. He went on to explain that the name God holds a special kind of life and danger to it. Once this scriptural word, God, is invoked, one can never truly be certain how resulting consequences might unfold. His lesson to me still rings true: words, especially when spoken by an unquestioned authority, are never just words, because they form the bodies of knowledge, faith, practice, and culture that create our realities. Christian themes, metaphors, and concepts influenced the projects of Euro-Enlightenment such as law, science, and history. All of these disciplines are tools used to justify and inscribe acts of imperialism onto the bodies of land and the land of bodies "discovered" in the Americas.[14]

The biblical text itself became a primary frame through which this New World reality could be interpreted and explained.[15] For example, Robert Warrior's significant work illustrates how the words of the Hebrew Testament are utilized as proof texts for the justification of murderous violence against Indigenous peoples in the role of the new Canaanites and land invasion perpetrated by God's Chosen people.[16] The words found in the Exodus and Conquest narrative organized the grammar of holy crusade, imperialism, and the continued occupation of stolen lands through the practices of colonialism and neocolonialism.[17] These scriptures became the nexus for the fifteenth-century papal decree that would become "the foundation of property law, nationhood, and federal Indian law in the early nineteenth century."[18]

The document that began the practice of discovery as a tool of empire was issued on May 4, 1493, by Pope Alexander VI in the form of a demarcation bull, which granted Spain possession of lands discovered by Christopher Columbus. The theocratic wedding of Christian and political authorities served to ensure Spain was granted ownership by papal bull proclaiming that "barbarous nations be overthrown and brought to the [Catholic] faith itself," and established "by the Authority of Almighty God conferred upon us in blessed Peter and the vicarship of Jesus Christ" then carved out territory discovered in the Western Hemisphere that was not in the "actual possession of any Christian king or prince."[19] The bull further stipulates that Spanish royalty must do the following:

> Moreover we command you in virtue of holy obedience that, employing all due diligence in the premises, as you also promise—nor do we doubt your compliance therein in accordance with your loyalty and royal greatness of spirit—you should appoint to the aforesaid mainlands and islands worthy, God-fearing, learned, skilled, and experienced *men*, in order to instruct the aforesaid inhabitants and residents in the Catholic faith and train them in good morals.[20]

To dispute or to infringe on this mandate would result in the offender "incur(ing) the wrath of Almighty God and of the blessed apostles Peter and Paul."[21] It is important to note not only the semantics of a political Christendom but also the emphasis on the male as bearing the divine right of conquest, possession, and moral authority. Like the new lands, the Indigenous bodies were taken charge of and made to conform by coercion and force. The Native peoples are marked by the Euro-colonial practices of domination and subjugation, which assume notions of "white" supremacy and technological superiority.[22] This hegemonic social illusion functions to keep Native peoples in the role of Canaanite or as the irredeemable other that must be managed or destroyed for the sake of civilization to progress away from the backwardness of the primitive condition.

The Doctrine of Discovery provided the United States government a foundation for its ideology of Manifest Destiny and solidified its presumptions of unquestioned authority into law with the 1823 Supreme Court case *Johnson v. McIntosh*.[23] Chief Justice John Marshall's opinion affirmed the feudal rights of conquest established by the Doctrine of Discovery's legitimizing of the European's superior rights in the New World for the public good that effectively denied the American Indian Nations's territorial sovereignty to lands they occupied from time immemorial.[24] The Supreme Court interpreted the Doctrine as "when European, Christian nations discovered new lands, the discovering nation automatically gained sovereignty and property rights in the lands of non-Christian, non-European Peoples" who were residing in and making use of the land. "This European title," the Court claimed, "granted the discovering nation the exclusive right to buy the land whenever the natives consented."[25] This title or granted right is formally known by the term "power of preemption." Only the United States is allowed to negotiate with Native peoples for land, and Native peoples cannot *sell* their land to any other nation but the discovering nation. By this logic, the United States guaranteed westward expansion and the means of deploying various treaties to purchase "European title."[26] Over time, this strategy assured a lack of competition with European nations and allowed the United States to concentrate its efforts on the practice of removing Indigenous opposition to the acquisition of the land. Despite the United States labeling of sparsely populated areas as terra nullius, or vacant lands, this land continued to be occupied and used as a source of spiritual and daily life by the Native peoples.[27] Under the conditions of the Discovery Doctrine, the land could be legitimately taken if the Native peoples consented through the use of contracts or treaties or if they were defeated in a "war."[28] This particular lexicon of colonialism gave rise to the genocidal projects of coercive treatises, military removals, reservations systems, and indoctrinations to Euro-American supremacy through formal education, including abusive, state-sponsored, Christian-run boarding schools.[29] These practices severely limited, and in some cases eradicated, the right to self-determination, property, commercial, and human rights for Indigenous peoples. All of these legal maneuverings work together to contribute to the misconception of the U.S. federal government as the guardian of Indigenous populations and natural resources.

This Christian Doctrine of Discovery is the basis for the regulation of Indigenous bodies discovered in the New World. Chief Justice Marshall appeals directly to this papal document in his formal legal opinion. Knowing how the Doctrine's language of supremacy works is critical to understanding the construction of this legal precedent as racist and self-aggrandizing. The federal government uses Marshall's reading to legitimatize a political agenda that is in direct violation of the U.S Constitution, which interprets the First Amendment as upholding a vitally necessary separation between church and state. A central argument against this hegemonic, theocratic interpretation may be based on the assertion that culturally derived metaphors, or words, construct a false literalism when interpreting social realities.[30] These cultural metaphors impact legally binding case law to sustain and fix social power in the United States by authorizing Euro-American white privilege and disenfranchising Indigenous peoples.[31] This disempowerment is the direct result of the predominate use of raced and sexualized Christian metaphors of chosenness and a God-given promised land to establish rule over Native Americans by a claim to a Christian/civilized Discovery.[32] *Johnson v. McIntosh* is foundational to the construction of settler colonialism as the primary mode of "meaning making" and the daily language within U.S. social reality. The reliance on the terms "Christians" and "heathens" in *Johnson v. McIntosh* is an illegitimate pretext for furthering legislation for the sake of domination. This willful blindness to the existence of separation between church and state allows the Court to blatantly ignore its founding dogma and to advance the colonial interests of the United States.[33]

The language of the Christian doctrine of sin as applied to Native identity being primarily heathen deeply impacted the legal discourse in the *Johnson v. McIntosh* case that came to shape U.S. Indian law. The presumptions of the Christianized, Manichean logic of righteous Christian versus sinning pagan in the legal code becomes so ingrained by usage that these classifications largely go unquestioned and are presumed to be literally the Truth. This analysis goes unrecognized as an artificial construct based on a very narrow Eurocentric context designed to set up an oppositional, binary relationship. This version of universal truth is then presented as the unquestioned standard for all people and in every circumstance because the words are couched in the seeming objectivity of legal discourse, lending the appearance of legitimacy. These binaries also utilize biblical language to systematize an unquestioned wounding of Indigenous peoples in the flesh by denying the sacredness of their humanity as well as their rights.

The conqueror-subjugated metaphors associated with the settlers acting in the role of the Israelites are used throughout U.S. policy development with modern Native nations.[34] The U.S. colonial agenda deploys Christian metaphors to legitimate and legalize the United States's or Christian European persons's theft of lands, resources, and to normalize the destruction of Native peoples, as the Canaanite, heathen, or pagan, in the name of God. The allegorical language of religion in the legal code also must be recognized in order to address the criminal impact it has not only on property rights and the resources of Native American Indians, but also the concrete affects to the spiritual and somatic lives of Indigenous communities. The use of Christian narratives and appeals made in the name of God in the Doctrine of Discovery's official pronouncement is undeniably at the heart of U.S. legal policy and practice. This profane practice is fundamentally what my grandfather and many Native Christians identify as the blatant, dangerous "misuse of the name of God." The biblical eisegesis of colonial legal discourse with its gendered binary and hetero-hierarchical hermeneutic continue to create a social reality where the violation of and lack of legal recourse for Indigenous peoples becomes an unavoidable certainty.[35] Specifically, colonial language narrating the conquest of Indigenous lands is also reflective of the United States's official management of and strategic disregard for the bodies of Indigenous peoples. This dominant Christian mindset can be traced to the writings of Puritan intellectuals like John Cotton, William Bradford, John Winthrop, and Increase Mather.[36] The influence of the Doctrine of Discovery on the journals, sermons, and historical literature of the time asserted "God had meant the savage Indian's land for the civilized English and, moreover, had meant the savage state itself as a sign of Satan's power and savage warfare as a sign of earthly struggle and sin. The colonial enterprise was in all ways a religious enterprise."[37] The Doctrine's ideology of white, Christian privilege attached to legal decisions continues to negatively impact Indigenous economic and cultural claims to their homelands. As recently as 2005, the case of *City of Sherrill v. Oneida Nation* came before the U.S. Supreme Court. The Court "ruled that land bought by the Oneidas does not fall under their sovereignty and therefore is not exempt from municipal taxation."[38] The majority opinion, given by Ruth Bader Ginsberg, acknowledged in the decision that the land was historically recognized as the property of the federally recognized Oneida "reservation" and unlawfully sold to whites in 1807. The Oneida pressured and eventually displaced by New York State and the federal government only became able to legally purchase back the land in 1997–1998. In his book, *Manifesting America*, Mark Rifkin notes that "Ginsberg invoked the 'impossibility doctrine' which refers to the 'impracticability of returning to Indian control land that generations earlier had passed into numerous private hands' particularly given its likely 'disruptive' effects in light of the 'justifiable expectations' of non-Indian residents (1490–92)."[39] The court applied on the "acquiescence doctrine" to establish that despite filing their claims promptly after reacquiring the property, following the legal process did not overcome the Oneidas's failure to reclaim ancient prerogatives earlier or lessen the problems associated with their relinquishment of the "reigns of government."[40] Essentially, the court ruling took the position that too much time had passed and implied that the dispossessed Oneida failed to overcome their subjugation soon enough to make a legitimate claim to self-determination, also known as tribal sovereignty. Despite the passage of time and a greater awareness of the historic wrongs against Indigenous nations, the settler sins of theft and violence continue to be forgiven and rewarded by the highest court in the land.

THE BLOOD AND THE BODY (POLITIC)

How is it that the sins of settlers are so readily forgiven and yet the Indigenous peoples continue to be judged harshly, as in the case of the Oneida? Interpretations of the world from the Euro-Christian context stand in sharp contrast to the Indigenous cosmologies that settlers encountered when they arrived in North America. The European West had a long history of theocracy as evidenced by the authority of the papacy's Doctrine of Discovery in dictating international law. By the time of the North American invasion, Christian theology had created well-defined and codified ideas about humanity's relationship to sin. The commitment to upholding the principles of the Christian God continued to hold sway even as theocracy gave way to the Enlightenment principles of democracy. The new Euro-American pursuit of a free and abundant New Jerusalem dictated that evil is to be subdued and converted or it must be destroyed for the sake of righteousness. The society of white mythology, as the bearer of the Truth, must defend itself against the contamination by cleansing itself of the parasitic danger of racial, sexual, economic, and cultural difference. The Euro-Christian convention historically retrofit scripture into the geopolitical narrative by describing the intrusion of sin on God's perfect creation to explicate its own white superiority.

This scripture is particularly interpreted through the work of the Christian theologian Saint Augustine of Hippo to establish many of the cultural presumptions about the nature of God and human beings that persist even today. Augustine's interpretation focused on the literal meaning of the first three books of Genesis to explicate the God-given order of all worldly things, as well as the appropriate gender roles for humanity, the origin of sin, and the inherited consequences of that sin.[41] Platonic principles of a created hierarchical order may be applied to this creation narrative to show that God is the unchangeable, perfect source of all life and goodness. The ranking of creation places God in the highest seat, followed by the heavenly hosts. Humans fall just below the angels. Augustine believed that "the pre-eminence of man consisted in this, that God made him to His own image by giving him an intellect by which he surpasses the beasts."[42] Animals fall below humanity but are placed above plants and inanimate objects.[43] Heteronormative patriarchy comes into play as woman is described as the "help" of man, meaning that she is created primarily for the purposes of procreation within marriage. Woman, embodied by Eve, is described as being physically weak and intellectually inferior to men. This inferiority goes unquestioned by Augustine, who takes for granted "that men are the measure of creation."[44] Augustine, having struggled with sexual desire as documented in his book, *Confessions*, attempts to justify the goodness of procreation that God intended with the uncontrollable lustful emotions he associates with the act of sex. This leads him to conclude that sex for the purpose of procreation in Eden was performed by an act of will and not irrational desire experienced by humans after the forbidden fruit was eaten.[45] Augustine sexualizes sin, which in his perspective functions as a kind of sexually transmitted disease of the soul that infects all persons generation to generation. He says of Christ's conception, "There was no desire of the flesh involved, which the rest of men who contract original sin are begotten and conceived by."[46] However, all hope is not lost because sin may be resisted/forgiven if the rational individual is or chooses to become a repentant Christian who seeks the goodness of God's grace.[47] Augustine's conflicted relationship with women and feelings of guilt about his carnal desires continue to influence contemporary views on sexuality as sin.[48]

Thomas Aquinas, another influential thinker in the formation of Christian thought, also contemplated the problem of sin and evil. He drew on the philosophies of Aristotle to construct his methodology. Unlike Augustine, Aquinas "does not believe that the reality of original sin is something empirically verifiable. . . . For him, belief in original sin can be based only on divine revelation. . . . Nor does he believe that people are now fundamentally corrupt or depraved."[49] Instead, he asserts that original sin "amounts to a falling short with respect to God" because people are "limited by their bodies and by material objects around them."[50] Aquinas's fundamental optimism about the goodness of people united to the grace that God offers would enable humans to rationally choose Christ.[51] Like Augustine, Aquinas also believed in a hierarchy in which men were ranked at the highest order of creatures made by God, above not only nature in Aristotelian "perfection," but also above women. Aristotle's understanding of biology may also have influenced him to believe that women resulted from a birth defect when male sperm were somehow interfered with in the act of fertilization. He also used the words of St. Paul to explain women's role as the helpmate who was created for the sake of man. Using this logic, Aquinas maintained that women are the physical and intellectual subordinates of men. [52]

Sin so narrowly read becomes the basis for the justified or righteous punishment/eradication in specific forms of racist and misogynistic colonial Christian narratives against Native American Indians.[53] Often equated with imagery of vicious "animalistic" beasts, as "demonic" children of the Devil, or willfully unrepentant pagans, Native peoples were subjected to coerced conversion or death.[54] Purification, or the washing away of sin manifested in Indigenous bodies (defined as peripheral, dark, sensory, anarchic, underdeveloped, and as female/penetrable), requires the shedding of blood. The Indian/Indigenous body is described as "dirty," "rapeable," and "not entitled to bodily integrity."[55]

The settler-colonial system rejected the validity or the existence of other Indigenous cosmologies and epistemologies that could be as complex, structured, and spiritually fulfilling as Western European-influenced Christianity. The colonial project denied the validity of Indigenous identity and social reality as legitimate. The Native American radical vision of creation as an interrelated kinship with no special hierarchy between living and non-living beings, as well as the deliberately non-anthropomorphic representations of the Divine, became branded as idolatry. These Native social structures gave its women property rights, sexual autonomy, and agency in domestic and political spheres, which threatened the objectives of white, male superiority while simultaneously giving rise to the fetishization of Native bodies.[56]

The European/Occident holds to a "white mythology," articulating Christian themes of *chosenness* and *godliness*. The language of oppositional dualism also enables imperial disciplinary discourse and the practice of binary absolutes, which fuel the engine of colonizing operations. For example, the idea of light being opposed to darkness. These Christianized metaphors literally function in the same treacherous manner as the language of the Doctrine of Discovery.[57] If the initial meeting of Native American Indian peoples did not begin with the immediate physical destruction of the Indigenous body, the introduction did begin with the intense observation, description, and classification of the Native land and body as an object for study. The Indigenous body existed as a foil to highlight the exceptionalism of the Euro-Christian body and its corpus of knowledge.[58] The language of conquest sought to define and name the reality of this *new* other being as hierarchically less-than the normative Christian human being and as incapable of possessing salvation or truth through Native epistemologies. The colonial project is centered on the deliberate misnaming and dismemberment of anything not grounded in a Christian, Western European/American origin. This process of "thing-ification," or equating Native peoples in theory and practice as objects, emerged early in the writings of Aimé Césaire, who coined the term.[59] The calculated eisegesis of the Euro-Christian enterprise traded on the multiple, popular treatises on race as a scientific, evolutionary fact in order to justify its acts of racist greed, theft, fraud, and violence inherent in its civilizing mission.[60] In such a setting, racism develops as "internal to the biopolitical state, woven into the weft of the social body, threaded through its fabric."[61] The repercussions of this Euro-American institutionalization of racism means that the specificity of bodies through the visible markers of race, gender, class, national/politico-religiosity, and sexuality collide in a manner so that perceived differences and similarities of culture and contextual knowledge become a pretext for invasion and regulation.[62]

The enduring Christian creation narrative's connection between the female form and metaphors about landforms begins graphically in the journal accounts of Columbus. Blessed and sanctified by Pope Alexander VI, Columbus reports, from his ship's vantage point, that the Earth is not round, as Europeans had supposed, but "was shaped like a woman's breast, with a protuberance upon its summit in the unmistakable shape of a nipple."[63] Within traditional Euro-Christian theology and the social milieu that it influences, there is a longtime association of the male as embodied in the god figure and the female embodied within human sin. This division serves to empower sexism and deny the full humanity of the female.[64] This unconscious acceptance of sexist metaphor as reality is clearly embedded in the words of the Doctrine of Discovery of 1493, as noted above, where men are called on to conquer and hold dominion over the Earth.

The subjugation metaphors of "virgin land" and the feminization of the New World are wrapped in the "metaphysics of gender violence." The violent penetration of the land is enacted through the Euro-American male perceived as figures of menace, given permission to plunder and rape. Furthermore, "in the minds of these men, the imperial conquest of the globe found both its shaping figure and its political sanction in the prior subordination of women as a category of nature."[65] If one doubts the unconscious acceptance of these metaphors as naturalizing violence against the female body, consider the image of the world as a terrestrial mother or Earth Mother. This longstanding image is used within our historic and contemporary societies. From Saint Francis of Assisi's "Canticle of the Sun," written at the end of his life in the thirteenth century, where he refers to "our sister Mother Earth," to the June 2015 publication of Pope Francis's environmental encyclical letter, Laudato Si, which quotes this reference to Mother Earth, we see a span of centuries where this metaphor of feminized land is used.[66] As early as December 28, 2008, Ecuador enshrined rights for nature/Pachamama as a part of its new constitution. Bolivia's Universal Declaration of the Rights of Pachamama, or "Mother Earth," was signed into their national law on Earth Day in April 2010. On December 22, 2010, the UN General Assembly, with all 192 member states in agreement, passed a resolution that put the issue of Mother Earth rights as an item on the UN agenda for debate.[67] China and Europe reaffirmed their commitments to the Paris Climate Accord to save "Mother Earth," as phrased by German Chancellor Angela Merkel in June 2017. This renewed commitment came in direct response to the U.S. withdrawal from the agreement announced by the Trump administration.[68] These references to the female Earth are most often linked to concern about environmental degradation, as "the rape of Mother Earth." This language naturalizes the violation of the Indigenous female (Pachamama), it appropriates the Indigenous name in a move that overlooks the role of colonial commerce progress as a driving force in her exploitation, and it falsely sets up the Western-created United Nations as her declared savior figure.

Persons who align self-identity with white mythology believe Euro-Christian Americans are superior and closer to all deemed closer to the divine. Men of God and the empires they built take these gendered demarcations of exclusionary language literally. The boundaries of inclusion and exclusion mark specific bodies as sinful and therefore as sites where violence can be righteously exercised without consequence. This language accomplishes the division of humanity and establishes the rules of what makes one human. Native bodies are rendered as sinful, soulless, feminized beings present but existing in a white, male-glorified culture without a viable claim to Indigenous land, history, religion, or future. Such bodies may be and are tortured, raped, neglected, imprisoned, pathologized, and murdered by good Christian citizens and their governments.

Those who record history, namely those who have won power, craft our social imagination in such a way that it is edited for content. Only certain colonial realities are possible and the oppressive conditions of settler occupation remain, seemingly unchangeable. In the colonized space, settler and Indigenous persons are made to forget the human capacity for imagination and creating decolonial possibilities. In these Christian and political spaces, the patriarchal voice continues to hold authority in such a way that remembrance is a potent apparatus in defying institutionally endorsed amnesia. Resistance can be enacted through the unfiltered communication of the experiences of multiply oppressed women and their communities.[69] For Indigenous women in the Americas, the feminized language of land seizure and sexualized violence renders them as ghosts who live and die with evil acts forcibly inscribed on their bodies. The acceptance of this Eurocentric reality necessitates the acceptance of the self as appropriately placed outside of society and labeled as evil or outside the bounds of legitimate existence.

During the time of American westward expansion, the literal genocide of Native bodies was the primary method for dealing with the "Indian problem." The closing of the U.S. frontier brought the notion of giving Christian *help* to the Indigenous peoples to assimilate into Euro-American culture and to improve their lives through interventions of the State with the Church. Christian missionaries sought to convert Native peoples from the earliest of colonial times. This process became more systematized as the nation became more domesticated. This partnership provided the government with the opportunity to engage in the humanitarian management of Indigenous bodies and Indigenous economic resources to shore up its power and wealth. The U.S. government and the Church could impose Eurocentric patriarchal discipline and guidance with traumatic and often deadly efficiency. The values of white supremacy and removal from one's family and extended community through missionary-run boarding school education were mandated by the government and imposed on Native children. Children who survived the disease, physical and sexual abuses, and emotional isolation spent years becoming further alienated from both the Native and non-Native society. The goal of this education of indoctrination required the most vulnerable of tribal members to be "completely transformed" into U.S. citizens by enforcing "militaristic discipline and regimented activities, from morning until prayers before bed."[70] Essential to this education was learning the appropriate social hierarchy demanded by the racism and sexism of Euro-American society. The curriculum consisted of the "boys being taught vocational and manual skills" and the "girls were trained to be wives and mothers or for work as domestics in middle-class white families' homes,"[71] ensuring that the students would not be equipped for or allowed to enter into American society as equals.[72] Essentially, the Church and the government utilized the biblical narrative of sin wed to the legal arguments related to the Doctrine of Discovery as mutual reinforcing methods aimed at exterminating Native communities and culture. The colonizer's educational program laid out an agenda to systematically gaslight the next generations of Indigenous peoples to accept societal marginalization and victimization as a result of their own inherent inferiority.

Given the Euro-American Christian milieu's historic infusion of race, gender, and sexuality into its language of sin, sexual violence cannot be ignored or reduced to only themes of patriarchy. Sexualized brutality must be seen for what it is: a strategic, militarized action. While Indigenous bodies are targeted for the economic and political benefit of the settler, it must be acknowledged that gender influences the sexual cruelty in a disproportionate manner. Therefore, as activist and scholar Andrea Smith puts it, "while both Native men and women have been subjected to a reign of sexualized terror, sexual violence does not affect Indian men and women in the same way. When a Native woman suffers abuse, this abuse is an attack on her identity as a woman and an attack on her identity as a Native. The issues of colonial, race, and gender oppression cannot be separated."[73] In the context of rape crisis counseling, Smith recounts how every Native woman who survived sexual assault said that she wished she was no longer an Indian.[74]

Contemporary sexual violence against Indigenous women is rarely investigated, and the perpetrators, if caught, seldom face criminal prosecution.[75] I am aware that Native American Indian women are not the only women to experience abuse; however, statistically Native Americans are twice as likely to experience rape/sexual assault compared to all other races in the United States.[76] This targeting of Indigenous women is not incidental but the result of sociopolitical efforts of colonizers and colonizing institutions who "use tactics that are no different from those of sexual perpetrators, including deceit, manipulation, humiliation and physical force."[77] The Western legal system does not view the crime of rape as a physical wounding not only of the individual woman but also a trauma inflicted on the entire community.[78] Instead, the criminal justice system's "rape law has its roots in European property law," which unites legal code with biblical and theological ideology where "women were conceived of as the property of men—and rape merely a trespass to chattels."[79] The well-documented and much-lamented histories of sexual violence in Native territory have not lessened current rape statistics. Contemporary sex trafficking and prostitution of Native women, especially in man camps located at fracking sites, stand out as being almost indistinguishable from colonial tactics of enslavement, exploitation, exportation, and relocation.[80] Even with President Obama's signing of the Violence Against Women Act in 2013, with provisions intact for Native nations to enforce criminal authority over non-Indigenous offenders, exemption from recrimination is still a standard outcome for even the most violent of rapes and murders in the case of Indigenous women.[81]

The Christian Doctrine of Discovery continues to function as the theoretical scaffolding, built on the bones of these ancestors, for all judicial claims for establishing and regulating the *borders* of Native lands and bodies. Placing and then cutting out these boundaries is actually accomplished under the purview of the massive, well-funded U.S. military.

Campaigns of "blood and soil" ideology are well documented in both historic and contemporary martial and local militia aggression.[82] Extensive accounts of the mutilation and extermination wed to sexual degradation are the underreported legacy of the colonizers who became popularized as heroes of American history.[83] The borders of the land that are confidently referred to as established by the U.S. colonial and neocolonial project are not stable. The internal contestations between contemporary Indigenous nations and government-backed corporations over the environmental abuse of treaty lands and tribal resources are an indicator of just how unstable legal borders are within the United States. This conflict was dramatically witnessed in the November 20, 2016 clash of the Indigenous water protectors with Energy Transfer Partners over the Dakota Access Pipeline's construction through the Standing Rock Sioux Reservation. The water protectors voiced concern for the main water source for the reservation, the destruction of cultural artifacts on the land, and the danger an oil leak posed to the ecosystem. The scene became violent when the Morton County Sheriff's Department assaulted the peaceful demonstrators with water hoses in subzero temperatures, tear gas, and sound weapons resulting in 160 people injured and seven activists taken to a local hospital.[84] This incident highlights the way in which U.S. settler-colonial narratives continue to project their violent, racist anxieties onto Indigenous peoples who practice agency and resistance to exploitation.

The work of creating the American national identity that conceals its Euro-Christian usurper status requires a complex matrix of boundaries, justifications, and categories to delegitimize the original peoples of the continent. The desire to build a wall, either literally or figuratively, does little to dissipate the cruel practice of racialized femicide inflicted on the bodies of Indigenous women and land. Along the national borders to the north and the south, the danger to women continues specifically within the boundaries of the Indigenous female body. Present-day demands for drone surveillance, armed guards, and physical barriers to prevent the flow of terrorism and *illegal* immigrants into suburbia serve to warp recognition of the actual flow of violent aggression from America outward. The United States uses the language of fear to demarcate *ownership* while demonizing the most powerless of populations—the women who experience a raced and gendered form of genocide.[85]

THE RIGHTEOUS CIVIL SWORD, RED AND BLOODY

On the borders, Indigenous women of color often but not always living in poverty experience unimpeded terror beneath the bystander gaze which see death and chose to do nothing to alleviate their suffering.[86] To the north, the Missing and Murdered Women's Movement highlights how the violence is spilling over the imagined dividing lines between the Canadian-American borders. Northern British Columbia's Highway 16, also known as the Highway of Tears, is a 724-kilometer stretch of road that ends at the Gulf of Alaska in the city of Prince Rupert, also called the Gateway to Alaska. This road is infamous for the dozens of women and girls who are missing or have been murdered in its vicinity.[87] In 2014, the Royal Canadian Mounted Police (RCMP) reported that nationally, 1,017 women and girls identified as Indigenous, First Nations, Inuit, or Métis were murdered between 1980 and 2012. This number reflects a homicide rate roughly 4.5 times higher than that of all other women in Canada.[88] As of this writing, the number has jumped to 1,200 and the murder rate is now six times higher. The police force states that of all the victims, only eighteen were found near the Highway of Tears. The local people in and around Prince Rupert believe the number is thirty-three, forty-three, perhaps even more.[89] In the highway murders, reluctance and even refusals on the part of the RCMP to investigate the murders involved deleting records requested by reporters and families under the Freedom of Information Act and actively discouraging family members from putting up flyers or utilizing private investigators.[90] Ominously, the Human Rights Watch documented the RCMP violations of the rights of Indigenous women and girls: young girls pepper-sprayed and tasered; a twelve-year-old girl attacked by a police dog; a seventeen-year-old punched repeatedly by an officer who had been called to help her; women strip-searched by male officers; women injured due to excessive force used during arrest; and other disturbing allegations of rape and sexual assault by RCMP officers.[91]

The unwillingness of the police to protect and willingness to engage in the victimization of women through sexual violence is in essence creating a state-sanctioned killing zone. This war zone is located in a remote region where poor women live without a viable and affordable public transportation system. The result is that many women hitchhike to travel Highway 16 to get basic necessities and services only found in the larger cities. This road is also home to out-of-state truckers further complicating investigations. Most of these cases obviously remain unsolved. However, in 2012, the RCMP utilized DNA testing to name trucker Bobby Jack Fowler, an American, as the killer of sixteen-year-old Colleen MacMillan who was found murdered after going hitchhiking on the highway back in 1974.[92] The police are not unaware that these Indigenous women are being systematically targeted. In fact, Wayne Clary, an RCMP sergeant who was once in charge of the investigative task force, believes many men are actively hunting Native women. Clary told the media, "We've uncovered men who drive vans with the door handles removed from the inside, duct tape, plastic wrist restraints, trap doors. It's incredible to me how many men are capable of doing this."[93] Despite the outrage, the efforts of a National Inquiry, and Indigenous and human rights groups's recommendations, the reports of the killings and the disappearances continue. [94]

The numbers in the South along the Mexican-American border are just as ferociously disturbing. The earliest reports of femicide came from Ciudad Juárez, just across the Rio Grande from El Paso, Texas, a factory town that ranks as the most populated U.S./Mexican border city. [95] The United Nations defines femicide as, "a crime involving the violent and deliberate killing of a woman because of her gender. Although femicide refers to cases resulting in deaths of women, other forms of gender discrimination include degradation of women on a physical, psychological, economic, or sexual level." [96] While not all of the women along the southern border are considered to be from Indigenous ancestry, there is a settler-colonial othering/exclusion that transpires with any group of people not seen as Anglo-American. This insistence on the U.S. Euro-American citizen as the only "legitimate" American ignores the historic invasion of Mexico to intensify U.S. economic and territorial power. Texas as well as California became states under this sweeping policy of expansion through a racialized rhetoric fused to warfare. Manifest Destiny is deployed in such a way that "This ideology normalizes the successive invasions and occupations of Indigenous nations and Mexico as not being colonialist or imperialist, rather simply ordained progress. In this view, Mexico was just another Indian nation to be crushed." [97] The characterization of the Mexican people as lacking the innate ability to benefit from the opportunity to be given them by liberating American armies could only result in being doomed to permanent inferiority and/or to extinction. [98] Racial discrimination against Mexicans also features the same gendered tropes used against Native American Indians, where men were described as lazy and shiftless while the women were cast as sexually exotic and available. [99] This history of white supremacy on the part of the U.S. government continues to impact the discourse and actions of its policy makers today.

The mid-twentieth century turn from colonization by direct rule to neocolonialism, later called globalization, led to further economic agreements that ratified the exploitation of the labor and resources of the former colonies to continue to benefit the rich, former colonizing nations of the world. [100] In this context, the North American Free Trade Agreement (NAFTA) was designed to "establish a free-trade zone in North America; it was signed in 1992 by Canada, Mexico, and the United States and took effect on Jan. 1, 1994. NAFTA immediately lifted tariffs on the majority of goods produced by the signatory nations. It also calls for the gradual elimination, over a period of 15 years, of most remaining barriers to cross-border investment and to the movement of goods and services among the three countries." [101] Juárez's location placed the city on

> the frontlines of globalization . . . well before NAFTA that began officially in 1994. In the mid-1960s, Mexico established the Border Industri-

alization Program to encourage foreign investment and job creation in what began as feminized assembly-line production. From modest beginnings, the labor force has grown to nearly a quarter-million workers in 300 plants in the city, most of them U.S.-owned. Many female workers migrated from Mexico's interior in hopes of finding wealth.[102]

With the introduction of NAFTA, more than three hundred *maquiladoras*, internationally owned factories, maintaining approximately 219,000 workers, moved to Juárez, including General Electric, Alcoa, and Du-Pont.[103] These U.S. corporations, however, did not bring the promised prosperity to Mexico and in some ways contributed to increasing national poverty.[104] In addition to the increase in poverty, the Human Rights Dossier reported, "A spike in female migration to Mexico's borders, stemming from the North American Free Trade Agreement (NAFTA) implemented in 1994, inflamed misogynistic sentiments among many men who saw the transition of women from the home to the workplace as threatening and has contributed to an unprecedented social pathology in which a misogynistic chain of homicides and impunity have occurred."[105] The corporations run constantly, which places the hundreds of (female) *maquila* workers in positions of increased vulnerability, as many are forced to commute to and from work at some of the darkest hours of the day and night. Workers still begin and end these shifts without police or security patrols provided by the factories.[106] Many of the women who were employed by *maquiladoras*, became victims of femicide: "Thus, as a result of the decade-long history of femicides in Juárez, large *maquilas* began to provide bus service to and from the *maquila*, but this has not been an effective preventive security measure."[107] In 2017, the UN Study on the Status of Women, Freedom of Religion or Belief, and Traditions reported,

> Women's bodies have been found riddled with stab wounds and bite marks, exhibiting signs of rape, mutilated breasts, chopped hair and facial disfiguration. Some women have been tied up with their own shoelaces and others have been stuffed into 55-gallon drums filled with acid. Despite intense outrage and public protests within the country and throughout the international community, the Mexican federal government has taken little decisive action in investigating the murders and preventing future ones.[108]

According to authorities, nearly 1,500 women have been murdered in the city, on the Mexican border with the United States, since the mid-1990s. However, the families, who are left to mourn and often search for the bodies without police support, believe the number to be much higher.[109] The women and girls whose bodies are found, caught in what Sergio González Rodriguez calls the femicide machine that he "locate[s] in the Mexican state of Chihuahua, Ciudad Juárez lies in the middle of the borderland that unites Mexico and the United States": an American area containing the "vector of oil fields, natural gas, solar and wind-energy exploitations, and first-class military bases and installations."[110] He goes on to describe how the "systematic actions against women bear the signs of campaign: They smack of turf war, of the land's rape and subjugation."[111] The women are reduced from complex human beings to narratives describing bones and bodies that have been wounded, marked, mutilated, and tortured.[112] While the situation speaks to Mexican government's failures to recognize the misogynistic aggression as multilayered, there is little doubt that the poverty, domestic abuse, drug trafficking, political corruption, and police indifference have contributed to a situation where women are targeted for death.[113] Media coverage and official governmental statements contribute to a tabloid story reminiscent of captivity narratives which entertained readers with stories of Indigenous cruelty, sexuality, paganism, and, I would add, a perceived, perpetual state of victimhood.[114] This calculated representation is a well-worn tactic that attempts to reinforce the ideology of *white* supremacy and to erase the establishment of U.S. geopolitical expansion and neocolonial economics's consequential obliteration of non-white communities.

These gruesome details about the missing, the murdered, and the femicides reenact the horrors of the evil of colonial conquest inflicted upon Native American women and girls. While all these women and girls are killed for reasons known only to their killers, Ann Laura Stoler suggests the details of the slaughter, which rupture into the everyday experience, register emotionally as shocking, yet the recovery comes quickly as a result of familiarity with a practice as old as the colonial encounter itself.[115] In the adventure tales of the conquistadores, we hear familiar resonances: "The Spaniards cut off the arm of one, the leg or hip of another, and from some their heads with one stroke, like butchers cutting up beef and mutton for market . . . Vasco ordered forty of them to be torn to pieces by dogs."[116] Likewise, conquistadores had their concubines's cheeks marked with hot irons as a sign of belonging to their masters.[117] All of the contemporary victims are also cut and often dismembered, mutilated, and sometimes placed methodically and displayed for shocking discovery. The control the killer exercised over their bodies is reminiscent of more than just the Spanish conquest. The connivance of the United States government's "Indian Wars" is vividly wed to a policy of degradation and extinction. One account, which is especially applicable, is of the massacres at Sand Creek in 1864 reported by Lieutenant James Connor. Connor describes a scene where the mutilation of Native female bodies and the removal of sexual organs for display on sticks or to be worn as hats by the soldiers became a source of heroic pride.[118] More accounts are recorded in Smith's work describing the perceived danger of how, "Native women are bearers of a counter-imperial order and pose a supreme threat to the dominant culture" that must be dealt with by those who live committed to the *white* mythology of Western Euro-centrism.[119]

U.S. military violence is routinely used to destroy an enemy by attacking its women, who bring life and security to their communities. As Martin Luther wrote, "No one need think that the world can be ruled without blood. The civil sword shall and must be red and bloody." [120]

The Christianized Doctrine emboldens notions of American exceptionalism and the sense of divine chosenness to vanquish any bodies that stand in the way of its economic and political interests. The same raced, gendered tropes used for Native American Indians are applied to the evil enemies of democracy not only in the past with conflicts within and outside our borders. The similarities between the atrocities of the past and the present are uncanny. The tools of racism and misogyny are still being employed, whether the perpetrator of these crimes is or is not of European descent. The violence weaves itself through and across boundaries to permeate the global cultural imagination in such a way that it infects the psyche of all who encounter it. The expansionistic tendencies that moved the United States from the Atlantic to the Pacific also wreaked havoc on the Inuit communities of Alaska and the Native Hawaiians and on into the Pacific Islands. The language of domestication was clearly present in the words of President McKinley when he named the Filipinos as "orphans of the Pacific" in need of Western education to "uplift, civilize and Christianize them." [121] In this manner, McKinley "eclipse[d] the brutality of the U.S. military campaigns that cost half a million Filipino lives and trivialize[d] ongoing independence struggles by suggesting that Filipinos were incapable of self-government or even understanding U.S. aims." [122] The threat of savage violence to the physical safety or to the economic interests of the United States becomes the vehicle for colonial military interventions abroad over time, including the Korean War, the Vietnam War, the First Gulf War, and the ongoing war on terrorism that brought occupying forces into Afghanistan and Iran. [123] The discourse that accompanies these interventions justifies the construction of military bases to ensure democracy and Christianized values can be fostered while the policing of any threats can be addressed immediately with force. The United States as the "world's sheriff" going into Indian country is a metaphor that is still used to describe the reenactment of discovering people in a state of savagery and delivering them to justice at the end of a gun. [124]

The internalized shame and rage of the experience of genocide and extended occupation by such hegemonic forces imposes a greater propensity toward self-destruction on the part of dominated Indigenous peoples. The concrete expressions of internalized shame that manifest in dysfunction keeps the dominant culture blind to how its systems are complicit in this destruction of Native peoples. [125] As stated in the quotes of the past religio-political leaders, the Native peoples are defined by their lack and their inevitable disappearance. John Eliot stated, "As for these poor Indians, they have no principles of their own, nor yet wisdom of their own, (I mean as other Nations have)."[126] Theodore Roosevelt would sum up his feelings at the death of Geronimo this way: "I don't go so far as to think that the only good Indians are dead Indians, but I believe nine out of ten are, and I shouldn't like to inquire too closely into the case of the tenth."[127] The idea that Native American peoples are primitive and destined for extinction is continually presumed and not just a relic of the distant past. In 1988, when addressing university students from Moscow, Ronald Regan is quoted:

> Let me tell you just a little something about the American Indian in our land. We have provided millions of acres of land for what are called preservations—or reservations, I should say. They, from the beginning, announced that they wanted to maintain their way of life, as they had always lived there in the desert and the plains and so forth. And we set up these reservations so they could, and have a Bureau of Indian Affairs to help take care of them. At the same time, we provide education for them—schools on the reservations. And they're free also to leave the reservations and be American citizens among the rest of us, and many do. Some still prefer, however, that way—that early way of life. And we've done everything we can to meet their demands as to how they want to live. Maybe we made a mistake. Maybe we should not have humored them in that wanting to stay in that kind of primitive lifestyle. Maybe we should have said, no, come join us; be citizens along with the rest of us. [128]

These presidential quotes that betray a negative view of Indigenous peoples that may not be dismissed as a relic of an antiquated past.

Internationally, Indigenous peoples are often characterized as a dying, primal curiosity, as a ghostly "present yet absent" people in the face of the onslaught of global capitalism's progress.[129] While Native peoples and cultures continue to live and thrive in their own communities in spite of hegemony, the predominant narrative of the Native remains one of disappearance. Indigenous women as carriers and inheritors of the future through their reproductive capacities are targets for extermination and sterilization. Hegemonic mythologies make the physical and cultural annihilation of Native nations an obligation and a bloody exercise accomplished through the bodies of their women.[130] This is the legacy of the Doctrine of Discovery, which lives on in our contemporary social imagination and religious political institutions. The language of the election of U.S. settler society by the divine hand of God to war against the sin of savage pagans functions to fulfill its destiny through military conquest. The feminized metaphors of the land normalize Native women bodies to be seen as sites where war is waged to protect American progress and Christian democracy. As a consequence of the push for economic largess and expansive power, evil is manifested within the bodies of Indigenous/Indigenized women not because they are inherently sinful but because they are conceived of as sites where sin can be performed without consequence for the righteous violator. The Doctrine of Discovery is not a dry brittle parchment from long ago; the Doctrine lives in the religious social conscience of white supremacist American identity as the thirsty false idol already distended with, but ever demanding of, fresh blood.

BIBLIOGRAPHY

Achtemeier, Paul J. *HarperCollins Bible Dictionary*. New York: HarperCollins Publishers Inc., 1996.

Adams, David Wallace. *Education for Extinction: American Indians and the Boarding School Experience 1875–1928*. Lawrence: University of Kansas Press, 1995.

Alexander, VI. "Demarcation bull, granting Spain possession of lands discovered by Columbus." The Gilder Lehrman Institute of American History. www.gilderlehrman.org/content/demarcation-bull-granting-spain-possession-lands-discovered-columbus. Accessed June 18, 2015.

Alfred, Taiaiake. *Peace, Power, Righteousness: An Indigenous Manifesto*. Oxford: Oxford University Press, 2009.

Althaus-Reid, Marcella. *From Feminist Theology to Indecent Theology: Readings on Poverty, Sexual Identity, and God*. London: SCM Press, 2004.

"The Ancient Song Behind the Title of Pope Francis' New Encyclical." ChurchPop. www.churchpop/2015/6/18/ the-ancient-song-behind-the-title-of-pope-francis-new-encyclical. Accessed August 16, 2018.

Aquinas, Thomas. *On Evil*. Translated by Richard Regan. Edited by Brian Davies. Oxford: Oxford University Press, 2003.

Augustine. *Confessions*. Translated by Henry Chadwick. Oxford: Oxford University Press, 2009.

———. *The Literal Meaning of Genesis*. Translated by John Hammond Taylor. New York: Newman Press, 1982.

———. *On the Free Choice of Will*. Edited by Thomas Williams. Indianapolis/Cambridge: Hackett Publishing Company, 1993.

———. *The Trinity: De Trinitate*. Translated by Edmund Hill. Edited by John E. Rotelle. Hyde Park: New City Press, 1991.

Barajas, Joshua. *Police Deploy Water Hoses Tear Gas Against Standing Rock Protestors*. Public Broadcasting Services. www.pbs.org/newshour/rundown/police-deploy-water-hoses-tear-gas-against-standing-rock-protesters. Accessed August 17, 2018.

Barnett, Victoria J. *Bystanders: Conscience and Complicity During the Holocaust*. Santa Barbara: Praeger, 2000.

Bellrichard, Chantelle. "Life and Death Along Canada's 'Highway of Tears.'" Vice News. www.news.vice.com/article/life-and-death-along-canadas-highway-of-tears. Accessed February 19, 2018.

Boburg, Shawn. "Donald Trump's Long History of Clashes with Native Americans." *Washington Post*. July 25, 2016. www.washingtonpost.com/national/donald-trumps-long-history-of-clashes-with-native-americans/2016/07/25/80ea91ca-3d77–11e6–80bc-d06711fd2125_story.html. Accessed March 12, 2018.

Brockhaus, Hannah. "The World Needs a Change of Heart on Environmental Issues, Pope Says." Catholic News Agency. www.catholicnewsagency.com/news/the-world-needs-a-change-of-heart-on-environmental-issues-pope-says-27137. Accessed July, 2018.

Brown, Peter. *St. Augustine of Hippo: A Biography*. Berkley and Los Angeles: University of California Press, 2000.

Calloway, Colin G. *First Peoples: A Documentary Survey of American Indian History*, Fifth Edition. Boston and New York: Bedford/St. Martin's, 2016.

Césaire, Aimé. *Discourse on Colonialism*. Translated by Joan Pinkham. New York: Monthly Review Press, 1972.

Charleston, Steven and Elaine Robinson. *Coming Full Circle: Constructing Native Christian Theology*. Minneapolis: Fortress Press, 2015.

Child, Brenda J. *Boarding School Seasons: American Indian Families, 1900–1940*. Lincoln: University of Nebraska Press, 2000.

Comin, Matthieu, and Laurence Cuvillier. "Mexico: Ciudad Juárez, the City of Missing Women." France 24 International News. February 19, 2016. www.france24.com/en/20160219-video-ciudad-juarez-mexico-city-missing-women-murders.   Accessed February 24, 2018.

Coulthard, Glen Sean. *Red Skins, White Masks: Rejecting the Colonial Politics of Recognition (Indigenous Americas)*. Minneapolis: University of Minnesota Press, 2014.

Dabashi, Haimid. *Post-Orientalism: Knowledge and Power in Time of Terror*. New Brunswick: Transaction Publishers, 2009.

Deer, Sarah. *The Beginning and End Of Rape: Confronting Sexual Violence in Native America*. Minneapolis: University of Minnesota Press, 2015.

Deloria Jr., Vine. *God is Red: A Native View of Religion 30th Anniversary Edition*. Golden: Fulcrum Publishing, 2003.

———. *Custer Died For Your Sins: an Indian Manifesto with a New Preface by the Author*. Norman: University of Oklahoma Press, 1988.

———, and David E. Wilkins. *Tribes, Treaties, and Constitutional Tribulations*. Austin: University of Texas Press, 1999.

Dorris, Michael. "The Cowboys and Indians: Reagan's Patronizing Remarks Add Insult to Injury." *Los Angeles Times*. June 12, 1988. articles.latimes.com/1988–06–12/opinion/op-7307_1_american-indian. Accessed March 10, 2018.

Dunbar-Ortiz, Roxanne. *An Indigenous Peoples' History of the United States*. Boston: Beacon Press, 2014.

Escritt, Thomas, and Phillip Blenkinsop. "World Pledges to Save 'Mother Earth' Despite Trump's Snub to Climate Pact." Reuters. www.reuters.com/articles/us-usa-climatechange/world-pledges-to-save-mother-earth-despite-trumps-snub-to-climate-pact-idUSKBN18T1M0. Accessed August 17, 2018.

Everett, Dianna. "Indian Territory." *The Encyclopedia of Oklahoma History and Culture*. www.okhistory.org. Accessed February 11, 2018.

Fassett, Thom White Wolf, and Brenda Connelly. *Giving Our Hearts Away: Native American Survival. A Mission Study 2008–2009*. United Methodist Church: Women's Division, General Board of Global Ministries, 2008.

"Femicides of Juárez: Violence Against Women in Mexico." Council on Hemispheric Affairs. August 3, 2009. http://www.coha.org/femicides-of-juarez-violence-against-women-in-mexico. Accessed on February 22, 2018.

Fink, Chelsea, Emily Bruce, and Denise Lopez. "Maquiladoras, Misogyny, and Migration: Exploring Femicide in Ciudad Juárez." Human Rights in Latin America, UC Davis. www.derechoslatinamerica.com/2015/05/31. Accessed on February 23, 2018.

Floyd-Thomas, Stacey M., and Miguel A. De La Torre, eds. *Beyond the Pale: Reading Ethics from the Margins*. Louisville: Westminster John Knox Press, 2011.

Gabor, Malone. "Femicide: Not One More." Council on Hemispheric Affairs. October 24, 2016. www.COHA.org/femicide-not-one-more.2016/10. Accessed February 10, 2017.

George, Marie I. "What Aquinas Really Said About Women." *First Things*. www.firstthings.com/article/1999/12/what-aquinas-really-said-about-women.   Accessed August 17, 2018.

Gomez, Isaac. "Mexico—The Women of Juárez: Inside the City's Mysterious Murders." Women's UN Report Network. www.wunrn.com/2017/01/mexico-let-us-not-forget-the-murdered-women-of-juarez. Accessed February 20, 2017.

Gonen, Jay Y. *The Roots of Nazi Psychology: Hitler's Utopian Barbarism*. Lexington: University Press of Kentucky, 2000.

Gonzalez Rodriguez, Sergio. *The Femicide Machine*. Translated by Michael Parker-Stainback. Cambridge: Semiotext(e), MIT Press, 2012.

Gordon, Avery F. *Ghostly Matters: Haunting and the Sociological Imagination.* Minneapolis: University of Minnesota Press, 1997.

Greenblat, Stephen. "How St. Augustine Invented Sex: He Rescued Adam and Eve from Obscurity, Devised the Doctrine of Original Sin-and the Rest is Sexual History." *The New Yorker.* www.newyorker.com/magazine/2017/06/19/how-augustine-invented-sex. Accessed August 17, 2018.

Hansen, Jackie. "Missing and Murdered Indigenous Women and Girls: Understanding the Numbers." Amnesty International CA Blog. www.amnestyca.org/2014/09. Accessed February 16, 2018.

Hedglen, Thomas L. "Midwest City." *The Encyclopedia of Oklahoma History and Culture.* www.okhistory.org. Accessed February 11, 2018.

Hixson, Walter L. *American Settler Colonialism: A History.* New York: Palgrave Macmillan, 2013.

Horsman, Reginald. *Race and Manifest Destiny: Origins of American Racial Anglo-Saxonism.* Boston: Harvard University Press, 1981.

Huhndorf, Shari M. *Going Native: Indians in the American Cultural Imagination.* Ithaca: Cornell University Press, 2001.

———. *Mapping the Americas: The Transnational Politics of Contemporary Native Culture.* Ithaca: Cornell University Press, 2009.

Kim, Nami, and Anne Joh. *Critical Theology Against U.S. Militarism in Asia: Decolonization and Deimperialization.* New York: Palgrave Macmillan, 2016.

King, Gilbert. "Geronimo's Appeal to Theodore Roosevelt." Smithsonian Institute Magazine. November 9, 2012. www.smithsonianmag.com/history/geronimos-appeal-to-theodore-roosevelt-117859516/. Accessed March 10, 2018.

Krieg, Gregory. "What Kind of Border Wall Does Trump Want? It Depends on Who's Asking." Cable News Network. www.cnn.com. Accessed January 17, 2018.

Kwok, Pui-lan. *Postcolonial Imagination and Feminist Theology.* Louisville: Westminster John Knox Press, 2005.

Larosa, Paul. "Mystery of Missing and Murdered Women Along 'Highway of Tears.'" CBS News, CBS Interactive Inc. www.cbsnews.com. Accessed February 20, 2018.

Luther, Martin. *Von Kaufhandlung und Wucher, Luther's Works Vol. 15.* Weimer: Weimer, 1524.

Mann, Barbara Alice. *Iroquoian Women: The Gantowisas.* New York: Peter Lang Publishing, 2004.

———. *Spirits of Blood, Spirits of Breath: The Twinned Cosmos of Indigenous America.* Oxford: Oxford University Press, 2016.

McClintock, Anne. *Imperial Leather: Race, Gender, and Sexuality in the Colonial Contest.* New York: Routledge, 1995.

Miller, Robert J. *Native America, Discovered and Conquered: Thomas Jefferson, Lewis and Clark, and Manifest Destiny.* West Port, CT: Praeger, 2006.

Morgan, Rachel E., and Grace Kena. "Criminal Victimization, 2016." U.S. Department of Justice, Office of Justice Programs, Bureau of Justice Statistics. www.bjs.gov/content/pub/pdf/cv16.pdf. Accessed September 6, 2018.

Morrison, Samuel E. *The Intellectual Life of Colonial New England.* New York: New York University Press, 1956.

Moya-Smith, Simon. "Trump's Disrespect for Native Americans is Nothing New." CNN Opinion. www.cnn.com/2017/11/29/opinions/trump-native-americans-moya-smith-opinion/index.html. Accessed March 12, 2018.

Muscati, Samer. "Those Who Take Us Away: Abusive Policing and Failures in Protection of Indigenous Women and Girls in Northern British Columbia." Human Rights Watch. February 13, 2013. www.hrw.org. Accessed February 15, 2018.

National Crime Victimization Survey. Violence Against Women Online Resources. www.vaw.umn.edu/documents/inbriefs/sexualviolence/sexualviolence. Accessed April 10, 2011.

Newcomb, Steven T. *Pagans in the Promised Land: Decoding the Doctrine of Christian Discovery.* Golden: Fulcrum Publishing, 2008.

"North American Free Trade Agreement." U.S. Customs and Border Protection, Department of Homeland Security. www.cbp.gov/trade/nafta. Accessed January 17, 2018.

Pearce, Roy Harvey. *The Savages of America: A Study of the Indian and the Idea of Civilization.* Baltimore: John Hopkins Press, 1965.

Piggott, Stephen. "Hatewatch: Anti-Immigration Round Up 2/14/2018." Southern Poverty Law Center. www.splcenter.org/hatewatch. Accessed February 15, 2018.

Rifkin, Mark. *Manifesting America: The Imperial Construction of U.S. National Space.* Oxford: Oxford University Press, 2009.

Ruther, Rosemary Radford. *Sexism and God-Talk: Toward a Feminist Theology.* Boston: Beacon Press, 1983.

Schilling, Vincent. "The True Story of Pocahontas: Historical Myths Versus Sad Reality." Indian Country Today. www.indiancountrymedianetwork.com/history/genealogy/true-story-pocahontas-historical-myths-versus-sad-reality. Accessed March 12, 2018.

Searchers: A Family's Desperate Search for a Missing Woman Police Can't Find. Vice Canada. 2015. www.video.vice.com/en_us/video/searchers-misty-potts/56002385288359da081ef41c. Accessed February 19, 2018.

Searchers: Highway of Tears. Vice Canada. 2015. www.video.vice.com/fr_ca/video/searchers-highway-of-tears/55f1d0cb2cafb83220be0f4e. Accessed February 19, 2018.

Searchers: Drag the Red. Vice Canada. 2015. www.video.vice.com/es_latam/video/searchers-drag-the-red/55959b5e238147364dbc2093. Accessed February 19, 2018.

Simpson, Audra. *Mohawk Interruptus: Political Life Across the Borders of Settler States.* Durham: Duke University Press, 2014.

Smith, Andrea. *Conquest: Sexual Violence and American Indian Genocide.* Cambridge: South End Press, 2005.

Spanos, William V. *America's Shadow: An Anatomy of Empire.* Minneapolis: University of Minnesota Press, 2000.

Staudt, Kathleen, and Howard Campbell. "The Other Side of the Ciudad Juárez Femicide Story." *ReVista Harvard Review of Latin America.* Winter 2008. www.revista.drclas.harvard.edu/book/other-side-ciudad-juarez-femicide-story. Accessed February 20, 2018.

Stiglitz, Joseph E. *Making Globalization Work.* New York: W.W. Norton and Company, 2007.

Stoler, Ann Laura. *Race and the Education of Desire: Foucault's History of Sexuality and the Colonial Order of Things.* Durham: Duke University Press, 1995.

Stratton, Billy J. *Buried in Shades of Night: Contested Voices, Indian Captivity, and the Legacy of King Phillip's War.* Tucson: University of Arizona Press, 2013.

Sugirtharajah, R.S. *Voices from the Margins.* Maryknoll: Orbis, 1991.

Taylor, Bron. "Debate Over Mother Earth's 'Rights' Stirs Fears of Pagan Socialism." *The Interfaith Observer.* www.theinterfaithobserver.org/journal-articles/2012/5/15/debate-over-mother-earths-rights-stirs-fears-of-pagan-social.html. Accessed August 15, 2018.

Tinker, George E. *Missionary Conquest: the Gospel and Native American Cultural Genocide.* Minneapolis: Fortress Press, 1993.

Tordorow, Tzvetan. *The Conquest of America: The Question of the Other.* Norman: University of Oklahoma Press, 1999.

Treat, James. *Native and Christian: Indigenous Voices on Religious Identity in the United States and Canada.* New York: Routledge, 1996.

"Trump's Wall: President Denies Changing View on Mexico Border Plan." British Broadcasting Company. www.bbc.com/news/world-us-canada-42724380. Accessed January 18, 2018.

"Victims of Sexual Violence: Statistics," Rape, Abuse, and Incest National Network, www.rainn.org/statistics/victims-sexual-violence. Accessed September 6, 2018.

Walker, Jana L. "Safe Women, Strong Nations Project: Ending Violence Against Native Women." Indian Law Resource Center. www.indianlaw.org/issue/ending-violence-against-native-women. Accessed February 11, 2018.

Waller, James. *Becoming Evil: How Ordinary People Commit Genocide and Mass Killing.* New York: Oxford University Press, 2002.

Warner, Meg. "Blood and Soil: Protestors Shout Nazi Slogan in Charlottesville." Cable News Network. www.cnn.com/2017/08/12/us/charlottesville-unite-the-right-rally/index.html. Accessed August 12, 2017.

Whitfield, Henry, ed. *The Light Appearing More and More Towards the Perfect Day. Or, a Farther Discovery of the Present State of the Indians in New England (1651).* Massachusetts Historical Society Collections, vol. 4. Cambridge: 1834.

Wilkins, David E. *American Indian Sovereignty and the U.S. Supreme Court: The Masking of Justice.* Austin: University of Texas Press, 1999.

———, and K. Tsianina Lomawaima. *Uneven Ground: American Indian Sovereignty and Federal Law.* Norman: University of Oklahoma Press, 2001.

Williams, Robert A., Jr. *The American Indian in Western Legal Thought: The Discourses of Conquest.* New York: Oxford University Press, 1990.

Young, Robert J.C. *Postcolonialism: An Historical Introduction.* Oxford: Blackwell Publishing, 2001.

Zinn, Howard. *A People's History of the United States 1492–Present.* New York: Harper Perennial Modern Classics, 1999.

NOTES

1. I will refer to the Doctrine of Discovery also by the names of Discovery or Doctrine to avoid repetition. Capitalization will be used to indicate it is the formal title.

2. America Ex Nihilo is a reference to the Christian concept of Creation Ex Nihilo or God creating the cosmos out of nothing. This idea emerged to establish God as "the sole, sovereign master of the universe directing the work of creation by verbal command and a freely determined plan." Joel W. Rosenberg, "Creation," in *HarperCollins' Bible Dictionary*, ed. Paul J. Achtemeier (New York: HarperCollins Publishers Inc., 1996), 209–210.

3. This notion of empty space where colonists made "America" out of nothing through hard work, bravery, and a vision for justice is reinforced using national anthems and well-rehearsed pledges that are widely recognized. This language serves to indoctrinate the citizens in believing the concept of the United States as a divinely ordained or fated and ethical inevitability.

4. Shawn Boburg, "Donald Trump's Long History of Clashes with Native Americans," *Washington Post,* July 25, 2016, www.washingtonpost.com/national/donald-trumps-long-history-of-clashes-with-native-americans/2016/07/25/80ea91ca-3d77–11e6–80bc-d06711fd2125_story.html (accessed March 12, 2018).

5. Simon Moya-Smith, "Trump's Disrespect for Native Americans is Nothing New," CNN Opinion, November 29, 2017, www.cnn.com/2017/11/29/opinions/trump-native-americans-moya-smith-opinion/index.html (accessed March 12, 2018).

6. Vincent Schilling, "The True Story of Pocahontas: Historical Myths Versus Sad Reality," Indian Country Today, September 8, 2017. www.indiancountrymedianetwork.com/history/genealogy/true-story-pocahontas-historical-myths-versus-sad-reality (accessed March 12, 2018).

7. Steven T. Newcomb, *Pagans in the Promised Land: Decoding the Doctrine of Christian Discovery* (Golden: Fulcrum Publishing, 2008), ix

8. "During the 1820s and 1830s dozens of tribes were removed by treaty under the 1830 Indian Removal Act, which authorized the president to force tribes to cede their

lands east of the Mississippi . . . In 1889 the government specified the enclosed boundaries for Indian Territory, now officially reduced to an area bounded by Texas on the south, Arkansas and Missouri on the east, Kansas on the north, and New Mexico Territory on the west. Soon this area was reduced again when the Organic Act created Oklahoma Territory in May 1890. The Act even more closely defined Indian Territory, reducing it to slightly more than the eastern half of the present state. In the 1905 Sequoyah Convention, Indian leaders sought to bypass the territorial process and bring about separate statehood for Indian Territory. However, with the 1907 union of the Indian nations and Oklahoma Territory as the State of Oklahoma, a separate, Indian-dominated territory/state was no longer viable. During the twentieth century, the generic term 'Indian Territory' came to represent the entire Oklahoma region during the pre-statehood period." See Dianna Everett, "Indian Territory," *The Encyclopedia of Oklahoma History and Culture*, www.okhistory.org (accessed February 11, 2018).

9. "Founded as a military support community in 1942 and located in Oklahoma County nine miles east of Oklahoma City, Midwest City retains that primary function in the twenty-first century. As the metropolis closest to Tinker Air Force Base (AFB), the community has residential, commercial, social, spiritual, educational, and recreational resources to serve the needs of one of the largest logistics and support activities in the U.S. Air Force . . . The impetus for building Midwest City began in 1940 when the U.S. War Department began expanding the U.S. Army Air Corps, constructing air bases around the nation in locations with good year-round flying weather." See Thomas L. Hedglen, "Midwest City," *The Encyclopedia of Oklahoma History and Culture*, www.okhistory.org (accessed February 11, 2018).

10. By "settler colonialism" I am referring to a form of colonialism where the invasion of a non-Indigenous population seeks to replace the original population by "a process that entailed the demarcation and control, boundaries, maps, surveys, treaties, seizures, and the commodification of the land," which ultimately drove an ethnic cleansing of the continent. Walter L. Hixson, *American Settler Colonialism: A History* (New York: Palgrave Macmillan, 2013), viii.

11. In this chapter, I will refer to the Indigenous peoples throughout the Americas as Native American Indians, or Native peoples, Indians, and/or Native Americans. The terms are used interchangeably to avoid tedium. Indigenous communities often self-identify by these titles or variations on these names, and/or a specific tribal affiliation.

12. In reality, all participants have complex and intersectional experiences despite the attempts of this ongoing, carefully constructed subliminal legacy of the Doctrine of Discovery. In order to show the oppositional binary of white, eurocentric supremacy, I acknowledge the error of this dichotomy but use its language to illustrate its ideology's destructive activities.

13. Matt. 28:19 (New International Version).

14. The emphasis is mine. I, like many Indigenous and non-Indigenous scholars and peoples, challenge the idea that our communities are the objects of discovery. I also will use emphasis with other words like civilizing, legal, chosen, and their derivatives, which create a lexicon to justify Euro-American supremacy and its hegemonic practices.

15. I am not saying that all European peoples or all peoples in general were devout, believing Christians. I am only saying that Christianity is such a part of the cultural milieu that its impact on meaning-making even reaches into disciplines that were labeled secular or rational during the Enlightenment and throughout Modernity.

16. Robert Warrior, "Canaanites, Cowboys, and Indians," in *Voices from the Margins*, ed. R.S. Sugirtharajah (Maryknoll: Orbis, 1991). I am aware of the other Indigenous, Christian scholars's criticism of Warrior's analysis. See: Robert Allen Warrior, William Baldridge, and Jace Weaver, "Canaanites, Cowboys, and Indians: Deliverance, Conquest, and Liberation Theology Today," in *Native and Christian: Indigenous Voices on Religious Identity in the United States and Canada*, ed. James Treat (New York: Routledge, 1996), 93–104. My intent is to illustrate how the narrative of conquest in Christian

identification with chosen-ness or entitlement is the narrative that Euro-American colonizers embraced. Native American Indians's ability to identify with the Canaanites has everything to do with our experience of genocidal treatment and the political reality of occupation.

17. Robert J. C. Young, *Postcolonialism: An Historical Introduction* (Oxford: Blackwell Publishing, 2001), 45. Young defines neocolonialism as a term for "formerly colonized territories" that "gradually had their political sovereignty returned to them, they nevertheless remained subject to the effective control of the major world powers" who ruled them and continue to be subject to a continuing economic hegemony that renders the postcolonial state still dependent on the systems that initially oppressed them.

18. Newcomb, *Pagans in the Promised Land,* ix.

19. Pope Alexander VI (1431–1503), "Demarcation bull, granting Spain possession of lands discovered by Columbus," The Gilder Lehrman Institute of American History, www.gilderlehrman.org/content/demarcation-bull-granting- spain-possession-lands-discovered-columbus (accessed June 18, 2015).

20. Pope Alexander VI, "Demarcation bull." The italics are my emphasis and will be important to remember at a later point in the chapter.

21. Pope Alexander VI, "Demarcation bull."

22. I use the term "white" here to describe the racist and hetropatriarchal hermeneutic, which is the ideological basis for claims of Western Euro-American superiority and not a descriptor for a specific phenotype/race of people.

23. The term Manifest Destiny, coined in 1845, was defined as the right of the United States to expand and take possession of the entire North American continent given by Providence/God to develop the great experiment of liberty and federated self-government without interference from other nations. Reginald Horsman, *Race and Manifest Destiny: The Origins of American Racial Anglo-Saxonism* (Cambridge: Harvard University Press, 1981), 219–220.

24. Robert A. Williams, Jr., *The American Indian in Western Legal Thought: The Discourses of Conquest* (New York: Oxford University Press, 1990), 231. For further reading on this subject, see David E. Wilkins, *American Indian Sovereignty and the U.S. Supreme Court: The Masking of Justice* (Austin: University of Texas Press, 1999). Also, David E. Wilkins and K. Tsianina Lomawaima, *Uneven Ground: American Indian Sovereignty and Federal Law* (Norman: University of Oklahoma Press, 2001).

25. Robert J. Miller, *Native America, Discovered and Conquered: Thomas Jefferson, Lewis & Clark, and Manifest Destiny* (Westport: Praeger, 2006), 9.

26. Miller, *Native America, Discovered and Conquered,* 9.

27. For a further explanation of property and its connection to labor in the colonial mindset, see George Tinker, "John Locke on Property," in *Beyond the Pale: Reading Ethics from the Margins,* ed. Stacey M. Floyd-Thomas and Miguel A. De La Torre (Louisville: Westminster John Knox Press, 2011), 49–59.

28. Miller, *Native America,* 64.

29. For further reading on the subject of boarding schools's impact on Native American and First Nation peoples, see David Wallace Adams, *Education for Extinction: American Indians and the Boarding School Experience 1875–1928* (Lawrence: University Press of Kansas, 1995); Brenda J. Child, *Boarding School Seasons: American Indian Families, 1900–1940* (Lincoln: University of Nebraska Press, 2000); Andrea Smith, "Boarding School Abuses and the Case for Reparations," in *Conquest: Sexual Violence and the American Indian Genocide* (Cambridge: South End Press, 2005), 35–54.

30. Newcomb, *Pagans in the Promised Land,* xxi.

31. I use the term "white" again to describe the racist and heteropatriarchal hermeneutic, which is the ideological basis for claims of Western Euro-American superiority and not a descriptor for a specific phenotype/race of people.

32. Newcomb, *Pagans in the Promised Land,* 51–52.

33. Newcomb, *Pagans in the Promised Land,* xxi.

34. Newcomb, *Pagans in the Promised Land*, 1–12. Newcomb draws his methodology from the scholarship of Steven L. Winter in applying cognitive theory to legal discourse.

35. Gendered binary refers to the divisions made along stereotypical male and female biological and social categories. Likewise, hetero hierarchy alludes to the privileged and sanctified status given to heterosexual relationships and procreation in the Christian tradition.

36. Billy J. Stratton, *Buried in Shades of Night: Contested Voices, Indian Captivity, and the Legacy of King Phillips War* (Tucson: University of Arizona Press, 2013), 1.

37. Roy Harvey Pearce, *The Savages of America: A Study of the Indian and the Idea of Civilization*, rev. ed. (Baltimore: John Hopkins Press, 1965), 20.

38. Mark Rifkin, *Manifesting America: The Imperial Construction of U.S. National Space* (Oxford: Oxford University Press, 2009), 3.

39. Mark Rifkin, *Manifesting America*, 4

40. Mark Rifkin, *Manifesting America*, 4.

41. For further explanation, see St. Augustine, *The Literal Meaning of Genesis, vol. 2*, bk.7–12 of *Ancient Christian Writers: The Works of the Fathers in Translation*, No. 42, ed. Johannes Quasten, Walter J. Burghardt, and Thomas Comerford Lawler (New York: Newman Press, 1982).

42. St. Augustine, *The Literal Meaning of Genesis*, 193.

43. St. Augustine, *The Literal Meaning of Genesis*, 96–7.

44. E. Ann Matter, "Christ, God, and Woman in the Thought of St. Augustine," in *Augustine and His Critics*, ed. Robert Dodaro and George Lawless (London: Routledge, 2000), 165.

45. St. Augustine, *The Trinity: De Trinitate*, bk. 13:23, ed. John E. Rotelle, trans. Edmund Hill (Hyde Park: New City Press, 1991), 362.

46. St. Augustine, *The Trinity*, 361.

47. For more in-depth detail, see St. Augustine, *On Free Choice of the Will*. ed. Thomas Williams (Indianapolis/Cambridge: Hackett Publishing Company, 1993).

48. Stephen Greenblat, "How St. Augustine Invented Sex: He Rescued Adam and Eve from Obscurity, devised the Doctrine of Original Sin—and the Rest is Sexual History," *The New Yorker* www.newyorker.com/magazine/2017/06/19/how-st-augustine-invented-sex. (accessed August 17, 2018).

49. Thomas Aquinas, *On Evil*. ed. Brian Davies, trans. Richard Regan (Oxford: Oxford University Press, 2003), 43.

50. Aquinas, *On Evil*, 44.

51. Aquinas, *On Evil*, 45–47.

52. Marie I. George, "What Aquinas Really Said about Women," *First Things*, www.firstthings.com/article/1999/12/what-aquinas-really-said-about-women (accessed August 17, 2018).

53. Lisa A. Dellinger, "Sin-Ambiguity and Complexity and the Sin of Not Conforming," in *Coming Full Circle: Constructing Native Christian* Theology, ed. Steven Charleston and Elaine A Robinson (Minneapolis: Fortress Press, 2015), 119–132. See this for more extensive discussion of the Western Euro-Christian doctrine of sin as it is interpreted from a Native American Indian, Christian context.

54. There is a whole literary history from Indian captivity narratives, sermons, newspaper accounts, letters, and fictionalized historical accounts taken from European adventurers that present American Indians as the menacing other. Stratton, *Buried in Shades of Night*, 35.

55. Smith, *Conquest*, 8–10.

56. See Barbara Alice Mann, *Iroquoian Women: The Gantowisas* (New York: Peter Lang Publishing, 2004); Barbara Alice Mann, *Spirits of Blood, Spirits of Breath: The Twinned Cosmos of Indigenous America* (Oxford: Oxford University Press, 2016).

57. Newcomb, *Pagans in the Promised Land*, 3–11.

58. Tzvetan Tordorow, *The Conquest of America: The Question of the Other*. (Norman: University of Oklahoma Press, 1999), 14–33.

59. Aimé Césaire, *Discourse on Colonialism,* trans. Joan Pinkham (New York: Monthly Review Press, 2000), 42. His anti-colonial writings along with that of Frantz Fanon and Albert Memmi, would become foundational to the development of postcolonial theory through the works of Homi K. Bhabha, Gayatri Chakravorty Spivak, and Edward W. Said, often referred to in that field as the holy trinity.

60. Ann Laura Stoler, *Race and the Education of Desire: Foucault's History of Sexuality and the Colonial Order of Things* (Durham: Duke University Press, 2000), 200.

61. Stoler, *Race and the Education of Desire,* 69.

62. Vine Deloria Jr.'s seminal work provides a detailed explanation for how Western interpretations of theological doctrine, social sciences, and greed for Native lands and resources were deliberately intertwined to make extermination and cultural genocide a sanctified and necessary form of public policy. See *God is Red: A Native View of Religion 30th Anniversary Edition* (Golden: Fulcrum Publishing, 2003). See also *Custer Died for Your Sins: an Indian Manifesto with a New Preface by the Author* (Norman: University of Oklahoma Press, 1988). George E. Tinker also provides important insights on how the United States and Christian Mission worked together blurring the line of church and state to missionize Indigenous peoples in a state-sanctioned civil religion. See *Missionary Conquest: The Gospel and Native American Cultural Genocide* (Minneapolis: Fortress Press, 1993).

63. Anne McClintock, *Imperial Leather: Race, Gender, and Sexuality in the Colonial Contest* (New York: Routledge, 1995), 21.

64. Rosemary Radford Ruther, *Sexism and God-Talk: Toward a Feminist Theology* (Boston: Beacon Press, 1983).

65. McClintock, *Imperial Leather,* 14, 22–25.

66. Hannah Brockhaus, "The World Needs A Change of Heart on Environmental Issues, Pope Says," Catholic News Agency, www.catholicnewsagency.com/news/the-world-needs-a-change-of-heart-on-environmental-issues-pope-says-27137 (accessed July, 2018); "The Ancient Song Behind the Title of Pope Francis' New Encyclical," ChurchPop, www.churchpop.com/2015/6/18/the-ancient-song-behind-the-title-of-pope-francis-new-encyclical (accessed August 16, 2018).

67. Bron Taylor, "Debate Over Mother Earth's 'Rights' Stirs Fears of Pagan Socialism," *The Interfaith Observer,* www.theinterfaithobserver.org/journal-articles/2012/5/15/debate-over-mother-earths-rights-stirs-fears-of-pagan-social.html (accessed August 15, 2018).

68. Thomas Escritt and Phillip Blenkinsop, "World Pledges to Save 'Mother Earth' Despite Trump's Snub to Climate Pact," Reuters, www.reuters.com/article/us-usa-climatechange/world-pledges-to-save-mother-earth-despite-trumps-snub-to-climate-pact-idUSKBN18T1M0 (accessed August 17, 2018).

69. Kwok Pui-lan, *Postcolonial Imagination and Feminist Theology* (Louisville: Westminster John Knox Press, 2005), 37.

70. Colin G. Calloway, *First Peoples: A Documentary Survey of American Indian History,* fifth ed. (Boston: Bedford/St. Martin's, 2016), 394.

71. Calloway, *First Peoples,* 397.

72. Calloway, *First Peoples,* 397.

73. Smith, *Conquest,* 8.

74. Smith, *Conquest,* 8.

75. Smith, *Conquest,* 30–33.

76. "Victims of Sexual Violence: Statistics," Rape, Abuse, and Incest National Network, www.rainn.org/statistics/victims-sexual-violence (accessed September 6, 2018); See also Rachel E. Morgan and Grace Kena, "Criminal Victimization, 2016," U.S. Department of Justice, Office of Justice Programs, Bureau of Justice Statistics, www.bjs.gov/content/pub/pdf/cv16.pdf (accessed September 6, 2018).

77. Sarah Deer, *The Beginning and End of Rape: Confronting Sexual Violence in Native America* (Minneapolis: University of Minnesota Press, 2015), xix–xx.

78. Deer, *The Beginning and End of Rape,* 109–110.

79. Deer, *The Beginning and End of Rape,* 133.

80. Deer, *The Beginning and End of Rape*, 75–79.

81. "Tribal participation in the new jurisdictional provisions is voluntary. Though tribes can issue and enforce civil protection orders, under VAWA 2013 tribes generally could not criminally prosecute non-Indian abusers until at least March 7, 2015. However, under a pilot project, a tribe can start prosecuting non-Indians sooner if the tribe's criminal justice system fully protects defendants' rights under federal law; the tribe asks to participate in the pilot project; and the Department of Justice grants the request and sets a start date." It is also problematic that "many Indian nations are developing the infrastructure for tribal justice systems to provide safety to Native women and girls within their territories, including tribal police departments, codes, and courts." See Jana L. Walker, "Ending Violence Against Native Women," Indian Law Resource Center, www. indianlaw.org/issue/ending-violence-against-native-women (accessed February 11, 2018).

82. Jay Y. Gonen, *The Roots of Nazi Psychology: Hitler's Utopian Barbarism* (Lexington: University Press of Kentucky, 2000), 69. Blood and Soil or "Blunt and Boden" is associated with the philosophy of Nazi Germany, which romanticized genetic heritage as a pretext for its territorial, eastward expansion through invasion. I am not asserting that the United States government is in fact a Nazi regime. I am saying that Manifest Destiny deploys a similar philosophy of racial superiority and entitlement to its own domestic expansion and its regulatory practices in the international sphere. The phrase even emerged as shouted chants by White nationalists marching with lit torches in Charlottesville at the University of Virginia campus on August 11, 2017. See Meg Warner, "'Blood and Soil': Protestors shout Nazi Slogan in Charlottesville," Cable News Network, www.cnn.com/2017/08/12/us/charlottesville-unite-the-right-rally/index.html (accessed August 12, 2017).

83. Heroes of U.S. history books include Columbus, George Washington, Andrew Jackson, and others who fought Native Americans and instituted policies to their detriment. I use American here as a pejorative . . . a term indicative to the ideology of U.S. exceptionalism and supremacy with progress and Manifest Destiny. By using the term American as an identifier of U.S. citizenship, the legitimacy of claims to American identity of other nations in the Western Hemisphere, especially in the South, is erased or marginalized.

84. Joshua Barajas, "Police Deploy Water Hoses Tear Gas Against Standing Rock Protestors," November 21, 2016, www.pbs.org/newshour/rundown/police-deploy-water-hoses-tear-gas-against-standing-rock-protesters (accessed August 17, 2018).

85. I am referring to the 2016 presidential race when the Trump campaign ran on promises to fix the borders with a wall and highlighted violent crimes committed by undocumented immigrants. The political promises at the Trump rallies invoked the raced and gendered themes of U.S. White supremacy and sought to unite America by returning it to a place of exceptionalism and entitlement. The wall is yet to be built but continues to be debated and championed by his administration. For context, see Gregory Krieg, "What Kind of Border Wall Does Trump Want? It Depends on Who's Asking," Cable News Network, www.cnn.com/2018/01/11/politics/donald-trump-positions-on-the-wall-daca/index.html (accessed January 17, 2018); "Trump's Wall: President Denies Changing View on Mexico Border Plan," British Broadcasting Corporation, www.bbc.com/news/world-us-canada-42724380 (accessed January 18, 2018); Stephen Piggott, "Hatewatch: Anti-Immigration Round Up 2/14/2018," Southern Poverty Law Center, splcenter.org/hatewatch (accessed February 15, 2018).

86. Victoria J. Barnett, *Bystanders: Conscience and Complicity During the Holocaust* (Santa Barbara: Praeger, 2000).

87. Samer Muscati, "Those Who Take Us Away: Abusive Policing and Failures in Protection of Indigenous Women and Girls in Northern British Columbia," Human Rights Watch, February 13, 2013, www.hrw.org (accessed February 15, 2018).

88. Jackie Hansen, "Missing and Murdered Indigenous Women and Girls: Understanding the Numbers," Amnesty International Amnesty CA Blog, September 2014, amnestyca.org.

89. Paul Larosa, "Mystery of Missing and Murdered Women Along 'Highway of Tears,'" CBS News, CBS Interactive Inc, May 27, 2016, www.cbsnews.com (accessed February 20, 2018).

90. Chantelle Bellrichard, "Life and Death Along Canada's Highway of Tears," Vice News, October 16, 2015, www.news.vice.com/article/life-and-death-along-canadas-highway-of-tears (accessed February 19, 2018); Aee also the three-part Vice Canada documentary, *Searchers: A Family's Desperate Search for a Missing Woman Police Can't Find, Searchers: Drag the Red,* and *Searchers: Highway of Tears,* 2015 (accessed February 19, 2018).

91. Samer Muscati, Human Rights Watch, 2013.

92. Paul Larosa, CBS News, 2016.

93. Paul Larosa, CBS News, 2016.

94. Samer Muscati, Human Rights Watch, 2013.

95. Isaac Gomez, "Mexico—The Women of Juárez: Inside the City's Mysterious Murders," Women's UN Report Network, January 20, 2016, www.wunrn.com/2017/01/mexico-let-us-not-forget-the-murdered-women-of-juarez (accessed February 20, 2017).

96. Malone Gabor, "Femicide: Not One More," Council on Hemispheric Affairs, October 24, 2016, www.COHA.org/femicide-not-one-more (accessed February 10, 2017).

97. Roxanne Dunbar-Ortiz, *An Indigenous Peoples' History of the United States* (Boston: Beacon Press, 2014), 118.

98. Horsman, *Race and Manifest Destiny,* 229–232.

99. Horsman, *Race and Manifest Destiny,* 233–234.

100. Young, *Postcolonialism,* 46–47.

101. "North American Free Trade Agreement," U.S. Customs and Border Protection, Department of Homeland Security, January 17, 2018, www.cbp.gov/trade/nafta.

102. Kathleen Staudt and Howard Campbell, "The Other Side of the Ciudad Juárez Femicide Story," *ReVista Harvard Review of Latin America,* Winter 2008, www.revista.drclas.harvard.edu/book/other-side-ciudad-juarez-femicide-story (accessed February 20, 2018).

103. "Femicides of Juárez: Violence Against Women in Mexico," Council on Hemispheric Affairs, August 3, 2009, www.coha.org/femicides-of-juarez-violence-against-women-in-mexico (accessed February 22, 2018).

104. Joseph E. Stiglitz, *Making Globalization Work* (New York: W.W. Norton and Company, 2007), 61–101.

105. Chelsea Fink, Emily Bruce, and Denise Lopez, "Maquiladoras, Misogyny, and Migration: Exploring Femicide in Ciudad Juárez," Human Rights in Latin America UC Davis, May 31, 2015, www.derechoslatinamerica.com/2015/05/31 (accessed on February 23, 2018).

106. Evelyn Nieves, "To Work and Die in Juárez," Mother Jones, May/June 2002. www.motherjones.com/politics/2002/05/work-and-die-juarez (accessed February 20, 2018).

107. "Femicides of Juárez."

108. Gomez, "Mexico."

109. Matthieu Comin and Laurence Cuvillier, "Mexico: Ciudad Juárez, the City of Missing Women," France 24 International News, February 19, 2016, www.france24.com/en/20160219-video-ciudad-juarez-mexico-city-missing-women-murders (accessed February 24, 2018).

110. Sergio González Rodriguez, *The Femicide Machine,* trans. Michael Parker-Stainback (Cambridge: Semiotext(e), MIT Press, 2012), 7.

111. González Rodriguez, *The Femicide Machine,* 7

112. González Rodriguez, *The Femicide Machine,* 12.

113. González Rodriguez, *The Femicide Machine,* 84.

114. Audra Simpson, *Mohawk Interruptus: Political Life Across the Borders of Settler States* (Durham: Duke University Press, 2014,) 96.

115. Stoler, *Race and the Education of Desire*, 89.

116. Todorov, *The Conquest of America*, 141.

117. Marcella Althaus-Reid, *From Feminist Theology to Indecent Theology: Readings on Poverty, Sexual Identity, and God* (London: SCM Press, 2004), 39.

118. James Waller, *Becoming Evil: How Ordinary People Commit Genocide and Mass Killing* (New York: Oxford University Press, 2002), 25–26.

119. Smith, *Conquest*, 15.

120. Martin Luther, *Von Kaufhandlung und Wucher, Luther's Works Vol. 15* (Weimer: Weimer, 1524), 302.

121. Shari M. Huhndorf, *Mapping the Americas: The Transnational Politics of Contemporary Native Culture* (Ithaca: Cornell University Press, 2009), 59.

122. Huhndorf, *Mapping the Americas*, 59–60.

123. For context, see Nami Kim and Wonhee Anne Joh, *Critical Theology Against U.S. Militarism in Asia: Decolonization and Deimperialization* (New York: Palgrave Macmillan, 2016); Howard Zinn, *A People's History of the United States 1492–Present* (New York: Harper Perennial Modern Classics, 1999); Haimid Dabashi, *Post-Orientalism: Knowledge and Power in Time of Terror* (New Brunswick: Transaction Publishers, 2009).

124. See William V. Spanos, *America's Shadow: An Anatomy of Empire* (Minneapolis: University of Minnesota Press, 2000), xvii, 126–169.

125. See Shari M. Huhndorf, *Going Native: Indians in the American Cultural Imagination* (Ithaca: Cornell University Press, 2001).

126. John Eliot in Henry Whitfield, ed., *The Light Appearing More and More Towards the Perfect Day. Or, a Farther Discovery of the Present State of the Indians in New England* (1651), Massachusetts Historical Society Collections, vol. 4. (Cambridge: 1834), 131.

127. Gilbert King, "Geronimo's Appeal to Theodore Roosevelt," *Smithsonian Institute Magazine*, November 9, 2012, www.smithsonianmag.com/history/geronimos-appeal-to-theodore-roosevelt-117859516/#mJTtf8qmb88wRDod.99 (accessed March 10, 2018).

128. Michael Dorris, "The Cowboys and Indians: Reagan's Patronizing Remarks Add Insult to Injury," *Los Angeles Times*, June 12, 1988, www.articles.latimes.com/1988–06–12/opinion/op-7307_1_american-indian. (accessed March 10, 2018).

129. Avery F. Gordon, *Ghostly Matters: Haunting and the Sociological Imagination* (Minneapolis: University of Minnesota Press, 1997), 6.

130. Smith, *Conquest*, 79.

THREE

From Mỹ Lai to Ferguson

Collaterality, Grievous Deaths,
Militarized Orientalism, Benevolence, and Racism

Mai-Anh Le Tran

"A TRAGEDY OF MAJOR PROPORTIONS"

On March 16, 1968, American GIs of the Charlie Company, First Battalion, Twentieth Infantry Regiment, Eleventh Infantry Brigade, Twenty-third Infantry Division, were dispatched to the Mỹ Lai 4 subhamlet in Sơn Mỹ village of Quảng Ngãi province, in what is now the central coast of the People's Republic of Vietnam. Operational under Task Force Barker, a five-hundred-member strike force (self-dubbed "Barker's Bastards") commanded by eighteen-year veteran Lieutenant Colonel Frank Barker of the Army's American Division, Company "C" was to engage in a "search-and-destroy" mission in what was reportedly a "VC hotspot," believed to be a stronghold of the forceful Forty-eighth Local Force Battalion of the People's Liberation Armed Forces of South Vietnam (PLAF, or "Viet Cong"). Just over a month earlier, American and South Vietnamese firepower had managed to suppress a surprise Communist offensive in late January during the Lunar New Year festivities called "Tet," in which Viet Cong and North Vietnamese troops attacked provincial capitals, major cities, dozens of American and South Vietnamese bases, and even infiltrated the U.S. Embassy in Saigon. Though the "Tet Offensive" was defeated militarily, the exhausting brutality of warfare and mounting casualties up to that point was turning 1968 into the "bloodiest year" of what many later would characterize as a "blood-soaked decade"

(1965–1975) of U.S. entanglements in and over Vietnam and Southeast Asia (from the 1940s to 1975). In March of 1968, Charlie Company comprised five officers and some 125 troops commissioned under Task Force Barker's Operation Muscatine to "locate and destroy" PLAF's Forty-eighth Battalion. Anticipating fierce confrontation with the enemy, the soldiers were "psyched" for combat and "revenge for fallen comrades." According to intelligence briefings, civilians had been warned to evacuate the area. It was customary for local civilians—mostly local farmers, many of whom could not read—to be warned of American incursions through dispersed leaflets. Those who remained were to be treated as Viet Cong combatants or sympathizers. Essentially, "Pinkville"—as the region was designated according to population color-coding on military maps—was enemy territory, and it was to be wiped out.[1]

As the world would eventually come to know about a year later, on March 16, 1968, more than five hundred people in Sơn Mỹ village were reportedly killed by the soldiers of Company "C." None of those killed had been armed, and nearly half were teenagers or younger. It took the letter-writing campaign of one veteran, Ronald Ridenhour, who wrote to thirty military and governmental leaders (including newly elected president Richard Nixon) in March of 1969, to generate a series of inquiries into the discrepant reporting of commanding officers involved in the actions on that one day of what was ninety days of search-and-destroy missions in areas designated as free-fire zones. An inquiry by the Army's Criminal Investigation Division (CID)—along with graphic evidence provided by army photographer Ronald Haeberle—confirmed suspicion of a high-level cover-up, and resulted in a commissioned panel of military and civilian attorneys, chaired by Lieutenant General William R. Peers, which took more than four hundred testimonies from military and civilian personnel. In a 225-page public report presented on March 17, 1970, "the Peers commission found that between March 16 and 19 [of 1968], American troops 'massacred' a minimum of 175 but perhaps more than four hundred civilians in the two subhamlets of Mỹ Lai 4 and My Khe 4." Under Pentagon pressure, the word "massacre" was replaced with "a tragedy of major proportions." The report pointed to evidence suppression by division-level officers, and recommended charges against a number of soldiers, including twenty-five officers. The list of crimes included murder, massacre, assault with a deadly weapon, rape, torture, and maiming.[2]

Among the officers eventually charged for war crimes were Captain Ernest Medina, leader of Charlie Company, for issuing the order to kill, and his Second Lieutenant, William Calley of the First Platoon, for ordering the roundup of noncombatants, including women and children, into a ditch for mass shooting, and for single-handedly executing individuals who had attempted to flee. Of the officers charged, all but one was acquitted. Lt. Calley was found guilty of "premeditated murder of at least twenty-two Vietnamese civilians" and sentenced to life in prison. With presidential intervention, Calley's sentence was eventually reduced to ten years, of which he served only four months in stockade before being released on parole in 1974.[3]

William Calley's conviction was met with mixed public reaction. On the one hand, there was already a decisive rise of antiwar sentiment and growing discontent with prolonged U.S. presence in Vietnam; on the other hand, support for a presumed scapegoat could be heard in such rallying cries as "kill a gook for Calley." Was he an exemplar of disciplined obedience to the chain of command, or was he someone who—in the words of lead Army prosecutor Captain Aubrey Daniel—failed to recognize the "fundamental moral principle" of "the inherent unlawfulness of the murder of innocent persons"? Their orders, Calley averred, were "to go in rapidly and to neutralize everything. To kill everything." A member of the Third Platoon corroborated with his version of the perceived mission: the objective was "to go in and destroy the whole thing—women, children, animals, throw bodies in wells, ruin their water supply, kill their work animals. Wipe it out; burn the village. Every living thing. Just kill it. Exterminate." Years later, Calley still insisted, "I did what I had to do."[4]

COLLATERAL DAMAGE: WHICH BODIES COUNT?

"How exceptional was Mỹ Lai?" ask historians attempting to parse the moral perversity of what had transpired. The unsurprising answer is that given the multi-century history of American embroilment in serial warfare—the Mexican War, the Civil War, the Spanish-American War, World War I, the Korean War, the wars in Iraq and Afghanistan, to list a few— Mỹ Lai was but "one of many" atrocities seemingly normalized by governmental policies.[5] Helmed by General William C. Westmoreland, the war in Vietnam—as realized on the ground—was guided by the principle of "attrition," the tactics of which included search-and-destroy missions into free-fire zones to amass victories calculable by sheer "body count," or confirmed enemy kills. In consequence, it was an operationalized "mere gook rule"[6] that made the *count* more valuable than the *body*. Records of the undisclosed Vietnam War Crimes Working Group declassified in 1994 revealed more than three hundred allegations of murder and assault during the war in Vietnam. In Pinkville, apparently more than forty soldiers had actively participated in the killings, and thirteen were accused of rape. Notably, on that fateful day, none of the ground troops tried to stop the crimes, and none reported back to their superiors this "tragedy of major proportions."[7] Following the Geneva Conventions and international laws in the aftermath of World War II, the U.S. Army Field Manual 27–10 of July 1956 instructed military personnel to recognize "certain fundamental human rights of persons who fall into the hands of the enemy"—combatants or noncombatants alike. Lt. Calley claimed no recollection of such training during his accelerated time in Officer Candidate School (OCS). What he testified to was memory of an initiation into fear and hatred for the enemy: "Treat every Vietnamese as an enemy, including the children."[8]

According to the Sơn Mỹ War Remnant Site in Quảng Ngãi, there were 504 alleged victims in the so-called massacre: 231 men, 273 women, seventeen of whom were pregnant, more than half were under twenty years of age, 160 were age four to twelve, fifty were three years or younger. These numbers remain imprecise, as their count was sketchy at best. Initially, Task Force Barker claimed 128 "VC" kills and three weapons capture, with Company "C" reporting roughly ten to eleven civilian casualties, all attributed to artillery and gunship fire. The numbers seemed immaterial; after all, it was an engagement in an enemy-controlled territory that had already been declared a free-fire zone and subjected to B-52 bombings and artillery fire. The objects of pursuit were VCs, and when "body counts became the only yardstick of victory, the rule of the bush was, 'If it's dead and Vietnamese, it's VC.'" The paradox of the body count rule is that it remained indeterminate *which* and *how* bodies counted. In the words of one soldier: "The trouble is, no one sees the Vietnamese as people. They're not people. Therefore, it doesn't matter what you do to them." Thus, while body count may have been a measurement of progress, sometimes bodies were a mere nuisance to mission objectives. More strikingly, the concept of "collateral damage" had mitigated the complicated matters of accounting: it had become the military's best euphemistic reference to the so-called "unintentional" harm brought upon noncombatants and civilian property as an "acceptable cost of war." Within this logic of collaterality, the soldiers of Charlie Company weren't aiming their M-16s at some*body*; they were shooting at some*thing*—as in the order, "kill every*thing*."[9]

The backdrop of the Mỹ Lai killings rescales their tragic proportionality. Lyndon B. Johnson's Operation Rolling Thunder, the authorized bombing of North Vietnam, had been ongoing since 1965; the number of U.S. military personnel in Vietnam had reached 536,100 by 1968; the "sideshow" of bombing in Cambodia begun in 1964 persisted (in which over 2.7 million tons of munitions were deployed between 1965 and 1973); and the covert war in Laos was not brought to light until 1969. In total, more explosives were dropped on Vietnam than in all of World War II—one million tons in the north, and four million in the south.[10] The toll of Vietnamese civilian deaths were later estimated at two million by the Vietnamese government. The number of U.S. casualties is recorded at 58,220. Numbers matter, though not as a gauge for determining the level of atrocity or the portion of appropriate dismay and outrage. Echoing the banality thesis, historian Howard Jones proffers this take on the tragic sublimity of the killings in Sơn Mỹ: "What is perhaps most disturbing about Mỹ Lai is not that it stands out in the annals of wartime atrocities in the American experience, but that the factors and elements that converged there in March 1968 have converged in all wars: debilitating panic, dehumanizing rage, dissociative confusion, the heady sense of power over life and death."[11]

MILITARIZED ORIENTALISM: THE BIO- AND NECRO-POLITICS OF *DOMINUS*

War may have had that "spiritual texture" of a "ghostly fog" that shrouded a soldier's ability to discern right from wrong,[12] but another force was perhaps more corrosive to the fibers of their moral net; or, more aptly, another force itself may have served as the very logic by which the troops in Mỹ Lai 4 and their American compatriots sitting in front of television sets back at home calibrated the ordinariness and rightness of collateral casualties. As John Rowe and Rick Berg argue, along with other commentators advantaged by hindsight, the United States "did not go to Vietnam in search of raw materials, cheap labor, new commercial markets. . . . [It] wanted something abstract, utterly immaterial, and (finally) fantastic: a 'sphere of influence,' a counterweight in the imaginary game of 'balance of power' politics."[13] It was *dominus*, they point out, the "master," who presumed control over his *dominos*. In this vein, American entanglement in Vietnam and Southeast Asia—beginning with its underwriting of France's colonial claims upon Indochina through foreign aid of up to $1 billion by 1954, fortified by an anticommunist "domino theory" of then-president Dwight D. Eisenhower—coheres sublimely with an enduring Orientalist project of Western imperialism.[14] The empire's project was one of liberating those it deemed to be inherently "less than," with a "vision of righteousness" that "glorified the devastation [it] wrought" and necessitated the subordination and subjugation of the beneficiaries of its rescue.[15] Thus, while the United States may reject in principle "the use of military force or the threat of military force to achieve . . . political objectives," America as "superpower," "emancipator," "defender of freedom" reserves the right to "use its influence and its power [read: military force], when necessary and where it could be effective, against any state that defied this principle."[16] Such racist ethos—a self-righteous superiority disguised as a reasoned political ideology of democracy against communism, sloganized into a militant "better dead than Red"[17]—was palpable in the "spiritual texture" of the killings in Pinkville.

On the trails and in the ditches of those subhamlets, this racist Orientalism was militarized, and with it came a militant regime of enemy-making and enemy-slaughtering. In this scheme, the "enemy" became conspicuously invisible, humanly and culturally. They were, at once, indiscriminately uncounted and undifferentiable: a heap of *things*, a civilian or combatant, villager or guerilla, South Vietnamese, North Vietnamese, member of the National Liberation Front, or Communist—the differentiating subtleties did not matter, for within a binary of menace or victim, there was little leeway to consider complicated, multidimensional actors in their own political and economic struggle. Through the magic of both mass and popular media, such projections ossified "Vietnam" for the American cultural imaginary, reinforcing simultaneously the reproduction of an American body politic (liberator and defender of freedom) and the regulation of patriotic citizenship back at home (performed, for example, by the figure of the heroic "political veteran"). Resistance against *dominus* results in extermination (of the foreign enemy) or exile (of the domestic enemy, as might be the plight of the "conscientious objector").[18]

Ironically, this racist, Orientalist project was also in full operation on the home front, as revealed in the racial and classist bias of the infamous draft system: "those likely to benefit least . . . made the greatest sacrifices." The average draft age was nineteen, and higher percentages of draftees were working class, unemployed, and racial/ethnic minorities. Among the men of Company "C," 61 percent were draftees, with an age range of eighteen to twenty-two, and about half were African Americans and Latinos. Against the currents of Civil Rights struggles at home, racial/ethnic minoritized soldiers returning from duty recognized how the purported liberation of oppression in the "third world" was effectively diverting attention from the racial and colonial oppression at home. Martin Luther King, Jr. called the nation's attention to this paradox in his speech "Beyond Vietnam" on April 4, 1967, at Riverside Church in New York City, and he swiftly faced cultural and political ostracization for it. He was assassinated on April 4, 1968, just nineteen days after the massacre in Mỹ Lai.[19]

MILITARIZED BENEVOLENCE:
FROM ENEMY-MAKING TO REFUGE(E) PRODUCTION

A well-camouflaged racist, Orientalist ideology may have fashioned foreign policies and military actions, but more insidiously, it persisted as a core fiber of the American cultural and moral imagination long after U.S. military withdrawal from Vietnam. An ambiguous end to a controversial war found ideological resuscitation almost immediately in the figure of the helpless but "good" Vietnamese refugee in need of American freedom and reformation. The "co-constitutive" nature of *refuge* and *refugee*, which both result from and enable the recasting of "military aggressor" into "magnanimous rescuer," is what Yen Le Espiritu terms "militarized refuge(es)." There are several key dimensions to Espiritu's elucidation of this "(by)product" of racialized U.S. militarism. First, she explicitly conceptualizes war as "militarized violence": it is "not only epistemic or symbolic violence but the actual physical violence of 'guns and bombs' [the technological advancement of weapons of mass destruction] unleashed on 'expendable nonpersons' ["things"], those devoid of names and faces, family and personal histories, dreams and hopes, politics and beliefs." It is the same "raw, brutal, and destructive forces that Western imperial powers unleash on the lands and bodies of racialized peoples across time and space." Remarkably, through the logics of a military complex, the trope of "refuge" and the figure of "refugee" function to rebrand the American soldier from aggressor to rescuer, thereby refocusing the object of war's violence from the rescued to the rescuer. The war itself is thus (re)storied as an "American tragedy," and the conspicuous invisibility of the Vietnamese people becomes an "organized and strategic forgetting" that renders them perpetual collaterals and ontologically immaterial to America's greater destiny.[20]

Second, in conjoining and unsettling the concepts of "refuge" and "refugee," Espiritu exposes the enduring nature of U.S. militarism abroad—specifically in Asia Pacific—and traces the footprints of its militarized colonialism along trans-Pacific itineraries of refuge-seeking. The early colonial "vision of righteousness" is thus contemporized through a humanitarian narrative that reinforces *dominus*'s sovereignty upon a new class of wretched "refuses"—the Vietnamese refugees. In this case, the humanitarian machination of "refuge-providing" is militarized, and it masterfully refracts attention from the military industrial complex of "refugee-producing." The distinction between violence and benevolence is blurred, especially as the military units that were dispatched for military missions ended up being the very same implements that provided the rescue. Not only that, within this grand-scale scheme of benevolence, additional collaterals were added to the acceptable cost of war—the collateral damage exacted upon previously colonized indigenous lands, resources, and peoples, deployed in the service of refuge-production. A few examples serve this point.

As the war drew to a bewildering end with the takeover of Saigon by the (northern) People's Army of Vietnam in April of 1975, Operation Frequent Wind went into effect for the evacuation of U.S. personnel and affiliated Vietnamese. An estimated 140,000 were evacuated within this first wave of refuge-seeking. Televised images of U.S. military aircrafts swooping flailing Vietnamese bodies from rooftops for transport to naval carriers awaiting at sea became the dramaturgies that made the real seemingly indistinguishable from cinematic reels. The feat of transporting over 3,000 Vietnamese on the naval aircraft carrier USS Midway out of Saigon on April 30, for instance, was heralded as a "remarkable rescue mission" in which American soldiers were seen as photogenic "gentle, tender giants" coming to the rescue of destitute, stateless refugees who exuded gratitude. Following this benevolent itinerary, rescued Vietna-

mese were transported to a temporary base in a U.S. territory—the Philippines, Guam, or Wake Island—and then transferred to one of four
military bases in the United States—Camp Pendleton, CA; Fort Chaffee,
AR; Eglin Air Force Base, FL; and Indiantown Gap, PA. The two major
transitional processing centers were Clark Air Force Base (AFB) in the
Philippines, and Andersen Air Force Base in Guam. [21]

In the 1940s, Clark AFB had been the headquarters of the Thirteenth
Air Force, which had figured a key role in supporting U.S. forces in the
Korean War (1950–1953). Between 1965 and 1975, it became the largest
overseas U.S. military base in the world. When the Philippines eventually
disallowed the usage of the base as a launch site for B-52 bombings,
Anderson AFB of Guam became the central station for major missions to
North and South Vietnam, serving as the largest U.S. base for the B-52
bombers featured in Nixon's Operation Linebacker II—the eleven-day,
round-the-clock "Christmas bombing" of the northern cities of Hanoi and
Haiphong in December 1972, with 729 sorties and 87 B-52s launched in
less than two hours on December 18 alone. The Paris peace talks and
cease-fire agreement forged in January 1973 were attributed to such
"carpet-bombing" tactics. The star of a new generation of "high-technolo-
gy brutality," the B-52s were "the eight-engine behemoths that attempted
to bomb the Vietnamese communists into submission." As Espiritu puts
it, "[t]he Nixon Doctrine was thus a racial project: by withdrawing
American troops but intensifying the air raid, the United States priori-
tized American lives over Vietnamese lives, preserving the former while
obliterating the latter, racialized to be dispensable, via carpet bombing." [22]

Thus, as one of a series of critical "nodes of U.S. colonial and military
empire in the Asia Pacific region," Guam was an exploitable "empty
land," a convenient reservoir of human and natural resources for a mili-
tary-turned-humanitarian "staging area." Within the first wave of evacuation in April of 1975, 115,000 refugees passed through the island, a number exceeding the local civilian population by at least twenty-five thousand. What was to be an expedient stopover became a "dumping
ground" for a large-scale colonial benevolence scheme in which Indigenous peoples saw their resources depleted without recompense, while
refugees strained for the deliverance they thought had been promised, as
resettlement became increasingly elusive and exacting. The violence of
militarized refuge/recovery production recurs at such sites as Camp Pendleton in San Diego, home of the decorated First Marine Regiment,
known for campaigns of 1,900 and 850 kills and for being the last marine
infantry unit to leave Vietnam in 1971. The 125,000-acre training base
housed fifty thousand refugees between April and August of 1975 under
Operation New Arrival. Often obscured is the fact that the carnage of war
and the first-rate ground fighting by units like the First Marines was what
had brought about refugee displacement to begin with. Another little-

known fact is that Camp Pendleton's facilities are located on traditional Juaneno, Luiseno, and Kumeyaay tribal land once "discovered" and later "owned" through Spanish and Anglo-American colonial conquest.[23]

Literature on Vietnamese refugee outflow in the aftermath of the war describes distinguishable waves and modes of departure. In the first period, an estimated 140,000 were evacuated by U.S. Navy and cargo ships. In subsequent waves, over 800,000 (839,228 registered by the United Nations High Commissioner for Refugees, or UNHCR) sought refuge by other means, including by sea (the wave of "boat people" in the late 1970s through mid-1980s) and through resettlement programs under the Refugee Act of 1980.[24] Here we focus on the militarized machination of refuge-producing and refugee-making, which complicates the introjection of the Vietnamese into American consciousness, and which yielded material and political consequences for the racialized adaptation of the earlier wave of refugees/asylees to American life.

The process of militarized-violence-turned-militarized-recovery is simultaneously redemptive and deceptive. On one hand, in redeploying his[25] militarized training and resources toward rescue and recovery, the soldier/veteran is "rehumanized" as heroic and innocent of war's criminality. Such redemption comes at the expense of the rescued, as Viet Thanh Nguyen points out, for the latter must remain a foil for the hero's "substantiation." Meanwhile, the liberated refugee must show indebtedness to their liberator's empire and its "gift of freedom" through a continuous performance of the role of grateful and deserving beneficiary—the successful, anticommunist "model minority." Ironically, the refugees's model minority performance both obscured and justified the category of "collateral damage." Not only that, their performance helped to mask the truer reality that many Americans did not welcome their arrival. That liberation is conditional upon *dominus*'s redemptive grace is further shown in the special dispensation given to the roughly 90,000 Amerasian children—born of Vietnamese mothers and American GIs—admitted into the United States between 1982 and 1999. The dangerous arbitrariness of it could be seen in the haphazard Operation Babylift, in which over 2,500 infants and children (many of whom were Amerasians) were airlifted in military cargo planes in April 1975, transitioned to orphanages, and granted parolee status. An investigation by the Immigration and Naturalization Service later found that over ten percent of those children were ineligible for adoption. Of the total number, only twelve children were later reunited with their Vietnamese parents.[26] The separation of brown children from their parents under the guise of state benevolence finds eerie recapitulation in current events.

Encapsulating her thesis, Espiritu writes: "The iconic images of desperate and frantic Vietnamese, wailing with pain, grief, and terror as they scrambled to escape 'communist Vietnam' at any cost, have visually and discursively transformed the Vietnamese from a people battered by decades of U.S. warfare in Vietnam to those persecuted by the Vietnamese communist government and rescued by the United States." Against such "revisionism," Espiritu "reconceptualizes 'the refugee' not as an object of rescue but as a site of social and political critiques, whose emergence, when traced, would make visible the processes of colonization, war, and displacement."[27]

MILITARIZED RACISM:
BODY COUNTS ON THE HOME FRONT

Militarized "refuge" and the militarized "refugee" as a co-constitutive (by)product of U.S. militarism is manufactured along the empire's colonial itineraries abroad, but it is also actively produced on the home front. In the fall of 2014, the sublimity of militarized state power was on a "dramatic show of force" in the streets of Ferguson, Missouri, when Americans saw on television screens "camo-wearing police carrying assault [weapons] and aiming high-powered rifles from sniper positions atop mine-resistant armored vehicles," directed at American civilians who took to the streets in protest of the fatal shooting of an unarmed eighteen-year-old African American named Michael Brown by white police officer Darren Wilson.[28] The concept of "military sublime" is described by Cathy Schlund-Vials as "a distanced aesthetic/political mode marked by 'dramatic, large-scale spectacles of war.'"[29] Diverting our gaze to a staged grandeur better witnessed from afar—as opposed to the "very real disorder, chaos, and destruction" on the ground—the sight described above induces a condition of vertigo, a "loss of balance,"[30] as Americans strained for comprehension of what appeared surreal before their eyes: teargas, flashbangs, rubber bullets, long-range acoustic devices, military-grade weapons, armored tactical vehicles, the wailing of pain, grief, and terror, a suburban "wasteland" not unlike the searched-and-destroyed hamlets of a haunting past, a lifeless body ditched on the ground, a "confirmed kill" in an enduring and expansive conflict between law enforcement and civilian bodies that do not count. In this scene, "[t]he line between law enforcement in a constitutional state and military action directed against an enemy became increasingly blurred."[31] The racialized war on communism abroad is brought home onto American streets in equally racialized wars waged in the name of "law and order" (the ideological banner for Richard Nixon's 1968 presidential campaign), first against the alleged threat of civil disobedience by racial minority groups, then against the purported menace of drugs and terrorism during the Reagan, Bush, and Clinton administrations. In what Henry Giroux has scathingly declared as a "lockdown state," a "militarized social logic" regulates obedience to and complicity with a regime of policed and militarized "security" across a wide range of social institutions, from neighborhoods, to schools, to public spaces.[32] As Barry Friedman puts it, "[p]olicing today is *regulatory*: it is about shaping behavior on the front end, not capturing crooks after the fact—and we have all become its targets."[33] With policing increasingly taking on the form of "paramilitary pacification," the prison eerily becomes a new dumping ground, tasked with a "waste management function" over lives rendered "disposable" by the state.[34]

While all citizens may be targets of the regulatory control of this new police state, the impact is distributed disproportionately against black and brown bodies. As Vietnamese American poet-activist Bao Phi intones in his spoken word on the sting of police brutality: "They told us the sky above our heads is the same / but we knew this wasn't true / the first time it rained / batons / we were the only ones getting wet."[35] The vertiginous sight of military-grade weapons and armored tactical vehicles in the streets of Ferguson called into scrutiny the existence of the "1033 Program" (Law Enforcement Support Program, or LESO), a federal initiative authorized initially by Congress in the National Defense Authorization Act of 1990 and made permanent in 1997, which "provides [military] property that is excess to the needs of the Department [of Defense] for use by agencies in law enforcement, counterdrug, and counterterrorism activities."[36] Under this 1033 program, "excess" military property amounting to more than $5.3 billion has been provided to approximately eight thousand federal and state law enforcement agencies across forty-nine states and three U.S. territories. Beyond usage of military equipment, however, hyper-policing of everyday racialized life is done through other legal and quotidian means. For instance, in an investigation of the Ferguson Police Department conducted by the Civil Rights Division of the Department of Justice, it was documented that "Ferguson law enforcement practices disproportionately harm Ferguson's African-American residents and are driven in part by racial bias."[37] Data showed that between 2012 and 2014, Black residents were the target of eighty-five percent of vehicle stops, ninety percent of citations, and ninety-three percent of arrests, even though only sixty-seven percent of Ferguson's population is Black. Between 2011 and 2013, Black residents were subjected to ninety-five percent of "Manner of Walking in a Roadway" charges (the reason Michael Brown was stopped in the first place by officer Darren Wilson) and ninety-four percent of "Failure to Comply" charges. In effect, aggressive ticketing and imposition of harsh penalties and fines served as tactics for a revenue-generating system, that many consider to be an active production of a "racial caste system" that "exploits and disqualifies" Black lives.[38]

Just as racialized militarism abroad requires a triangulation of colonized and indigenous peoples, militant racialization within the United States entails active triangulation of peoples of color. Today, scholar-activists recognize the historical arc that connects Vietnam to Iraq and

Afghanistan, Selma to Ferguson, the Kerner report with the Ferguson report, the earlier liberation fronts of the two-thirds world and contemporary global movements for human rights.[39] However, confrontations with law enforcement in everyday life still frequently result in public and divisive debates over who are the "good" victims, who are deserving targets, and who are mere collaterals. When New York Police Department officer Peter Liang was convicted and found guilty in 2016 of the shooting death of Akai Kareem Gurley in 2014, questions arose as to whether Officer Liang was a racialized scapegoat punished for simply "doing what he had to do," or a model minority privileged by "adjacent whiteness"[40] whose actions betrayed a fundamental disregard for human life. Ironically, in their very personhood as immigrants from Hong Kong and the Virgin Islands, respectively, both Liang and Gurley present a less-discussed substantiation of America's enduring colonial footprints.

On a different scale, just as Vietnamese bodies were acceptable collateral damage in the fields of Vietnam, they continue to be collaterals upon resettlement in the land of the free, the land of opportunity. The successful model-minority myth disallows the possibility for complexities and complications in the resettlement and adaptation trajectories for Vietnamese Americans, along with other Southeast Asians. Despite such realities as downward social and economic mobility, income disparity, rising poverty, unequal educational achievement, unemployment and underemployment, racial discrimination, generational tensions, and war traumas, Vietnamese refugees are stereotypically assumed to be "better off" and even "naturally suited" for harrowing social and economic conditions in the United States. Espiritu asserts, "Such tidy conclusions dispense with questions about U.S. power structures that continue to consign a significant number of Vietnamese Americans to unstable, minimum-wage employment, welfare dependency, and participation in the informal economy years after their arrival."[41] Engrafted alongside other Asian American groups to the model minority myth—originally contrived for Japanese Americans to laud post-internment rebound and thereby obscuring its unconstitutionality—the Vietnamese refugee community serves as collateral foil within a post-civil rights, neoconservative backlash against the so-labeled "underclass"—poor and non-white communities that make up the alleged morally deficient "culture of poverty."[42]

(RE)CALLING DISPLACED SPIRITS

In recent years, scholars have pushed beyond the former analytic categories of "identity, assimilation, and the recuperation of history" to probe more expansive, multi-century, "multiscalar," "pan-category" explorations of empire, war, race, and their impact on the "joint and disjointed lives" of Vietnamese and Southeast Asian refugees in the United States.[43] Guided not so much by academic ingenuity, and despite the institutional impulses toward the "planned obsolescence"[44] of racial/ethnic studies, this new wave of inquiry models after what is described as a movement toward transnational, intersectional, comparative, and connective activism and allyship by emerging generations of students on college campuses and in the streets. Perhaps it is an advancement of what Martin Luther King, Jr. had attempted when he broke from single-issue concerns and named the triple threat of racism, materialism, and militarism that connected the "fortified hamlets" of Vietnam with the neighborhoods of southwest Georgia and East Harlem. It is this same comparative and connective inquiry that allows us to link the streets of Mỹ Lai with those of Ferguson as vertiginous sites of militarized violence, the collateral damage of which is often dismissed as negligible, acceptable, inevitable. Entwining the life of the Vietnamese refugee with other racialized lives in the United States is a beginning step towards remembering the *disremembered*[45]—those conspicuously invisible, forcibly forgotten, "displaced spirits" who are "missing from one place and unknown in another."[46]

Writing on the Vietnamese mortuary and Indigenous religious tradition, Heonik Kwon discovers the notion of "grievous death" (*chết oan*) suffered by "displaced spirits," whose sudden and violent death prevents "the possibility of ritual appropriation and transformation of the deceased into an ancestral entity." In this conceptualization, "the souls of the dead can suffer from the enduring effects of a traumatic historical experience," and their continuous comingling with the living through haunting apparitions calls for anamnestic consolation and intervention. At sites of mass deaths such as Mỹ Lai, the ghosts appear as "vital historical witnesses, testifying to [a] war's unjust destruction of human life." Through social rites of death commemorations and ritual offerings, the living participate in the "disentangling from grievance" of these wandering ghosts.[47]

Such notions of a continuum of life and death that makes permeable the spiritual and material, this-worldly and ghostly, invite the Christian practical theologian to ponder a theological anthropology that challenges the logics of grievous, unjust collaterality, in which some humans are "de-realized" for the substantiation of others and some victims are more "grievable" than others.[48] If we follow Espiritu—who follows Judith Butler's conceptualization of "grief" as political and Avery Gordon's notion of ghostly apparition "as the principal form by which something lost or invisible or seemingly not there makes itself known or apparent to us,"[49]—then perhaps we might begin to see a Jesus who suffered a sudden, violent, grievous death, who keeps appearing as a wandering spirit, insisting that the living testify to the unjust violation of his body and spirit. This ghost (a variation of the Christian person of "Holy Ghost"?) and other lives invoked in these pages may very well be attesting to what

Neferti Tadiar describes as "alternative ways of becoming human"—both living and dead. They are the ones who, "despite being continuously impeded, and made illegible by dominant ways of being human," manage to exercise those "insurrectionary creative social capacities . . . in their very effort of living, in their making of forms of viable life."[50]

"Cầu Xin Hồn Của Bạn Đồng Hành Giúp Đỡ"[51] . . .
(May the Displaced Spirits of Companions Help)

Between November 14, 1985, and April 15, 1986, the Philippines Refugee Processing Center (PRPC) near Morong, Bataan, Philippines, was "home" for my family of five—Mom (Lê Hoàng Mai), Dad (Trần Văn Sánh), younger sister (Hoàng-Anh), brother (Tuấn-Anh), and myself (see figure 3.1). More precisely, unit 512-A, lower level, was our assigned residence for what was to be an indeterminate length of stay to process our transition from Ho Chi Minh City, Vietnam, to resettlement in Northern California. What I did not know until recently but should have guessed long ago is that Bataan had been the site of a key battle between American and Filipino forces against the Japanese between 1941 and 1942.[52] Our family was part of the Orderly Departure Program (ODP), an initiative instated after the United Nations Geneva Convention on "refugees and displaced persons in Southeast Asia" in 1979, which allowed for the authorized departures of Vietnamese for resettlement in a designated country under UNHCR coordination. The three authorized categories for resettlement in the United States were: 1) those with family members

Figure 3.1. Philippine Refugee Processing Center, Morong, Philippines. Public domain. Project Ngoc, Photographer.

already in the country; 2) those formerly employed by U.S. government agencies; and 3) those "closely identified" with U.S. presence in Vietnam before 1975.[53] We belonged to the first category, having had extended relatives already settled in the United States in earlier waves, including relatives who fled by boat. Ten years prior, my parents had also tried to venture out to sea, but after fourteen months in detention for the failed attempt, Dad figured he would try the "orderly" route.

Surely, the shrewdest of ideologues and political strategists must know that war seldom ends upon declaration of ceasefire or troops withdrawal, even as they debate whether warfare is a regenerative solution to a people's unfathomable social, economic, and political duress. What happened in Vietnam (or what happened *to* it) was not a singular war, as some now admit; it was a thirty-year "revolutionary struggle" against colonial occupation, a "civil war," a "domestic confrontation," a fratricide, a "Vietnamese war" to some, an "American war" to others.[54] The classification of "winner" and "loser" in the aftermath of such trauma is farcical, and the management of refuge for winners and losers alike requires more than a few planes and ships shuttling back and forth across the Pacific. The limits of paternal compassion were thus tested severely when the refugee, that the West had helped to mass-produce, took on life forms and kept showing up in the flesh. Unsurprisingly, benevolence's borders quickly shut down on many, as international "disenchantment"[55] resulted in literal "pushbacks" of boats that drifted ashore, in denials of entry visas to those who queued up for their turn, in strategic forgetting of those who languished in detention centers awaiting global legitimization of their fate, in political quibbling amongst Eastern and Western countries over the burden of protracted rescue. It would not be so exceptional to hear stories like that of the "Bolinao 52," survivors of a refugee boat that originally carried 110 refuge-seekers, who drifted to the shores of the Philippines after thirty-seven days at sea. As one captain's court martial later would reveal, they had been refused rescue by the USS Dubuque, which had been under order to join Operation Free Will in the Persian Gulf.[56]

We had it easy, people would say when they learned of the year and mode of my family's departure and location of our transitional period. Vietnamese refugees in the United States identify each other by wave of refuge-seeking, and with some generalization, they can tell a lot about you just by year and location. "Bataan in 1985." Those were easier times, they would say. My parents remain unsure as to why we only had to stay for roughly five months—just long enough for Christmas (Thanksgiving hadn't really registered for us), the Lunar New Year, Easter, and a couple of birthdays. My father had been a minister in the Evangelical Church of Vietnam, and there was a chapel in our residential zone, so between "church" activities, classes for basic English (from which I can only recall learning the days of the week), cultural orientation (from which my father remembers a frantic attempt to offer totally made-up translations for *The Sound of Music*), weekly compound clean-up duties, ration collection, fetching water for daily use, and generous neighbors quietly pressing small amounts of cash into my mother's hand so that she could secure more food for three ravenous mouths, time was whatever you made of it.

I was already old enough to have remembered much, but the writing of this short chapter became a surprising reminder of how much I do *not*, and a realization of how I have never puzzled over such a glaring autobiographical void. I have read and written about the Vietnamese refugee and immigrant experience as an academic, but the research has always been piecemeal and more self-taught than an explicit curriculum in my own scholarly formation. A "null curriculum" of (neo)liberal *theological* education—the other side of "planned obsolescence," if you ask me now. But despite all these years of catch-up, there remains a persistent psychic dissonance when it comes to reckoning with "Vietnam" as subject matter, even as I intellectually concede that it does *matter*. What if it is a spiritual captivity of sorts that has kept me a wandering ghost all this time, estranged from an "at-home-ness" with recollections of my disjointed traverse along the itineraries of empire, war, U.S. race relations, as a refugee-turned-naturalized-citizen who still gets asked whether I go "home" regularly . . . ?

We never found Uncle 8 after the war. Uncle 7 tried to desert and lost a toe. Uncle 2 never came out the same. Aunt 3 waited nearly a decade for her husband to be released from "re-education camp." Dad was kept for how long? And Mom, too? Who else had been detained? Wait, that relative of ours was a "VC"?! Such memory work would come in bits and pieces, spurts and stops during family conversations. While cathartic, these moments would remain fragmented. No household shrines and ritualistic offerings to conjure or honor wandering ghosts, for we are "good" Christians. We came from the former South Vietnam, which no longer exists. These tidbits alone might allow a discerning reader knowledgeable about Vietnam as "subject matter" to speculate a few other things—such as what I might have been taught to remember and to forget, or whom might have figured as "enemy," "hero," and "victim" in the lessons that I had learned in my youth and the lessons not learned in my adult life in the United States. In all of this, a self-conscious awkwardness lingers, as I am told by the eyes of Americans that my presence over here as a former refuge-seeker reminds them of the pain that they had experienced or witnessed over there.

For Espiritu, the U.S. invasion of Iraq served as that "shock of recognition" which made "Vietnam" reappear before her eyes: "the spectacle of violence; the 'we need to destroy it in order to save it' mandate; the ways that peace could only come in the form of a 'war without end'; and the brutal displacement of thousands of Iraqi men, women, and children from their homes and neighborhoods."[57] For me, the flash point was August 9, 2014, and the vertiginous sight/site was Canfield Drive, Ferguson, roughly fifteen miles north of where I was living and teaching. For in the days following the shooting death of Michael Brown on August 9, a lifeless body on the ground became a "displaced spirit" (*hồn chết oan*) that haunted my thana-voyeuristic imagination, beckoning me to reckon with the spirits of other "grievous deaths" whom I, for one reason or another, had managed to ignore.

In the months that followed, I wrote the following words in a presidential address to the Religious Education Association, an international academic organization for the study of religion and education:

> We Religious Educators teach in a conjuncture in which blood- and rain-soaked streets give off ghost flames, haunting the public imagination with quiet grief and resounding rage for a more just, less violent world. If Religious Education is "the reshaping of life's forms with end and without end," "[t]o link lives of individuals and communities to larger, ultimate realities and purposes," if it is necessarily an "intervention in the world" as Paulo Freire announced long ago, then we need Religious Educators who are deeply attuned to ghostly apparitions of suppressed memories and subjugated experiences, and are committed to resurrecting deadened spirits. Against the enduring "pathological praxis of hostile passion and cruelty," embedded within what theologian Dorothee Sölle calls "structures of violence that rule this world," we need pedagogies that help us to narrate the anguish, to ritualize principled protest, and to reinvest in what Evelyn Parker calls "emancipatory hope" in the future.[58]

Against the pathological praxis of racialized militarism and militarized racism exercised along the relentless itineraries of empire(s), perhaps a promise of theological refuge and rescue lies in a reimagined calculus of *collateralis*: a rejection of any count that renders bodies as "less than," for commitment to an accompaniment "alongside," no matter how exhaustingly prolonged it might be.

BIBLIOGRAPHY

Allison, William Thomas. *My Lai: An American Atrocity in the Vietnam War*. Baltimore: Johns Hopkins University Press, 2012.

Bilton, Michael, and Kevin Sim. *Four Hours in My Lai*. New York: Viking, 1992.

Boyle, Brenda M., and Jeehyun Lim, eds. *Looking Back on the Vietnam War: Twenty-First Century Perspectives*. New Brunswick: Rutgers University Press, 2016.

Butler, Judith. *Precarious Life: The Power of Mourning and Violence*. London: Verso, 2004.

Caputo, Philip. *A Rumor of War*. New York: Holt, Rinehart and Winston, 1977.

"Charlie Company and the Massacre," PBS.org, www.pbs.org/wgbh/americanexperience/features/my-lai-charlie-company-and-massacre/.

Chan, Sucheng. *The Vietnamese American 1.5 Generation: Stories of War, Revolution, Flight, and New Beginnings*. Philadelphia: Temple University Press, 2006.

Chomsky, Noam. "Visions of Righteousness." In *The Vietnam War and American Culture*, edited by John Carlos Rowe and Rick Berg, 21–51. New York: Columbia University Press, 1991.

"DCAS Vietnam Conflict Extract File record counts by Casualty Category (as of April 29, 2008)." www.archives.gov/research/military/vietnam-war/casualty-statistics#category

"Department of Defense Excess Property Program in Support of U.S. Law Enforcement Agencies: An Overview of DOD Authorities, Roles, Responsibilities, and Implementation of Section 1033 of the 1997 National Defense Authorization Act." U.S. House Committee on Armed Services, Subcommittee on Oversight and Investigations, November 13, 2014, https://www.hsdl.org/?view&did=760378.

Do, Hien Duc. *The Vietnamese Americans*. Westport: Greenwood Press, 1999.

Duc, Nguyen Huu. "Bolinao 52." San Francisco: Right Here In My Pocket, and Kanopy, 2017.

Espiritu, Yen Le. *Body Counts: The Vietnam War and Militarized Refuge(es)*. Berkeley: University of California Press, 2014.

Friedman, Barry. *Unwarranted: Policing without Permission*. New York: Farrar, Straus and Giroux, 2017.

Giroux, Henry A. *The Violence of Organized Forgetting: Thinking Beyond America's Disimagination Machine*. San Francisco: City Lights Books, 2014.

Gordon, Avery. *Ghostly Matters: Haunting and the Sociological Imagination*. Minneapolis: University of Minnesota Press, 1997.

Hayton, Bill. *Vietnam: Rising Dragon*. New Haven: Yale University Press, 2010.

"Investigation of the Ferguson Police Department." United States Department of Justice, Civil Rights Division. March 4, 2015. www.justice.gov/sites/default/files/opa/press-releases/attachments/2015/03/04/ferguson_police_department_report.pdf.

Jones, Howard. *My Lai: Vietnam, 1968, and the Descent into Darkness*. Oxford: Oxford University Press, 2017.

Kiernan, Ben. *Việt Nam: A History from Earliest Times to the Present*. Oxford: Oxford University Press, 2017.

Kwon, Heonik. "Missing Bodies and Homecoming Spirits." In *Looking Back on the Vietnam War: Twenty-First Century Perspectives*, edited by Brenda M. Boyle and Jeehyun Lim, 126–139. New Brunswick: Rutgers University Press, 2016.

Le Tran, Mai-Anh. *Reset the Heart: Unlearning Violence, Relearning Hope*. Nashville: Abingdon, 2017.

Lee, Shelley Sang-Hee. *A New History of Asian America*. New York: Routledge, 2014.

Moore, Mary Elizabeth. *Teaching as a Sacramental Act*. Cleveland: Pilgrim Press, 2004.

Palumbo-Liu, David. *Asian/American: Historical Crossings of a Racial Frontier*. Stanford: Stanford University Press, 1999.

Passavant, P.A. "I Can't Breathe: Heeding the Call of Justice." *Law, Culture and the Humanities* 11, no. 3 (2015): 330–339.

Peers, William R. *The My Lai Inquiry*. New York: Norton, 1979.

Phi, Thien-Bao. "For Colored Boys in Danger of Sudden Unexplained Nocturnal Death Syndrome and All the Rest for Whom Considering Suicide Is Not Enuf," in *The Way We Pay: Poetry by Thien-Bao Phi*, 2011. baophi.com/the-way-we-pay/.

"The Philippines (Bataan) (1942)." PBS. September 2007. www.pbs.org/thewar/detail_5209.htm.

Rogers, Robert F. *Destiny's Landfall: A History of Guam*. Honolulu: University of Hawai'i Press, 1995.

Rowe, John Carlos, and Rick Berg. *The Vietnam War and American Culture*. New York: Columbia University Press, 1991.

Schlund-Vials, Cathy J. "Re-Seeing Cambodia and Recollecting the 'Nam." In *Looking Back on the Vietnam War: Twenty-First Century Perspectives*, edited by Brenda M. Boyle and Jeehyun Lim, 156–174. New Brunswick: Rutgers University Press, 2016.

———, ed. *Flashpoints for Asian American Studies*. New York: Fordham University Press, 2018.

"State of the World's Refugees, 2000." UNHCR. www.unhcr.org/3ebf9bad0.html.

Tadiar, Neferti. "Lifetimes in Becoming Human." Keynote panel address, presented at "Angela Davis: Legacies in the Making." 2009. University of California, Santa Cruz.

Tang, Eric. "Collateral Damage: Southeast Asian Poverty in the United States." In *Asian American Studies Now: A Critical Reader,* edited by Jean Yu-wen Shen Wu and Thomas C. Chen, 454–474. New Brunswick: Rutgers University Press, 2010.

Taub, Amanda. "Why America's Police Forces Look Like Invading Armies." *Vox.* August 19, 2014. www.vox.com/2014/8/14/6003239/police-militarization-in-ferguson. Accessed July 24, 2018.

Tran, Mai-Anh Le. "To Set One's Heart in a Violent World." *Religious Education* 110, no. 4 (2015): 358–373. dx.doi.org/10.1080/00344087.2015.1063960.

NOTES

1. William Thomas Allison, *My Lai: An American Atrocity in the Vietnam War* (Baltimore: Johns Hopkins University Press, 2012), 31; Bill Hayton, *Vietnam: Rising Dragon* (New Haven: Yale University Press, 2010), xiii; Ben Kiernan, *Việt Nam: A History from Earliest Times to the Present* (Oxford: Oxford University Press, 2017), 444; Howard Jones, *My Lai: Vietnam, 1968, and the Descent into Darkness* (Oxford: Oxford University Press, 2017).

2. Jones, *My Lai,* 1–5, 245, 252–253, 268. William R. Peers, *The My Lai Inquiry* (New York: Norton, 1979), 14, 16–17, 211.

3. Jones, *My Lai,* 285. See also "Charlie Company and the Massacre," PBS.org, www.pbs.org/wgbh/americanexperience/features/my-lai-charlie-company-and-mas-sacre/.

4. Jones, *My Lai,* 43 (emphasis added), 304, 311, 339–340.

5. Jones, *My Lai,* 340.

6. Allison, *My Lai,* 12.

7. The exceptions seemed to have been found in the actions of helicopter pilot Hugh Thompson and his door-gunner Lawrence Colburn. With Colburn's assistance, Thompson landed his helicopter in the field to provide coverage and rescue of civilians being rounded up by the American troops. Enduring public backlash and labeled "traitor" and "sympathizer," the men were eventually awarded the Soldier's Medal in 1998. Jones, 105–111, 344.

8. Jones, *My Lai,* 3–4, 18, 178.

9. Allison, *My Lai,* 52; Jones, 3–4, 18, 25, 24, 178, 226; Michael Bilton and Kevin Sim, *Four Hours in My Lai* (New York: Viking, 1992), 60; Philip Caputo, *A Rumor of War* (New York: Holt, Rinehart and Winston, 1977), xviii.

10. Cathy J. Schlund-Vials, "Re-Seeing Cambodia and Recollecting the 'Nam," in *Looking Back on the Vietnam War: Twenty-First Century Perspectives,* ed. Brenda M. Boyle and Jeehyun Lim (New Brunswick: Rutgers University Press, 2016), 162; Yen Le Espiritu, *Body Counts: The Vietnam War and Militarized Refuge(es)* (Berkeley: University of California Press, 2014), 30; See brief chronology in Brenda M. Boyle and Jeehyun Lim, *Looking Back on the Vietnam War: Twenty-First Century Perspectives* (New Brunswick: Rutgers University Press, 2016), ix–xiv.

11. Shelley Sang-Hee Lee, *A New History of Asian America* (New York: Routledge, 2014), 287; Boyle and Lim, *Looking Back on the Vietnam War,* xii; Jones, *My Lai,* 353. Some estimates put the number of Vietnamese civilian deaths closer to three or four million. See "DCAS Vietnam Conflict Extract File record counts by Casualty Category (as of April 29, 2008)," www.archives.gov/research/military/vietnam-war/casualty-statistics#category.

12. Jones, *Mỹ Lai,* 342.

13. John Carlos Rowe and Rick Berg, *The Vietnam War and American Culture* (New York: Columbia University Press, 1991), 3.

14. Rowe and Berg, *The Vietnam War and American Culture,* 8; Hien Duc Do, *The Vietnamese Americans* (Westport: Greenwood Press, 1999), 22.

15. Noam Chomsky, "Visions of Righteousness," in *The Vietnam War and American Culture*, ed. John Carlos Rowe and Rick Berg (New York: Columbia University Press, 1991), 25, 29. Citing Francis Jennings, *The Invasion of America* (Chapel Hill: University of North Carolina Press, 1975), 6.

16. Chomsky, "Visions of Righteousness," 33, 43. Referring to a *New York Times* commentary by James Reston, February 26, 1965.

17. Rowe and Berg, *The Vietnam War and American Culture*, 13.

18. Rowe and Berg, *The Vietnam War and American Culture*, 4, 7, 10.

19. Rowe and Berg, *The Vietnam War and American Culture*, 4–5; Jones, *My Lai*, 20.

20. Espiritu, *Body Counts*, 14, 22, 29, 31, 38. Citing David Palumbo-Liu, *Asian/American: Historical Crossings of a Racial Frontier* (Stanford: Stanford University Press, 1999), 235. See also Henry A. Giroux, *The Violence of Organized Forgetting: Thinking Beyond America's Disimagination Machine* (San Francisco: City Lights Books, 2014).

21. Espiritu, *Body Counts*, 55–56.

22. Espiritu, *Body Counts*, 49–51. Citing Sucheng Chan, *Asian Americans: An Interpretive History* (Woodbridge: Twayne, 1991), 51; Robert F. Rogers, *Destiny's Landfall: A History of Guam* (Honolulu: University of Hawai'i Press, 1995), 242.

23. Espiritu, *Body Counts*, 44–46, 187.

24. Espiritu, *Body Counts*, chapter 3; Sucheng Chan, *The Vietnamese American 1.5 Generation: Stories of War, Revolution, Flight, and New Beginnings* (Philadelphia: Temple University Press, 2006).

25. The pronoun "his" is used intentionally to foreground the hyper-masculinist representations of military actions in Vietnam, as pointed out by Espiritu. According to Carol Lynn Mithers, there were about ten thousand women military personnel who served in the war. Most were nurses or low-ranking officers; some served in communications, intelligence, language specialty, air-traffic control, and aerial reconnaissance photography. As Mither puts it, ". . . there has always been a place for women to serve in war, but there is no place for them in its mythology." See Rowe and Berg, "Missing in Action: Women Warriors in Vietnam," 75–91.

26. Espiritu, *Body Counts*, 47, 53–54, 57–58, 96–97, 123; Chan, *The Vietnamese American 1.5 Generation*. The Gallup poll in May 1975 indicated that fifty-four percent of Americans were against refugee settlement. Espiritu, 47.

27. Espiritu, *Body Counts*, 178.

28. Amanda Taub, "Why America's Police Forces Look Like Invading Armies," *Vox*, August 19, 2014, www.vox.com/2014/8/14/6003239/police-militarization-in-ferguson (accessed July 24, 2018).

29. Schlund-Vials, in *Re-Seeing Cambodia and Recollecting the "Nam,"* 159. Citing Samina Najmi, "Naomi Shihab Nye's Aesthetic of Smallness and the Military Sublime," *MELUS: Multi-ethnic Literatures of the United States* 35, no. 2 (Summer 2010): 151–171.

30. Schlund-Vials, *Re-Seeing Cambodia and Recollecting the "Nam,"* 157–158.

31. P.A. Passavant, "I Can't Breathe: Heeding the Call of Justice," *Law, Culture and the Humanities* 11, no. 3 (2015): 333.

32. See Giroux, *The Violence of Organized Forgetting*.

33. Barry Friedman, *Unwarranted: Policing without Permission* (New York: Farrar, Straus and Giroux, 2017), 18.

34. Passavant, "I Can't Breathe," 333, 37.

35. Thien-Bao Phi, "For Colored Boys in Danger of Sudden Unexplained Nocturnal Death Syndrome and All the Rest for Whom Considering Suicide Is Not Enuf," in *The Way We Pay: Poetry by Thien-Bao Phi*, 2011, baophi.com/the-way-we-pay/.

36. "Department of Defense Excess Property Program in Support of U.S. Law Enforcement Agencies: An Overview of DOD Authorities, Roles, Responsibilities, and Implementation of Section 1033 of the 1997 National Defense Authorization Act." U.S. House Committee on Armed Services, Subcommittee on Oversight and Investigations, November 13, 2014, https://www.hsdl.org/?view&did=760378.

37. "Investigation of the Ferguson Police Department," United States Department of Justice, Civil Rights Division, March 4, 2015, www.justice.gov/sites/default/files/opa/press-releases/attachments/2015/03/04/ferguson_police_department_report.pdf

38. Passavant, "I Can't Breathe," 336–337.

39. Cathy J. Schlund-Vials, ed., *Flashpoints for Asian American Studies* (New York: Fordham University Press, 2018), 2.

40. Schlund-Vials, *Flashpoints for Asian American Studies*, 10.

41. Espiritu, *Body Counts*, 19.

42. See Eric Tang, "Collateral Damage: Southeast Asian Poverty in the United States," in *Asian American Studies Now: A Critical Reader*, ed. Jean Yu-wen Shen Wu and Thomas C. Chen (New Brunswick: Rutgers University Press, 2010).

43. Espiritu, *Body Counts*, 202. See Nitasha Sharma, "The Racial Studies Project: Asian American Studies and the Black Lives Matter Campus," in *Flashpoints for Asian American Studies*, ed. Cathy J. Schlund-Vials (New York: Fordham University Press, 2018), 48–65.

44. See Cathy J. Schlund-Vials, "Planned Obsolescence, Strategic Resistance," in *Flashpoints for Asian American Studies*, ed. Cathy J. Schlund-Vials (New York: Fordham University Press, 2018), 66–81.

45. See Mary Elizabeth Moore, *Teaching as a Sacramental Act* (Cleveland: Pilgrim Press, 2004).

46. Heonik Kwon, "Missing Bodies and Homecoming Spirits," in *Looking Back on the Vietnam War: Twenty-First Century Perspectives*, ed. Brenda M. Boyle and Jeehyun Lim (New Brunswick: Rutgers University Press, 2016), 133. See a fuller treatment in the author's book, *After the Massacre: Commemoration and Consolation in Ha My and My Lai* (Berkeley: University of California Press, 2006).

47. Kwon, "Missing Bodies and Homecoming Spirits," 133, 36–38.

48. Espiritu, *Body Counts*, 97.

49. Judith Butler, *Precarious Life: The Power of Mourning and Violence* (London: Verso, 2004), 30; Avery Gordon, *Ghostly Matters: Haunting and the Sociological Imagination* (Minneapolis: University of Minnesota Press, 1997), 63.

50. Neferti Tadiar, "Lifetimes in Becoming Human," Keynote panel address, presented at "Angela Davis: Legacies in the Making," 2009, University of California, Santa Cruz, 5–6.

51. A line from the prayer of Ms. Tung Trinh, whose story was retold in the documentary *Bolinao 52*. The film follows her journey back to the island in the Philippines where she and other survivors had been rescued, to set up an altar of food offerings for the "displaced spirits" of her deceased companions.

52. "The Philippines (Bataan) (1942)," PBS, September 2007, www.pbs.org/thewar/detail_5209.htm.

53. Chan, *The Vietnamese American 1.5 Generation*.

54. Kwon, "Missing Bodies and Homecoming Spirits," 132.

55. "State of the World's Refugees, 2000," UNHCR, www.unhcr.org/3ebf9bad0.html.

56. See Emmy-winning documentary by Nguyen Huu Duc, "Bolinao 52," (San Francisco: Right Here In My Pocket, and Kanopy, 2017). See also my discussion of the event in *Reset the Heart: Unlearning Violence, Relearning Hope* (Nashville: Abingdon, 2017).

57. Espiritu, *Body Counts*, 176.

58. Mai-Anh Le Tran, "To Set One's Heart in a Violent World," *Religious Education* 110, no. 4 (2015), dx.doi.org/10.1080/00344087.2015.1063960.

FOUR

The Shame Culture of Empire

The Chrysanthemum and the Sword *as Handbook for Cold War Imperialism*

B. Yuki Schwartz

Shame is Asian, at least according to popular wisdom. When I tell people that I research shame, it's not uncommon for someone to reply, "Of course you would, you're Asian, shame is important in Asian culture." Unspoken in this assumption is that shame, like Asians in the United States, is a perpetual foreigner that will never fully belong in the United States. Guilt is the quintessentially American affect, tied to U.S. values of citizenship, thrift, and moral character. According to shame researchers June Price Tangney and Ronda L. Dearing, people who are guilt-prone are less likely to engage in criminal activities or drug use, and more likely to practice safe sex, go to college, and be active members of their communities. "In short," they write, "given a choice, most parents would prefer to raise a guilt-prone child,"[1] rather than a shame-prone child.

I was a shame-prone child. Popularly defined as the experience of having a flawed, incorrect, or undignified identity or sense of being, shame signals the incongruity between self and social identities. Brené Brown defines shame as "the intensely painful feeling or experience of believing we are flawed and therefore unworthy of acceptance and belonging."[2] While her definition has taken root in the popular consciousness of the 2010s, it doesn't tell the whole story of shame. Rarely raised in definitions of shame is how the experience of acceptance and belonging are not just psychologically determined, but also politically and historically ordained. These definitions also rarely speak of how shame works to create or prevent that belonging and acceptance. My proneness toward shame as a biracial Japanese American child raised in the rural Southern United States came most often through the question Asian Americans are often asked: "Where are you really from?" My "Asian shame" arose around the question of who really belongs within the psychic and political boundaries of the United States. This shame isn't Asian, but Asian American, rearing up in the space between two adjectives of impossible identification, both of which are defined and shaped by racism, militarism, and imperialism in Asia and in the United States. "Asian American shame" irrupts from the demand that we blush at our histories, our culture, our food, our languages, our accents, our stories of survival, and our faces, whose skin tones may or may not betray that blush.

The United States and its subjects whose belonging aren't questioned have yet to blush at the reason why many Asian Americans are here in the first place: the wars, occupations, economies, and political imperial ambitions that linked Asia to the United States decades before many of us were even born. According to Victor Bascara, Asian Americans are "living proof of America's expansionist history,"[3] our presence shining a light on the half-truths about why people from Asia migrated to the United States, not just for a "better life" but as a result of U.S. global ambitions. Asian American presence in the United States exposes U.S. transgressions against its own stated democratic values, and its unmet responsibilities toward its Asian American subjects.

The myth of "Asian shame" covers over this reminder, essentializing shame as part of a perpetually foreign culture that gives U.S. imperialism free rein for its acts. Yet shame is often multiple, sometimes legitimating empire and sometimes resulting in what Paul Gilroy describes as productive shame, which critically examines the traumas of the past, and their effects on policy and identity in the present. For Gilroy, productive shame is "conductive to the building of a multicultural nationality that is no longer phobic about the prospect of exposure to either strangers or otherness."[4] It contests the type of shame theories that produced the idea of "Asian" or "primitive" shame, calling for a decolonial/deimperial politics based on shared values, where those wounded by the politics of empire can share blushes and identify their shames's sources. Rather than seeing shame as the longing for acceptance and belonging, Gilroy defines shame as the space where "identification is complicated by a sense of responsibility."[5] Instead of identity existing autonomously, shame illuminates the complications of relationships, policies, histories, politics, narratives, and contingencies that go into making identity—particularly national identity. To imagine shame in this way aids in an "understanding of the different psychic lives of postcolonials,"[6] providing a critical perspective from which to act in ways that takes the pain of shame seriously and responsibly.

Shame isn't usually theorized in this way. Many texts on shame, particularly those written for popular markets, focus on shame's elimination, or as something that one must be healed from. This perspective forecloses possibilities for productive relational responsibility, and for the building of community or a politics that embraces the otherness that shame often centers around. It also withholds shame as a tool through which sites of injustices, past and present, can be identified, recognized, and responsibly worked through. However, theorizations on shame have had long histories with imperialism, functioning alongside military, political, and economic maneuvers and policies to legitimate and justify imperial ambitions and violence. In her work to "world," or provincialize and contextualize the so-called "universal truths" of psychoanalytic theory, Ranjana Khanna explicates how psychoanalysis colluded with imperialism and colonization to produce the civilized subject of the European nation-state. Khanna describes how psychoanalysis aided in the nationalist and imperial process of unconcealing or bringing into existence the national-colonial self, and "it situated itself, with fascination, in opposition to its repressed, concealed, and mysterious 'dark continents': colonial Africa, women, and the primitive."[7] Deeming shame as associated with the primitive and female other, psychoanalytic and anthropological theories also cast those associated with shame—women, racialized colonial subjects, people in poverty—as primitive and feminized as well, rendering them the dark and uncivilized counterpart who threatened the male, middle-class, and white Western subject. This relegation to the non-European subject left shame neglected as a topic for Christian theology. Theologies stemming from Western Europe and North America tend to focus on guilt, the psychic experience that Sigmund Freud named as essential for the development of a civilized subjectivity, as site for theological reflection on sin and salvation.[8] Though feminist theorists have taken up the issue of shame and its occurrence in women's lives as a result of patriarchal systemic oppression, and pastoral theologians recognize shame as painful experience of marginalization, shame has only recently begun to be a site for systematic or constructive theological reflection.[9]

This essay seeks to explore shame, particularly the myth of "Asian shame," and its relationship with U.S. imperialism. I will contextualize the text that popularized this concept in the U.S. imagination, Ruth Benedict's *The Chrysanthemum and the Sword*, placing its genesis and its influence within the site of U.S. imperialism at the beginning of the Cold War. It will examine what this text says about shame, Asian and otherwise, to investigate how the idea of "Asian shame" functions in order to promote a political eschatological vision of a world under democracy that is free of shame, and one where empires can act without judgment. I will conclude with a gesture toward claiming productive shame as a necessary site for theological reflections that seek to contest and challenge imperialism and militarism.

WORLDING COLD WAR SHAME

According to Jodi Kim, the Cold War was not just a historic era but "an epistemology and production of knowledge,"[10] one that fashioned the globe in the postwar era along Manichaean lines of good and evil, American and Soviet, capitalist and communist, but more significantly, male and female, white and nonwhite. Asia was the specific geographic site where the United States produced and carried out many of its Cold War policies and movements. In Asia, the United States worked to embed itself economically, politically, and militarily within territories that had been former sites of European and Japanese colonization, intervening or interrupting emerging nations's attempts at decolonization in some cases, or outright opposing it in others. In contrast to European or Japanese colonization, however, U.S. imperialism in Asia relied less on military conquest of peoples and territories in campaigns of outright warfare by the United States alone, and instead focused on economic, social, and cultural persuasion and coercion, in addition to overt and covert U.S. military operations.[11]

As part of that strategy of cultural persuasion, multiple and various discourses and texts aided the U.S. project of Cold War empire, working to both construct and enlist subjects in the United States and within U.S.-occupied nations in Asia in the project to reimagine the world along U.S. imperial contours. According to Kim, Cold War discourses functioned to structure geopolitical space, craft ideology, and reimagine culture in specific, strategic ways. "Produced in multiple sites and in a variety of forms and genres, Cold War [discursive] compositions give witness to how the Cold War is a multivalenced object of analysis that exceeds its apparent containment by the Manichaean logics of good and evil."[12] Christina Klein also argues for analyzing Cold War cultural productions as partners in U.S. Orientalist imperialism, including popular "middlebrow"[13] magazines, literature, theatrical productions, movies, and other meaning-making discourses, as contributing to this Manichaean division in service to the U.S. empire. According to Klein, U.S. foreign policy and popular cultural productions functioned in tandem to reflect and support one another, serving as "a cultural space in which the ideologies undergirding [U.S. foreign] policies could be, at various moments, articulated, endorsed, questioned, softened, and mystified."[14] Popular discourses consumed by middle-class, middlebrow U.S. subjects at home and overseas participated in the U.S. project of global imperial conquest that was an "anti-conquest" or a "system of reciprocity" with Asian nations that "benefitted all parties."[15] Instead of copying the European system of colonization, the United States engaged in a multipronged, multifaceted strategy of affective sentimentality that stressed a narrative of global integration that employed the metaphors of family, togetherness, culture, and community. Rather than relying on outside force, "the global imagi-

nary of integration generated an inclusive rather than a policing energy."[16] Alongside policies of containment, narratives of integration aided
in the advancement of U.S. policy worldwide and in garnering support in
the United States for international development agencies such as the
International Monetary Fund, NATO and SEATO, and the Marshall
Plan.[17] Texts on shame began to emerge in this era, helping to define and
import mainstream U.S. values during the Cold War and producing national subjects—both U.S. citizens as well as the subjects of decolonizing
lands who were being integrated into the U.S. imperial economic, military, and political order—along specific racialized and gendered lines.

While the majority of texts about shame produced during this time
period do not explicitly or emphatically address these international goals
or imperial priorities, instead implicitly supporting those agendas
through their descriptions of healthy psychic development that fall in
line with U.S. morality systems, there is one particular text that was overt
in its use of shame to craft U.S. foreign policy, and in fact, was commissioned by the U.S. government for that purpose: Ruth Benedict's *The
Chrysanthemum and the Sword: Patterns of Japanese Culture*. This text is
often mentioned as one of the first texts of the twentieth century to address shame, but is rarely cited as a definitive source for shame theory,
likely because of what John Lie describes as the "unduly essentialist and
culturalist" nature of the book and its descriptions of Japanese character
and national identity.[18] Despite these problems with the text, Benedict
and her best-selling book popularized both shame and the idea of shame
cultures for a mass audience. Benedict made shame accessible, not just for
the generals and politicians in Washington who were overseeing Japan's
defeat and occupation, but also for middlebrow readers in the United
States and Japan.[19] By crafting shame in order to contain its use and its
irruptions, *The Chrysanthemum and the Sword* demonstrates a Cold War
symptomaticity between psychoanalysis, anthropology, and U.S. foreign
policy in Asia that worked together to manage and produce the subjectivities in the United States and Japan through which military, economic,
and political influence could manifest and could have "at once consolidated, destabilized and reconstituted America's self-identity and identification."[20] Klein points out that cultural productions abetting U.S. imperial hegemony don't need to be explicit in order to function. Rather, cultural texts paraphrased U.S. international policies, making them accessible
to mainstream readers, and replacing abstract concepts with character
types or models of behaviors that were hailed as suitable for life at home
and abroad. According to Klein, these texts "formed the intellectual wing
of the postwar hegemonic bloc and as such they promoted political and
ideological positions that harmonized with those held by political leaders."[21] *The Chrysanthemum and the Sword* is a site where ideology, policy,
and the production of culture intersect in order to construct and uncon-
ceal specific national identities—for both U.S. citizens and their occupied

Asian subjects—within the site of the new world order implicitly ruled over by a U.S. global empire. In this text, shame and its associated affect, guilt, function in a kinder, gentler Manichaean division, advocating tolerance and moral uplift for those trapped within shame culture while at the same time providing cover and disavowal for actions that the United States took during World War II, especially as U.S. citizens during the Cold War began to express feelings of guilt about the atomic bombings of Japan that killed and maimed hundreds of thousands of Japanese people. This rejection of shame culture also served to cover and disavow the Japanese empire's responsibility and shame for the atrocities it committed before and during the war, encompassed in Japan's rehabilitation as a junior partner in U.S. Cold War ambitions.[22] In utilizing the myth of Asian shame, *The Chrysanthemum and the Sword* aided in unconcealing Cold War national identities to serve the United States's anti-conquest projects of global hegemony.

THE SHAME OF
THE CHRYSANTHEMUM AND THE SWORD

The Chrysanthemum and the Sword was commissioned by the U.S. government in 1944 as a handbook to help military and diplomatic leaders to understand "what the Japanese were like"[23] so that U.S. policymakers could predict the Japanese behavior in the event of Japan's defeat and occupation by Allied forces. Benedict describes the Japanese in the book's very first sentence as "the most alien enemy the United States had ever fought in an all-out struggle,"[24] and whom Marilyn Ivy notes were, by the time the book was published in 1946, being rehabilitated as a democratic and capitalist partner to the United States.[25] Despite her professed respect and admiration for Japanese culture, Benedict consistently identifies shame as the main problem for Japanese culture and the defining characteristic for Japanese otherness.[26] Unlike modern definitions of shame and guilt that equate guilt with transgressive action and shame with transgressive being, Benedict determines that what separates Christian-influenced guilt from Asian shame is the location of the judgment upon individual or community action. In psyches formed through guilt culture, judgment stems from an internally developed conscience, whereas in a shame culture the behaviors of the individual or community are managed by external communal judges who are always on the lookout for a social error. According to Benedict, this Japanese belief that "the eyes of the world are upon you," and the anxiety that the rest of the world was judging the Japanese as a nation for any loss, mistake, or humiliation, were related to the Japanese cultural emphasis on hierarchy, which played out socially, politically, and in the case of the war, globally.

According to Benedict, this is one rationale for Japan's wartime aggressions: to create a world safe for its communal morality based on shame.

It must be noted that Benedict doesn't explicitly call Japan a shame culture, nor does she imply that the two cultures she describes in the book are binary opposites of one another. Benedict doesn't explicitly recommend turning the Japanese into guilt-ridden mimickers of American values, but instead proclaims what she sees as the eschatology of Japanese moral development: a life free from shame, an experience that Japanese experience as children before their societal and moral training begins. According to Benedict, the greatest desire of the Japanese individual is "his 'self without shame.' In the mirror he sees his own eyes as the 'door' of his soul, and this helps him to live as a 'self without shame.' He sees there the idealized parental image. . . . There their selves are spontaneously good as they were in childhood, without the mentor of 'shame.'"[27] This is the self that exists before a Japanese individual becomes formed and shaped into the rigid hierarchy of Japanese culture, a process she compares to the practice of Japanese gardening through training and shaping chrysanthemums through wires and meticulous trimming. For Benedict, the true test of whether Japan will be able to take its place as an approved actor in the new world order is whether it will be able to let go of both its dependence on shame as a method of shaping individual and global hierarchies—and in fact, entirely relinquishing its dependence on hierarchies as a way of ordering the world—and instead adopt the free and "natural" way of being that she describes as part and parcel of U.S. "de-mok-ra-sie,"[28] in which one may "act quite simply and innocently as one pleases."[29] The book ends on this cautious note, hopeful for that change but doubtful that the psychological development put in place through the shame culture of Japan will allow that transformation to happen. In tracing the pattern of Japanese culture, Benedict identifies two conjoined avenues that are now open for the Japanese in the postwar era. The first is that of the chrysanthemum now freed from its imprisoning constraints, standing in for the individuals suffering under the weight of an unbearable system and culture of shame, and one that they may now throw off in favor of "de-mok-ra-sie." The other is the sword, a symbol of self-responsibility and individual moral action. She notes the irony of advocating for the sword as a symbol for the future of a defeated and presently occupied enemy, but for Benedict, it is only through prioritizing the values of the sword as they exist in Japanese culture that Japan may move from a confining shame culture to the freedoms of a culture that exists without shame.[30] Benedict theorizes that by questioning the role that shame plays in their culture, and turning away from it, the Japanese under U.S. occupation "hope for a new growth of freedom among their countrymen: freedom from fear of the criticism and ostracism of 'the world.'"[31]

A LACK OF EMPIRICAL AND IMPERIAL SHAME

Chrysanthemum has both its defenders and detractors, but there are two critiques of the text that are rarely mentioned, both of which address the text's relationship to shame and imperial militarism in Asia. The first is the source of Japanese shame that Benedict assigns to culture. The second is the relationship between shame and empire, which she and her supporters often overlook. To create a theory of Japan's shame culture, Benedict did not rely on her own observations, explaining in the first chapter of the book that, because of the war, she could not travel to Japan to do anthropological fieldwork. Her research relied on texts and media, including novels and parenting manuals, written by Japanese and translated into English, and Western analyses of Japanese culture. She additionally relied upon interviews with native informants, including *kibei*, or individuals of Japanese ancestry who had been born in the United States and held U.S. citizenship, but had grown up in Japan; *nisei*, or individuals of Japanese ancestry who had been born in the United States from parents who were immigrants from Japan and held U.S. citizenship; Japanese POWs; and Westerners who had lived in Japan. Emily Roxbury theorizes that because many of Benedict's textual sources were plays or books about Japanese theater written in the early twentieth century by British scholars of drama, her understanding of "shame culture" is framed through a theatrical or specular lens.[32] Although Benedict asserted that this theatricality and specularization expressed in the feeling of being watched is absent in the "guilt culture" of the United States, Roxbury argues that Japanese American life at the time of Benedict's research was tinged with a particularly theatrical flavor. The surveillance, arrests, corralling, and internment of the 120,000 Japanese Americans and Japanese resident aliens in the United States was dramatically shaming, following a theatrical discourse that cast Japanese Americans and Japanese U.S. residents as enemies to gain public consent for their incarceration. According to Roxbury, "At the center of this overdetermined theatricalization of Japanese ethnicity, Benedict researched and wrote the most influential Western assessment of Japan whose conclusion circulated to the highest levels of power in the U.S. government, military and academy."[33]

That theatricalization and specularization was still at work as Benedict interviewed her research subjects: Japanese Americans who had been incarcerated in the internment camps but had been released and were living in Washington, DC. Benedict also was working in Washington, DC, as the head analyst for the Overseas Intelligence Division of the U.S. Office of War Information, which contributed to the development of U.S. psychological warfare tactics in Europe and Asia.[34] Although the interviews were not mandatory, Ezra Vogel reported in the foreword to the original publication that the interviewees felt that their cooperation was "compulsory," without feeling free to leave the interviews until they had answered Benedict's questions with as many details as possible, repeatedly, particularly about Japanese wartime propaganda.[35] Roxbury argues that Benedict had determined the nervousness and feeling of "being watched" that the interviewees displayed came not from any social or political setting—in this case, a racist setting that had determined that they needed to be watched—but from their inherent shame culture that had psychologically trained them toward the feeling of perpetual judgment.[36] Roxbury argues that other explanations for the interviewees's feeling of being watched include the likelihood that they still had friends and relatives interred in the camps and might have feared for their safety if they did not cooperate with Benedict. That Benedict specifically references the slogan "the eyes of the world are upon you,"[37] a slogan internees took up as an attempt to bear witness to the trauma of their incarceration and surveillance by the U.S. government and its public, indicates the ghostly traces of the internment in Benedict's thesis. It comes as no surprise, then, that the Japanese American stand-ins for Benedict's anthropological study of the enemy Japanese might have the experience of having the shame culture's "judgment of the public upon his deeds." As David Palumbo-Liu remarks about early sociological studies of Japanese Americans that also described them as a people who always felt like they were being watched, "One could not ask for a better example of how body, psyche and space converge in mapping out the coordinates of Asian/American social ontology—why does it surprise these sociologists that racially marked people might have a particular intuition of being watched?"[38] If one is always being watched, and has been psychically conditioned to feel that surveillance in the psyche, the experience of shame stems not just from culture, but from the experience of surveillance and policing. Shame pervades Benedict's text, not as a cultural sanction based in a judgment of peers, but as an imperial strategy meant to force passivity and stifle a population's agency, power, and ability to act, and to justify military actions against a racialized enemy at home and abroad.

Benedict's emphasis on culture as a source of shame also affected her understanding of the constructedness of Japan's society, one created along imperial lines. This oversight can be traced to her main native informant, Robert "Bob" Hashima, whose name doesn't appear in Benedict's text but appears in her notes. Hashima was a *kibei* who was born in the United States and went to Japan at thirteen-years-old for education. In 1941, he returned and was immediately sent to an internment camp before getting a job with the Office of War Information (OWI) as Benedict's research assistant. As a *kibei*, an English-speaking U.S. citizen who could interpret for Benedict what she could not, Hashima occupied a liminal space between the "most alien enemy" and the too-familiar home, through which Benedict could both gather information about Japanese society she needed while retaining her critical distance. He could explain for her the small details she couldn't understand, including the concepts of *giri* (obligation) and *haji* (shame). However, according to C. Douglas Lummis, Hashima's credibility as an interpreter for Japanese cultural values was problematic at best, as Hashima's task was to explain to Benedict a culture that he himself wasn't altogether well-versed in, an ambivalence that Lummis reported was still apparent years later when Lummis interviewed him. Himself an outsider to Japan and its culture, Hashima entered Japanese society that had been organized and structured for war under Japanese imperial politics and assumed that it was "natural" Japanese society. What he took for Japanese culture was in fact Japan under militaristic ideology, an interpretation that suited the needs of both Benedict and the OWI. According to Lummis:

> *The Chrysanthemum and the Sword* is the product of a remarkable convergence of conceptions. Benedict, Hashima, and Japan's wartime militarists—though each for entirely different reasons—all promoted the myth that Japanese society was something like a family or tribe, that there were no functional class differences within it, that the ideas of democracy and rebellion were inconceivable within it, that its value system was traditional, that the core of its values was unchanged over the millennia, resulting in a national identity that was culturally determined and immutable, at least in the absence of powerful external force—in short, that the system was not the product of state or class oppression and that it was incomprehensible in terms of such categories as capitalism, colonialism, militarism which were being applied to other societies. To be totalitarian and to be Japanese were one in the same.[39]

By removing the political and social forces surrounding the experience of shame, making it a product of cultural training that shaped the psyche and the moral character of "the most alien enemy," Benedict uses "shame culture" to overshadow shame's role in empire building. That Japan had been embarking on its own imperial civilizing project throughout Asia is something entirely missing from Benedict's text. Sonia Ryang and Lummis both point out that Japan's identity as a military and political force attempting to secure its position in a world of competing Western empires is absent from her construction of the nation's shame culture. While Benedict does refer to Japan as an imperial state, this description is usually in regard to its head of state, Emperor Hirohito, rather than any other hallmarks typically relied upon to define an empire, such as political, military, economic, and cultural occupation and conquest over lands and peoples inside and outside national borders. Also, Benedict's focus on Japan assumes a homogeneity that doesn't exist, as part of what made up the "Japanese culture" included its dependence on and justification of lands it had colonized and occupied, including Korea, parts of China, Taiwan, the Ryukyu Islands, which includes Okinawa, as well as lands that had been former colonies of European nations, such as Vietnam, Indonesia, the Philippines, and Singapore, that it occupied during the war. *Chrysanthemum* also ignores the diversity in the population in Japan itself, completely disregarding the Indigenous Ainu as well as subjects from colonized territories who were, at the time of the war's end, living in Japan and serving the empire, either by choice or by force.[40] According to Ryang, "This omission granted the Japanese state a perfect alibi for World War II. This is not a coincidence—*Chrysanthemum* effectively presents Japan to its readers as a self-contained entity, having no link to any of the societies it colonized."[41] This omission also contributes to what Lummis diagnoses as a fundamental error of the book itself: Benedict's assumption that the culture she encountered in her research was a "natural" one, not one that had been constructed out of Japanese imperial goals and ambitions, which themselves specifically were crafted to mirror Western ones, including reliance on and exploitation of colonial territories and subjects.[42]

Kim argues that the United States during the Cold War didn't overlook Japanese imperial ambitions but ignored them as irrelevant because they were not antithetical to U.S. goals and the white supremacist, imperial taxonomies that undergirded them. The U.S. occupation of Japan was part of a strategy of "gendered racial rehabilitation" that sought to convert a former competitor for resources and territory in Asia into a junior partner and assimilated subject of strategic value in the new Cold War world order. As a nation of "honorary whites," Japan transformed from a most alien enemy to a necessary staging ground for U.S. economic and military expansion into Asia and a site of experimentation for building capitalist economies necessary for U.S. and European prosperity. Kim writes:

> Thus, liberal reforms, plans to try Emperor Hirohito as a war criminal, and the payment of war reparations to Japan's Asian conquests were eschewed in favor of building Japan's industry and developing a strong export-led economy, while at the same time expanding American military bases on the island. In this way, Japan's Asian neighbors were subjugated once again, this time as a 'quasi-colonial source of raw materials' for both Japan and its U.S. Cold War sponsor.[43]

As one of the key participants of the U.S. gendered racial rehabilitation of Japan, Benedict contributed to this project of disconnecting culture from empire, and, as a result, provides a foundation to delink shame from political and social forces that supported the ambitions of the empire. In addition to the racialized, gendered rehabilitation she performs in her own text, specifically gendering the nation of Japan as feminine and emasculating Japan and Asia as a deviant and weaker other,[44] she constructs a political eschatological vision of a world to come that has no place for shame. An affect traditionally associated with the feminine other, shame appears in *Chrysanthemum* as incongruent with the affective sentimentalities of integration that the United States was implementing at home and abroad, a project that *Chrysanthemum* itself, "the bible of American troops who undertook the occupation of Japan,"[45] was commissioned to help bring about. More than just describing the differences between two different cultures, Benedict outlines the differences between two empires and dictates the shape of empire for the Cold War era that is coming into focus. Simultaneously exposed and foreclosed, shame—or more precisely, shame and freedom from shame—become the vehicles for building nations in a new world order. As Ivy puts it, *Chrysanthemum* justifies and overlooks the atrocities of Japanese empire, allowing both nations to forget their imperial and colonizing ambitions under the forgiveness of the United States's paternalistic embrace. "By arguing that the notion of 'shame' could describe an entire culture, and that culture itself could account for the ethico-political actions of a modern nation-state, Benedict let the Japanese off the historical hook."[46] According to Ryang, *Chrysanthemum* presents a justification of Japan's past, disconnected from political ambitions that mirror those of the United States at the start of the Cold War and that will carry the United States and its Asian younger siblings into a new world order.[47] By placing cultural shame at the heart of Japanese national subjectivity, *Chrysanthemum* allows Japan to disavow the role that its former colonized territories and its present-day occupied lands play in both the nation's economic and political security, and in its understanding of what it means to be Japanese. "In this process, the marginals inside and outside Japan, including Koreans, Chinese, Ainu, Okinawans, the economically disposed (the homeless, day laborers, etc.), the socially disenfranchised (the disabled, women who did not fit the standard middle-class norms, the elderly, etc.), have been systematically silenced."[48] Much as Freud ignored differences within European empires in order to craft a European citizen subject formed through guilt, Benedict and those who championed her book in Japan used shame to construct a homogenous Japanese subject and dangled freedom from shame in the postwar period as an eschatological escape that also promised pardon, forgiveness, and forgetfulness for any atrocities committed under empire, particularly against those who were marginalized and oppressed by the nation's political and economic policies at home and abroad, past and present. Ryang argues:

> It is another paradox of Japanese society that the conventional understanding that Japanese are shame-oriented is blatantly contradicted by the Japanese state's ongoing refusal to grant citizenship and/or voting rights to former colonial subjects who continue to live in Japan. Whether Benedict intended this ugly reality or not is irrelevant, for the situation transcends the intention of any one author. *Chrysanthemum* is a text produced within the field of historically conditioned power relations

between the United States and Japan. The postwar military occupation helped to create the amnesia of Japan's former colonial oppression and aggression in Asia, while imposing on Japan the American logic of the Cold War and its power games.[49]

For the United States, this use of shame and freedom from shame was useful in ordering U.S. public opinion and affective responses for its actions in Asia both during the war and during its Cold War imperialism across Asia. Rather than being constrained by either guilt or shame, a world free of shame allows the United States to disavow responsibility for its actions in using atomic bombs on Hiroshima and Nagasaki, instead focusing on any potential future that could happen based on its principles and potential for moral good. According to Kim, this movement allows the United States to disavow any judgment for its past actions and rather occupy a space within the logic of the "future anterior," where what has happened becomes displaced by the possibility of what will have happened, if the United States hadn't checked Soviet power through those atomic bombings.[50] In attempting to manage its own reputation on the world stage as it worked to export free-market democracy worldwide, especially to decolonizing nations on the Asian and African continents, U.S. foreign policy officials had in *Chrysanthemum* a playbook on how to strategically utilize shame for purposes of national security and global integration. Rather than operating just as an Orientalist text, *Chrysanthemum* functioned as what Klein describes as a postorientalist text, operating not with the binary of Orientalism, but the fluid, complex, and intertwined affective logics of "American investment in, affiliation with, and appropriation of"[51] so-called Oriental countries, using shame and freedom from shame to demonstrate the simultaneous difference-yet-potential-for-sameness that existed between the Unites States and its new and future partners in the global political economy. In doing so, *Chrysanthemum* identifies a key similarity between the United States and Japan that marks both nations's imperial goals: A Cold War world to come, based in "de-mok-ra-sie" that is free of and free from shame, where difference is contained and integrated, lest it become a threat.

After the publication of *Chrysanthemum*, popular psychoanalytic and self-help theories on shame continued to define shame as a condition incompatible with democracy, particularly the global institution of democracy that the United States was attempting to install in nations around the world during the Cold War. These theories follow *Chrysanthemum*'s lead, describing shame as an experience of feminine passivity resulting from having one's being or innate identity looked at, judged, exposed, and found wanting or lacking, but also a condition that an individual (and nation) could heal from or, more vitally, escape from into a world free of shame, judgment, and critique.

THEOLOGICAL REM(A)INDERS OF COLD WAR SHAME

However, shame didn't disappear in this new world order, but remained for *Chrysanthemum*'s native informants, and for other Japanese and Japanese American citizens who were incarcerated for racial difference. Shame remains, especially for those within the U.S. borders who cannot be fully assimilated to the racial, gendered rehabilitation that takes place during the Cold War at home and abroad. Shame remains for those victims of both Japanese and U.S. imperialism whose sufferings and subjectivities are concealed by framings of shame that ignore political and lived contexts. According to Kim, "Survivors of the bomb and Japanese American subjects . . . are both constituted by and objects of gendered racial rehabilitation, which functions at once to heighten gendered racial shame and weaken it by holding Japanese and Japanese Americans at a certain, seemingly, proximity to whiteness."[52] Rather than disappearing from the world, shame instead falls upon those who are vulnerable, whose identities are suspect, and who are foreclosed from full participation in U.S. society through political, economic, social, and imperial strategies.

As a topic for theology, shame can be positioned as a remainder and a reminder of Cold War politics, policies, and worldviews. One example of this Cold War remnant lies in traditional biblical studies that rely upon the "shame culture" and "guilt culture" divisions of historical anthropological studies, continuing to position shame with the feminine, related to passivity and otherness that cannot be fully understood in the shame-free West.[53] As I began to research shame as a topic for theology, I began to question the distinctions between shame theories that emphasized a shame-free existence, and theories advocated by decolonial and queer theorists who advocated shame as a strategy of subversive identity and memory that points to the presence of those silenced or concealed by imperial shame, and opens possibilities for responsibility and relationships based on shared pain and shared hopes. Yet the distinctions between these theories are not absolute. Shame functions ambivalently and multiply, aiding in the oppressions that exile and silence those who pose a problem for empires, yet flashing up at inconvenient moments to remind those within imperial systems of their responsibilities and solidarities to and with one another. Shame is exposure; the question is what's being exposed, and by whom? Sociologist Helen Merrell Lynd, rejecting the traditional definitions of shame found in psychoanalytic and anthropological literature, defined shame as an interruption of the unquestioned self, an unexpected confrontation with who one is and who one has the potential to become. "Fully faced, shame may become not primarily something to be covered, but a positive experience of revelation."[54] Beyond Benedict's political eschatology of a world to come that's free from shame, Lynd points to shame's apocalyptic or messianic power to shake and remake one's inner and outer worlds. For Merrell Lynd, shame coupled with love that makes the revelation or exposure bearable, "makes possible the discovery of an integrity that is peculiarly one's own and of those characteristically human qualities that are at the same time most individualizing and most universal."[55]

As an affect traditionally assigned to women and so-called primitive others, and one wielded and repressed by imperial powers who also sought protection from it, shame has been shamefully avoided in theological reflection. For Christian theologians who are attempting to seriously reckon with the presence of empire in our sacred texts and our ways of understanding our relationship to the divine and one another, a theological turn toward shame invites encounters with multiple and myriad revelations, rem(a)inders, and responsibilities. For me, living in the midst of U.S. empire where Cold War logics still operate under new guises, reimagining shame—not only as flawed identity to be healed away through the embrace of individualistic resilience, and instead as a tactic for identifying injustices and breaks in relationships or away from cherished values—reorients me toward spaces where political and militaristic forces functioned to shape my identity and identifications. Ryang advises reading *Chrysanthemum* alongside works of decolonial writers such as Frantz Fanon and Jean Améry, "and many others whose writings would bring our understanding one step closer to the pain of the colonized, the persecuted, oppressed, and exterminated. Then—and only then—can *Chrysanthemum* become a text that speaks to humanity at large rather than just a graceful license of self-obsession and self-consolation by the victor on the vanquished."[56] Following Ryang's advice, I seek in investigating shame as a topic for political theological reflection, not the eschatology of a shame-free world, but the apocalyptic revelations of shame that overturns, reveals, and remakes me along with the worlds I inhabit with others, whose sufferings and blushes we share.

BIBLIOGRAPHY

Arel, Stephanie N. *Affect Theory, Shame, and Christian Formation.* New York: Palgrave MacMillan, 2016.

Bascara, Victor. *Model Minority Imperialism.* Minneapolis: University of Minnesota Press, 2006.

Benedict, Ruth. *The Chrysanthemum and the Sword: Patterns of Japanese Culture.* Boston: Houghton Mifflin Company; reprinted by Mariner Books, 2005.

Brown, Brené. *I Thought It Was Just Me (But It Isn't): Making the Journey from "What Will People Think?" to "I Am Enough."* New York: Avery Books, 2008.

Burrus, Virginia. *Saving Shame: Martyrs, Saints and Other Abject Subjects.* Philadelphia: University of Pennsylvania Press, 2008.

———, Mark D. Jordan, and Karmen Mackendrick, eds. *Seducing Augustine: Bodies, Desires, Confessions.* New York: Fordham University Press, 2010.

Chung Simpson, Caroline. *An Absent Presence: Japanese Americans in Postwar American Culture, 1945–1960.* Durham: Duke University Press, 2001.

Gilroy, Paul. *Darker than Blue: On the Moral Economies of Black Atlantic Culture*. Cambridge: The Belknap Press of Harvard University Press, 2010.

———. *Postcolonial Melancholia*. New York: Columbia University Press, 2005.

Ivy, Marilyn. "Benedict's Shame." *Cabinet*, no. 31. Fall 2008. www.cabinetmagazine.org/issues/31/ivy.php. Accessed October 24, 2018.

Khanna, Ranjana. *Dark Continents: Psychoanalysis and Colonialism*. Durham: Duke University Press, 2003.

Kim, Jodi. *Ends of Empire: Asian American Critique and the Cold War*. Minneapolis: University of Minnesota Press, 2010.

Klein, Christina. *Cold War Orientalism: Asia in the Middlebrow Imagination, 1945–1961*. Berkeley: University of California Press, 2003.

Lie, John. "Ruth Benedict's Legacy of Shame: Orientalism and Occidentalism in the Study of Japan." *Asian Journal of Social Science*, vol. 29, no. 2 (2001): 249–261.

Lummis, C. Douglas. "Ruth Benedict's Obituary for Japanese Culture." *The Asia-Pacific Journal: Japan Focus*, vol. 5, issue 7. July 3, 2007. www.apjjf.org/-C.-Douglas-Lussmis/2474/article.html. Accessed August 9, 2018.

Malina, Bruce J. *The New Testament World: Insights from Cultural Anthropology*. Louisville: Westminster John Knox Press, 2001.

Merrell Lynd, Helen. *On Shame and the Search for Identity*. London: Routledge, 1958.

Palumbo-Liu, David. *Asian/America: Historical Crossings of a Racial Frontier*. Stanford: Stanford University Press, 1999.

Pattison, Stephen. *Shame: Theory, Therapy, Theology*. Cambridge: Cambridge University Press, 2000.

Price Tangney, June, and Ronda L. Dearing. *Shame and Guilt*. New York: The Guilford Press, 2002.

Roxbury, Emily. *The Spectacle of Japanese American Trauma: Racial Performativity and World War II*. Honolulu: University of Hawai'i Press, 2008.

Ryang, Sonia. "*Chrysanthemum*'s Strange Life: Ruth Benedict in Postwar Japan." *Japan Policy Research Institute Occasional Paper* 32. July 2004. www.jpri.org/publications/occasionalpapers/op32.html. Accessed October 25, 2018.

Shannon, Christopher. "'A World Made Safe for Differences': Ruth Benedict's *The Chrysanthemum and the Sword*," In *Reading Benedict, Reading Mead: Feminism, Race, and Imperial Visions*, edited by Dolores Janiewski and Lois W. Banner, 70–85. Baltimore: Johns Hopkins University Press, 2004.

Stille, Alexander. "Experts Can Help Rebuild a Country." *The New York Times*. July 19, 2003. www.nytimes.com/2003/07/19/arts/experts-can-help-rebuild-a-country.html. Accessed October 25, 2018.

Yoneyama Lisa. *Hiroshima Traces: Time, Space, and the Dialectics of Memory*. Berkeley: University of Calilfornia Press, 1999.

Yoshihara, Mari. *Embracing the East: White Women and American Orientalism*. Oxford: Oxford University Press, 2003.

NOTES

1. June Price Tangney and Ronda L. Dearing, *Shame and Guilt* (New York: The Guilford Press, 2002), 137.

2. Brené Brown, *I Thought It Was Just Me (But It Isn't): Making the Journey from "What Will People Think?" to "I Am Enough"* (New York: Avery Books, 2008), 5.

3. Victor Bascara, *Model Minority Imperialism* (Minneapolis: University of Minnesota Press, 2006), 8.

4. Paul Gilroy, *Postcolonial Melancholia* (New York: Columbia University Press, 2005), 99.

5. Paul Gilroy, *Darker than Blue: On the Moral Economies of Black Atlantic Culture* (Cambridge: The Belknap Press of Harvard University Press, 2010), 77.

6. Ranjana Khanna, *Dark Continents: Psychoanalysis and Colonialism* (Durham: Duke University Press, 2003), 17

7. Khanna, *Dark Continents*, 6.

8. Stephen Pattison describes the "pitifully few straightforwardly theological responses to shame" in the canon of European and U.S. theology as unsubstantial and unhelpful in any project to take shame seriously as a topic for systematic theological reflection. See Pattison, *Shame: Theory, Therapy, Theology* (Cambridge: Cambridge University Press, 2000), 190

9. Major texts relating to shame and Christian studies include Pattison, *Shame*; Virginia Burrus, *Saving Shame: Martyrs, Saints and Other Abject Subjects* (Philadelphia: University of Pennsylvania Press, 2008); *Seducing Augustine: Bodies, Desires, Confessions*, ed. Virginia Burrus, Mark D. Jordan, and Karmen Mackendrick (New York: Fordham University Press, 2010); and Stephanie N. Arel, *Affect Theory, Shame, and Christian Formation* (New York: Palgrave MacMillan, 2016).

10. Jodi Kim, *Ends of Empire: Asian American Critique and the Cold War* (Minneapolis: University of Minnesota Press, 2010), 3.

11. According to Andrew Hammond, what was a Cold War for the United States and Soviet Union was a "hot war" that was fought in multiple territories and nations, resulting in the deaths of more than twenty million people—eleven million in Asia alone. See Kim, *Ends of Empire*, 17.

12. Kim, *Ends of Empire*, 11.

13. Christina Klein defines "middlebrow" culture as being made up of the activities, texts, and institutions that were popular with and consumed by mainstream Americans, and specifically instructed this population about their identities and responsibilities as American citizens. Themes of tolerance, acceptance, and universalism were common themes that middlebrow intellectuals encouraged U.S. citizens to embrace. "The producers of middlebrow culture . . . sought to situate their audience in relation to a world increasingly as interconnected, whose ligatures were defined by the logic of the Cold War." See Christina Klein, *Cold War Orientalism: Asia in the Middlebrow Imagination, 1945–1961* (Berkeley: University of California Press, 2003), 13.

14. Klein, *Cold War Orientalism*, 9.

15. Klein, *Cold War Orientalism*, 13.

16. Klein, *Cold War Orientalism*, 23.

17. Klein, *Cold War Orientalism*, 26.

18. John Lie, "Ruth Benedict's Legacy of Shame: Orientalism and Occidentalism in the Study of Japan," *Asian Journal of Social Science* vol. 29, no. 2 (2001): 254.

19. As Mari Yoshihara observes, "Benedict's book was popular in Washington because, according to Margaret Mead, 'It was the kind of book that colonels could mention to generals and captains to admiration without fear of producing an explosion against "jargon,"' and was also 'safe to put in the hands of congressmen alert to the resist the 'schemes of long-haired intellectuals.'" See Mari Yoshihara, *Embracing the East: White Women and American Orientalism* (Oxford: Oxford University Press, 2003), 188

20. Kim, *Ends of Empire*, 10.

21. Klein, *Cold War Orientalism*, 63.

22. Caroline Chung Simpson describes this guilt and anxiety in reference to the Hiroshima Maidens project of the 1950s. See Chung Simpson, *An Absent Presence: Japanese Americans in Postwar American Culture, 1945–1960* (Durham: Duke University Press, 2001), 115. Kim also addresses the guilt in the U.S. populace regarding the Hiroshima and Nagasaki atomic bombings. See Kim, *Ends of Empire*, 113–114.

23. Ruth Benedict, *The Chrysanthemum and the Sword: Patterns of Japanese Culture* (Boston: Houghton Mifflin Company; reprinted by Mariner Books, 2005), 5.

24. Benedict, *The Chrysanthemum and the Sword*, 1.

25. Marilyn Ivy, "Benedict's Shame," *Cabinet,* no. 31, Fall 2008, www.cabinetmagazine.org/issues/31/ivy.php (accessed October 24, 2018).

26. Christopher Shannon argues that Benedict's main perspective on the Japanese was not that they needed to develop themselves along the lines of a guilt culture in order to be more like the United States, but rather that both the United States and Japan could benefit from being more like anthropologists. That is, the only way both cultures could develop and progress civilizationally would be by adopting a kind of anthropological professional distance from their cultures as she was doing as their anthropological interpreter. See Shannon, "'A World Made Safe for Differences': Ruth Benedict's *The Chrysanthemum and the Sword,*" in *Reading Benedict, Reading Mead: Feminism, Race, and Imperial Visions,* ed. Dolores Janiewski and Lois W. Banner (Baltimore: Johns Hopkins University Press, 2004), 81.

27. Benedict, *The Chrysanthemum and the Sword,* 288–289.

28. C. Douglas Lummis observes that "Benedict's attempt to render the word 'democracy' into the Japanese phonetic system is an embarrassing reminder of her ignorance of the basics of that language." See Lummis, "Ruth Benedict's Obituary for Japanese Culture," *The Asia-Pacific Journal: Japan Focus,* vol. 5, issue 7, July 3, 2007, www.apjjf.org/-C.-Douglas-Lussmis/2474/article.html (accessed August 9, 2018): 14n.

29. Benedict, *The Chrysanthemum and the Sword,* 294.

30. Benedict, *The Chrysanthemum and the Sword,* 296.

31. Benedict, *The Chrysanthemum and the Sword,* 315.

32. Emily Roxbury, *The Spectacle of Japanese American Trauma: Racial Performativity and World War II* (Honolulu: University of Hawai'i Press, 2008), 52.

33. Emily Roxbury, *The Spectacle of Japanese American Trauma,* 52.

34. Emily Roxbury, *The Spectacle of Japanese American Trauma,* 53.

35. Ezra Vogel in Roxbury, *The Spectacle of Japanese American Trauma,* 53.

36. Roxbury, *The Spectacle of Japanese American Trauma,* 54.

37. Roxbury, *The Spectacle of Japanese American Trauma;* Benedict, *The Chrysanthemum and the Sword,* 29.

38. David Palumbo-Liu, *Asian/America: Historical Crossings of a Racial Frontier* (Stanford: Stanford University Press, 1999), 301.

39. Lummis, "Ruth Benedict's Obituary for Japanese Culture," 12.

40. Lisa Yoneyama reports that at the time of the U.S. atomic attack on Hiroshima, records report that out of the 350,000 to 400,000 people in Hiroshima who were killed by the bombing itself or lethally exposed to radiation, at least 45,000 were Koreans. Japanese records report that between 1939 and 1945, the Japanese government imported more than 700,000 Koreans as forced laborers to work in Japanese war efforts. See Yoneyama, *Hiroshima Traces: Time, Space, and the Dialectics of Memory* (Berkeley: University of Calilfornia Press, 1999), 152.

41. Sonia Ryang, "*Chrysanthemum's* Strange Life: Ruth Benedict in Postwar Japan," Japan Policy Research Institute Occasional Paper 32, July 2004, www.jpri.org/publications/occasionalpapers/op32.html (accessed October 25, 2018).

42. Lummis, "Ruth Benedict's Obituary for Japanese Culture," 8.

43. Kim, *Ends of Empire,* 105.

44. Benedict consistently writes about the nation itself through feminized pronouns; Japan is always "she." While Japanese women appear periodically in the text, Japanese individuals tend to take the form of the literal "everyman." While Benedict is likely following the practices of her era, Yoshihara describes this practice as significant and original to Benedict in regard to Western analysis of Japan. According to Yoshihara, Benedict was the first to feminize Japan not by focusing on Japanese women, which was common in the literature of the era, but to take models of Japanese men and emasculate or feminize them, thus reinforcing and reinscribing Western imperial notions. See Yoshihara, *Embracing the East,* 172.

45. Alexander Stille, "Experts Can Help Rebuild a Country," *The New York Times,* July 19, 2003, www.nytimes.com/2003/07/19/arts/experts-can-help-rebuild-a-country.html (accessed October 25, 2018).

46. Ivy, "Benedict's Shame."

47. Ryang, "*Chrysanthemum*'s Strange Life," 7.

48. Ryang, "*Chrysanthemum*'s Strange Life," 9.

49. Ryang, "*Chrysanthemum*'s Strange Life," 10.

50. Kim quotes a line from the comedian Rod Corddry on *The Daily Show with Jon Stewart* to sum up the logic of the future anterior in regard to U.S. imperialism. Referring to the U.S. torture of inmates at Abu Ghraib prison in Iraq, Coddry argues, "We (the United States) shouldn't be judged on our actions. . . . It's our *principles* that matter, or inspiring, abstract notions. Remember, remember, Jon, just because torturing prisoners is something we *did* doesn't mean it's something we *would* do." See Kim, *Ends of Empire*, 110.

51. Klein, *Cold War Orientalism*, 15.

52. Kim, *Ends of Empire*, 125–126.

53. For example, see Bruce J. Malina, *The New Testament World: Insights from Cultural Anthropology* (Louisville: Westminster John Knox Press, 2001), a still-influential text on the social worlds of the New Testament.

54. Helen Merrell Lynd, *On Shame and the Search for Identity* (London: Routledge, 1958), 20.

55. Merrell Lynd, *On Shame and the Search for Identity*, 257.

56. Ryang, "*Chrysanthemum*'s Strange Life," 10.

FIVE

The Remains of the War Ruins

A Palimpsest of Necropolitics — America's Genocide and Military Prostitution in South Korea

Keun-Joo Christine Pae

A ROAD TO CAMP STANLEY: OPENING

It takes less than an hour by subway to get to Uijeongbu from old town Seoul, the capital city of South Korea. Uijeongbu is the largest satellite city north of Seoul, where it is not far from the border with North Korea. Prior to the Korean War (1950–1953), Uijeongbu was a sparsely populated farming village: a village of ten thousand with only one silk mill representing all of the industry in the area.[1] With the Korean War, hundreds of people, including gangsters and UN forces, swarmed in and created a netherworld.[2] Today Uijeongbu's skyline does not show any trace of the war. However, a ten-minute taxi ride from the Uijeongbu Station is Bbaetbeol, a small rural village where Camp Stanley has existed for more than fifty years. The longtime residents of the village still remember the bloody Korean War, the construction of the American base, bars and clubs along the hilly main road, and the modernization of the village in the 1970s.

In Bbaetbeol, *Durebang* (known as "My Sister's Place" to the English-speaking world), an organization founded by two Christian women, has advocated for the human rights of Western princesses (or *yanggongju* in Korean) for more than thirty years. "Western princess" is a derogatory term referring to the Korean women who sexually cater to American servicemen. When I visited *Durebang* in the summer of 2013, Camp Stan-

105

ley prepared its relocation to Pyeongtaek, a satellite city south of Seoul, where U.S. army, navy, and air force bases would be concentrated in a new military garrison. Bbaetbeol, facing the vast rice fields, did not look bucolic or peaceful, but odd. The village's serpentine and narrow main road began from *Durebang*'s cemented building through the top of the hill. Along the road were nightclubs with shuttered doors scattered among red-brick family houses. Streets were empty in the middle of one hot and humid summer day. It was not easy to imagine the lives of Western princesses in the heydays of the Bbaetbeol camptown. However, my journey to search for them had begun a long time ago, as Korean American Sociologist Grace Cho says that the Western princess is "a shadowy figure hidden in the collective psyche of the Korean diaspora."[3] No matter how comfortably I forget about Western princesses, they have lived in my psyche through my awareness of secrecy in my own family: one of my father's cousins was married to an African American GI and gave birth to a black daughter. My family has never talked about the black girl. I do not even remember her face. In our silence, however, we all know where she comes from, and how my aunt has lived since she came back to Korea with a black girl in her arms. Aunt S worked at a PX store on a U.S. military base in Uijeongbu when she met her ex-husband. As soon as she started dating a black man from the base, she was called a Western princess—the tag has followed her ever since.

This essay studies U.S. military prostitution in South Korea as feminist praxis to resist the U.S.-led militarization of the world. The study first questions why certain experiences of colonialism, war, and militarized violence have been silenced for a long time, and why these silenced and suppressed memories cannot be linearly retrieved. With a focus on two particular historical contexts—U.S. military occupation in South Korea (1945–1948) and the Korean War (1949–1953), this chapter delineates what the Western princess embodies. The two historical events, however, are not the beginning or the end of U.S. military prostitution in South Korea. Rather, they are placed in the endless cycle of past, present, and future in the larger human history of militarized suffering, always invoking different memories of war. In other words, militarized violence at the present moment can access the conscious experience only through the temporality where the past and the future collide with each other.

According to M. Jacqui Alexander, "time is neither vertically accumulated nor horizontally teleological."[4] Hence, she proposes the idea of the palimpsest: "the previous text having been imperfectly erased and remaining, therefore, still partly visible."[5] The palimpsestic time always offers the present as the meeting point between the past and the future, leading one to consciously look at what has been erased and what will leave traces. By framing time as that of a palimpsest of the patriarchal nation-building, heterosexual militarization, and colonialism, we can look at the stories of Western princesses from multiple angles and through many nameless victims of Japanese colonialism in South Korea, U.S. military occupation, the Korean War, and America's wars abroad. These stories appear familiar and unfamiliar, historically specific and transcendental, visible and invisible, and after all, ambiguous.

This chapter first engages the contemporary memories of U.S. military prostitution. These memories read a palimpsest of the institution of prostitution, developed and maintained during Japanese colonialism and U.S. military occupation in South Korea and consolidated through the Korean War. The body of the Western princess, thus, projects the silenced memories of history's victims, such as those who were massacred during the Korean War. Toward the end of this chapter, as a Christian feminist social ethicist, I argue why studying military prostitution is an important process of analyzing gendered and militarized American politics from a transnational feminist perspective and of developing gender- and sexuality-sensitive Christian discourse on war and peace.

THE GHOST OF CAMPTOWN: CONTEMPORARY MEMORIES OF U.S. MILITARY PROSTITUTION

It took more than fifty years for Koon-Ja Ha, survivor of the Japanese military "comfort women" system, to break the silence about her experience. Shaming Korea, Japanese colonizers, and even herself in public, Ha exhumed the traumatic deaths and silence of countless Asian women who were sexually enslaved by Imperial Japan at its bases.[6] The Japanese military "comfort women" system ended with World War II in the Pacific. When the survivors of the "comfort women" system finally broke their silence in the early 1990s, however, their stories became contemporary. The stories are still alive in the twenty-first century because the Japanese government refuses to officially acknowledge the presence of the forced "comfort women" system and to apologize for the sexual exploitation of colonized women. At the same time, the comfort women's breaking silence brought "the haunting presence" of the dead Western princess, such as Geum-i Yun, whose death became a spectral force that made visible "the continuing traumas of U.S. military domination."[7]

Yun was not the first Western princess whose body was mutilated and murdered by an American soldier in South Korea. Differently from other Western princesses' deaths, Yun's sparked a national movement against GI crimes and spread anti-American sentiments in Korea. This mass movement was the expansion of Koreans's collective response to Imperial Japan's "comfort women" system, which finally emerged in public consciousness.

In October 1992, Private Kenneth Markle from West Virginia murdered a twenty-six-year-old camp town prostitute, Geum-i Yun, in cold blood. Markle was one of her clients who had last been seen fighting with another GI over Yun before he killed her. Markle beat Yun to death and mutilated her dead body, leaving a Coca-Cola bottle and beer bottles in her womb and vagina, an umbrella in her rectum, and the powder of laundry detergent all around Yun's room to clean up her blood.[8] The grotesque body of Yun translated into the unilateral relationship between Korea and the United States. The heart of her death lies in the violence against the sexualized body of poor Korean women, who were neglected at the bottom of the social ladder in Korea. While alive, Yun was a part of one of the most despised groups in Korea due to her sexual labor for American soldiers. While dead, she became everyone's sweetheart, an innocent sister, or a girl next door, who sacrificed her body to feed her family. She was subsequently turned into an icon of Korean national-ism—her rape and death were equated with those of Korea by (neo)colonialists. The nationalists made Yun's gender and sexuality irrel-evant to their social activism against U.S. (neo)colonialism.[9] According to Hee-jin Jeong, a Korean feminist scholar and activist, the male-dominated Korean nationalist movement treated Yun's mutilated body as the prop-erty of Korea in the power struggle with the United States.[10] The flip side reveals the dark realities of wartime sexual violence against women and military prostitution justified by male groups: since women are seen as the carriers of culture and as the property of the nation, gender-based sexual violence has been the systematic weapon of war.

Yun's death raised social awareness of camptown prostitution in South Korea on a popular level. Since the Korean War, Koreans have known the presence of camptown prostitution, but the majority of them avoided speaking about the institution until Yun's case. The mass anti-U.S. movement in Korea in response to Yun's death reveals one crucial truth: when society is forced to excavate the traumatic memories of war, it selects only certain truths, just as the gender and sexuality of Yun were erased, and the public knew nothing about Yun except for her tragic death. Only the remaining partial truth allows us to trace the Western princess in the history of U.S.–Korean relations, while the unknown and untold truth continues to haunt us, whether we are conscious or uncon-scious of her presence.

According to Cho, the Western princess is a ghost composed of the material remains of the Korean War and the "residues of the daily prac-tices of war."[11] Camptown prostitution reminds the world that the war is still going on in the Korean Peninsula. Its own presence further disinte-grates Korea's dramatic economic development and America's narrative of saving Third World countries from poverty, tyranny, and gender op-pression. Cho further argues that the haunting effect of the Western prin-cess is produced not so much by the original trauma but "by the fact of being kept hidden precisely within the gaps in conscious knowledge about history."[12] Being the forgotten war in the United States, the Korean War has created a big hole in the collective American psyche. The disavowal of Americans's sexual exploitation of Korean women and mass killings of Korean civilians during the Korean War has a haunting force over the American public while silencing Korean Americans's traumatic memories of the war. For Cho, writing about the ghost (Western princess) is traumatizing the text (the official narrative of war) and projecting itself into a future haunting, because just as a new trauma can trigger an old one (a flashback), it can also flash forward.[13]

Cho's work sheds important light on my Christian, feminist consciousness. Writing about war and its deadly impact on humanity requires any ethicist of spiritual strength, moral courage, and intellectual rigor to face the haunting power of war. Namely, the important ethical tasks are how to rememorialize history's phantomlike victims and how to heal our past, present, and future traumatized by war.

SUFFERING PAST: U.S. MILITARY OCCUPATION OF SOUTH KOREA

U.S. military prostitution in Korea began when the Twenty-Fourth Army Corps, consisting of some seventy-two thousand men, arrived in Korea to transfer power from the crumbling Japanese empire to Korea, a supposedly independent country. Due to the sudden surrender of Japan, General Douglas MacArthur selected the units to deploy from Okinawa to South Korea by availability and transport.[14] The primary purpose of this deployment was to stop the Soviet Union from expanding its power to Northeast Asia. Soviet armies were already present in the north of the thirty-eighth parallel of the Korean Peninsula, disarming Japanese soldiers.[15] Unlike the Soviet Union, which did not attempt to establish its occupant government in North Korea, the United States immediately founded its military government and would rule over the southern part of the Korean Peninsula.

By the end of 1945, Bupyeong, a small town near Incheon, became the first entertaining camptown, where American soldiers sought out liquor and women for recreation. Bupyeong had public brothels around one of the important military bases of Imperial Japan.[16] U.S. military prostitution in Korea is a continuation of Imperial Japan's system of public prostitution. The Japanese colonial government (1910–1945) constructed red light districts, prohibiting people from selling and buying sex outside of these districts. Japan's carefully installed system of public prostitution was the backbone of militarized prostitution in modern Korea.

It was not a coincidence that Korean women's first organized movement after independence was to pressure the U.S. military government (USMG) to prohibit prostitution. In response to women's movements, the USMG banned public prostitution in South Korea in 1947. However, privatized prostitution became popularized due to pandemic poverty in the country. Service clubs and dance halls for American soldiers were quasi-public brothels where buying and selling sex were available and where the U.S. military monitored sex workers for venereal disease control.[17] The USMG suppressed unregulated prostitution to control the spread of venereal disease while regulating prostitution as "an expedient means of entertaining and controlling male soldiers."[18]

The foreign army's use of Korean women's bodies was not new to Koreans, who had survived through thirty-five years of Japanese colonialism. Military prostitution catering to Japanese soldiers began after Japan had forcefully opened the Korean market in 1876, bringing a growing influx of Japanese merchants, soldiers, and laborers. The first red light districts in Korea were founded in a Japanese residential area, the District of Hell (*jiokgolmok*), in Busan in 1902.[19] Japanese prostitutes, who were brought into Korea, worked at special bars and restaurants called *Yu-kwak* for Japanese customers. The public brothels were divided into Japanese and Korean brothels based on discrimination against Koreans, ethnic hierarchy, and racial purity.[20] Throughout the Japanese colonial period (1910–1945), the number of public prostitutes increased. For example, in 1937, 14,618 Korean women worked in public brothels due to poverty, while countless women were working in private brothels.[21]

Although the Japanese colonial government claimed that the public brothels were necessary to maintain a robust custom and to control venereal disease, both public and private brothels were hotbeds for venereal diseases across Korea. In 1928, the chair of the Public Health Division of the Japanese colonial government stated that fifty percent of Korean adults were infected with venereal disease. According to his claim, venereal disease was civilized disease, and this percentage was lower than that of Japanese adults with VD.[22] This odd claim rationalized Koreans's lack of civilization compared to their Japanese counterparts. Certainly, seen through Japan's system of public prostitution, the imperial ruling of Japan was gendered and sexualized.

During its military expansion between 1930 and 1945, Imperial Japan actively consumed women's bodies through the military "comfort women" system. At first, private businesses recruited Japanese women from poor rural areas for "military comfort stations" in China and other areas where large numbers of Japanese soldiers were stationed.[23] After the Sino-Japanese War in 1937, the Japanese military directly managed the comfort stations in order to control the rampant spread of venereal disease. The military drafted a large number of Korean women, mostly in their teens and twenties, because young Korean women in the Confucian society were "chaste enough to be free of venereal disease and young enough to endure disease if it developed."[24] The "comfort women" system was an integral part of Japan's military expansion, just as camptown prostitution is a fixed nature of the American military empire.

The post-colonial Korean society saw prostitution as the legacy of Japanese colonialism. From a nationalist perspective, the society depicted prostitutes as innocent victims of poverty and colonialism. However, after public prostitution had been outlawed, mainstream Korean society criticized all prostitutes and their male clients for deteriorating social morale and for neglecting their duties, such as looking after the poor and the hungry, as poverty was pandemic during the American military occupation.

Not only Imperial Japan's military "comfort women" system but also Japan's carefully planned public brothels are a palimpsest of U.S. military prostitution in South Korea. The USMG's lack of desire to protect Korean women from poverty, sexual exploitation, and public and private prostitution added more secrecy and shame to the Western princess. The Western princess represents that Korean women have been sexually exploited by colonial powers, their bodies condemned to death, while their sexualized labor was extracted for the fostering life of empire, and that these bodies have also been used to disease colonized men and to invoke feelings of guilt, humiliation, and powerlessness among these men.

Korean Women's Movement for Anti-Prostitution during American Military Occupation

It is worth exploring why Korean women's organizations pressured the USMG to abolish prostitution because their perspectives on prostitution are still prevailing in current Korean society. On May 17, 1946, the USMG announced Military Law Article 70, which prevented trafficking of girls and women.[25] Although Koreans interpreted this law as the closing of public brothels, the law prevented only quasi-slavery-type human trafficking rather than prostitution per se. Since most prostitutes were illiterate, this law did not help them free themselves even in the case that they were trafficked.[26] The inadequacy of Military Law Article 70 led Korean women's organizations to deliver a unified voice of anti-prostitution to the USMG, regardless of their different political ideologies. On February 14, 1947, the USMG announced an anti-prostitution law.[27]

Most leaders of the women's organizations agreed that any form of prostitution should be stopped immediately. However, their perspectives on prostitution differed, according to their political and religious positions. Socialist feminists understood prostitution within the larger socioeconomic structure, while rightists saw it in terms of a personal choice and a moral issue. These socialists argued that human trafficking was caused by deficiencies in the social system, such as poverty, and thus, economic reform for the poor must accompany the prohibition of prostitution.[28] Although women's activist groups shared compassion for prostitutes, accentuating their human dignity, most Christian female leaders believed that a woman entered into prostitution because of her ignorance. Politically conservative Christian leaders argued that because prostitution undermined (heteropatriarchal) family values, brothels must be shut down immediately in order to protect families and children from sexual corruption and venereal diseases.[29] These politically and religiously conservative women's organizations, favored by the USMG, opened shelters and rehabilitating facilities for the prostitutes who subsequently lost economic means after anti-prostitution laws had been enacted. However, most shelters and facilities were ineffective because the women leaders were ignorant of prostitutes's social backgrounds, and later because they lacked funding resources.[30]

After the anti-prostitution law was enacted, the owners of many public brothels turned their businesses into private bars and restaurants where selling and buying sex was secretly available. No records were found showing where public prostitutes went or what happened to them after the government had dismissed them. Nine months after the public brothels were closed down, the number of women involved in prostitution increased by more than fifty thousand from only two thousand before their closing.[31]

The Korean women's anti-prostitution movement in post-colonial Korea shows the historical root of elite women activists's ambiguous relationships with prostitutes. Female prostitutes are often objectified by women activists or targeted by human rights organizations. Unfortunately, there are no easy answers for how to understand prostitution, how to be in solidarity with prostitutes, or how to identify with them in social activism. The ghost of the Western princess has haunted Korean women's activism, too. No matter how hard they try to change social structures for gender equality and anti-violence against women, they may find their activism to be jeopardized by the presence of structured prostitution, aided by the institutionalized military and the masculinist government.

KOREAN WAR, FORGOTTEN WAR, UNFORGETTABLE WAR: CIVILIAN MASSACRES AND PROSTITUTION

Korean American critical theorist Jodi Kim defines the Korean War as "an arrested project of decolonization."[32] The Korean War (1950–1953) might have begun as a local civil conflict and an attempt to reunify Korea in the aftermath first of Japanese colonialism and then of American and Soviet division and occupation. Korea's nonaligned "third way" gets derailed, interpellated, and superseded by the two Cold War superpowers with China later added to the constellation.[33]

During the first month of the war (July 1950), the North Korean Army pushed the South Korean–U.S. defense line southward all the way to Busan, the southeastern tip of the Korean Peninsula. The United States acted quickly upon North Korea's crossing of the 38th parallel. However, the Truman administration did not have the proper system of knowledge to interpret North Korea's attack as "part of a continuum in Korea's own local efforts at reunification and decolonization."[34] In the larger context of Cold War politics, North Korea was merely seen as a proxy of Stalin, who was perceived as trying to expand Soviet power to Asia. At the beginning of the Korean War, "Korea" was insignificant to the United States, but the prevention of the Soviet expansion was crucial for the rest of the world from an American perspective.

The United States intervened in the war first by bringing the case of the Korean War to the United Nations. While the Soviet Union was absent at the United Nations Security Council meeting, the United States urged the UN to enter the Korean War to defend South Korean civilians. A UN resolution for a "police action" turned into a "de facto U.S. operation in Korea."[35] The U.S. forces, under the banner of the UN, took control of Seoul from North Korean forces (September 28, 1950) and pushed the North Korean People's Army to the border with China. Soon the Chinese troops entered the Korean War and defeated the United Nations Allied Army (November 1950–January 1951). The United States withdrew from North Korea (January 4, 1951), and Seoul fell into the hands of the North Korea's Chinese allies (January 4, 1951).

In March 1951, Seoul was recaptured by the United Nations Allied Army and the Korean War fell into a stalemate along the 38th parallel. On July 23, 1953, the armistice between North Korea/China and the United States/the UN was signed, and the current demilitarized zone between the Koreas confirmed for an indefinite period. The Korean War physically ended where it had begun without solving anything. As Bruce Cumings points out, "only the status quo ante was restored, only an armistice held the peace."[36] The Korean War has allowed the division and political tension between North and South Korea to continue until now. South Korea still experiences ideological conflict and division among the citizens: political conservatives have blindly labeled any progressive political movement as a communist movement, whether for the democratization of the country, reunification, anti-war, labor justice, or the LGBT movement.

For the United States, the Korean War was an opportunity to congeal its Cold War logic. The Korean War catalyzed a "Cold War consensus" and set a precedent for "how the United States would interpret and intervene in civil wars and anticolonial movements in Asia and elsewhere."[37] Furthermore, the consolidated U.S.–Korean relations through the Korean War became the constitution of Korean America as "an imperial and gendered racial formation."[38] No matter how hard America has tried to forget about its less-than-successful military operation in the Korean Peninsula, the very presence of Korean America inside the United States has always reminded the American public of the war. At the same time, the U.S. military's presence in South Korea makes Koreans always feel the war. U.S. military prostitution signifies the intimate and violent nature of U.S.–Korean relations.

America's Korean War and Civilian Massacres

The Korean War was the main force is creating the ghost of the Western princess, especially because the war shed too much blood of the innocent. Mass killings, massacre, or what Korean Sociologist Dong Choon Kim does not hesitate to call "genocide," is the crucial character of the Korean War. Kim offers three categories of mass killings of civilians: (1) U.S. troops's direct killings of civilians as part of their military operation, (2) South Korea's executions of "suspicious civilians" or political prisoners, and (3) state-sponsored political or personal reprisals committed by irregular right-wing youth groups and civilians.[39] Since those who were killed by American and South Korean soldiers were blindly labeled as communists, civilian massacres committed by the said parties have been rarely known to the public.

One of the early massacres of civilians happened at Nogeun-Ri, Chungchung Province, the central part of South Korea between July 25 and 29, 1950. The Nogeun-Ri massacre (also written as the No Gun Ri massacre) became known to the public in 1999 when the Associated Press started uncovering the U.S. army orders to shoot the approaching refugees.[40] The press released a series of interviews conducted with the survivors of the massacre and the Seventh Cavalry veterans who were ordered to shoot the refugees indiscriminately at the twin-underpass railroad bridge at Nogeun-Ri. The refugees were hiding there from the U.S. air bombing that instantly killed more than one hundred refugees. The survivors of the air strikes would be shot to death by American soldiers inside the underpass. More than four hundred refugees in total were killed at Nogeun-Ri.[41]

Grace Cho says that Nogeun-Ri evokes the future of the My Lai massacre in Vietnam in 1968.[42] Nogeun-Ri also evokes the past of Wounded Knee. On December 29, 1890, the U.S. Seventh Cavalry, that same regiment later responsible for the Nogeun-Ri massacre, slaughtered as many as three hundred mostly unarmed and defenseless Lakota men, women, and children at snowy and icy Wounded Knee.[43] Since the present moment of militarized violence happens too quickly to be perceived, it is accessible to conscious experience only through its traces. Since the trauma of militarized violence can traverse the boundaries of time and space (for example, Wounded Knee in 1890, Nogeun-Ri in 1950, and Mỹ Lai in 1968), the present becomes the temporality in which past and future collide. In the history of America's wars, someone's past is always somebody's future and vice versa.

During the first year of the Korean War, the number of Korean civilian victims surpassed that of soldiers particularly because of America's "rooting out" operations, accompanied by saturation bombing, strafing, and extensive shootings. Additionally, America's use of napalm in the Korean War brought massive destruction into the lives of Koreans. According to Korean journalist Gi-jin Kim, the U.S. Army used 32,357 tons of napalm. Among them, 4,313 tons were dropped during "Operation Strangle" between August 1951 and June 1952: the carpet bombing over North Korean towns nearby the Thirty-eighth parallel whenever the truce talks were at a stalemate. [44] Korea was the testing site for napalm, a newly developed weapon of mass destruction at that time. Several years later, based on its testing and observation of napalm, the United States more systematically used napalm along with Agent Orange in order to scorch the jungle, the forest, and the guerrillas in Vietnam (such as Operation Rolling Thunder in 1965). [45]

More than sixty cases of U.S. troops being involved in mass killings were reported in the aftermath of the news of Nogeun-Ri. A week before the Nogeun-Ri massacre, about one hundred refugees were killed by napalm and machine gun when they tried crossing the river at Chungwon, not far from Nogeun-Ri. In early August and September 1950, a few weeks after the Nogeun-Ri massacre, about eight hundred refugees were killed in Pohang by bombs simply because they stayed near the military line. [46] Similar stories of civilian massacres by U.S. soldiers are found all over Korea.

One might wonder why American soldiers perpetrated the high level of atrocity toward ordinary Koreans at the beginning of the Korean War while claiming to protect Korean civilians from communist enemies. Plausibly, as Dong Choon Kim argues, these mass killings by American soldiers were related to a combination of their deep racism against Koreans and the relative isolation of the incidents. [47] The Korean War was the first war for the United States to participate in nation-building and civil war in a post-colonial Third World country without understanding the country's historical complexity or the people's desires. Lack of knowledge of Korea and unwillingness to learn about Korea inevitably led Americans to treat all Koreans as potential collaborators with communists. In the American eye, Koreans were "gooks" without history who were not capable of determining their destiny but were tricked into dynamic communism. [48] The U.S. government also controlled the Western media tightly at the peak of McCarthyism. [49] As a result, ordinary American citizens rarely knew what happened in the Korean Peninsula or questioned the legitimacy of U.S. involvement in the war or U.S. responsibility for civilian deaths.

However, during and after the Korean War, the dominant images of American soldiers were associated with the benevolent givers who distributed chewing gum, chocolate, candy bars, and lollipops to destitute

Korean children in the war zone. No images showed why Americans were there in the first place. These images have spread notions of American benevolence, freedom, and generosity in Korea since the Korean War. However, those who witnessed and experienced the brutality of American soldiers could not reconcile the saint-like faces of the Americans who fed them during the daytime with the faces of the merciless killers who attacked their villages and raped women at night. Perhaps the collective psyche of the Koreans struggles with "the conflation of American rescue and annihilation in the body memory of the War."[50]

The survivors of the massacre can hardly retrieve what they experienced during the war. However, their bodies remember the smell of burning corpses and decaying bodies full of worms, the ear-splitting sound of bloody screams, warplanes, machine guns, and soldiers's yelling, the sight of open-bellied corpses and the sea of fire. No one can translate her or his sensory memories of war only to create silence and absences in her or his stories of war. The gaps along with the fragments of the war memories have the power to survive intergenerationally and transnationally. Just as Jews always remember the Holocaust, whether they physically experienced the tragedy or not, Koreans always remember the Korean War with its secrets, silence, absences, and tragedy. The body of the Western princess becomes the screen that projects the sensory memories, fragments, silence, and absences of the War.

U.S. Military Prostitution during the Korean War

During the Korean War, the Korean government adopted the Japanese institution of "comfort stations" to serve UN Allied Forces and Korean soldiers in the name of "protecting respectable women and rewarding soldiers for their sacrifice."[51] Since their arrival on Korean soil, the U.S. military had fought two wars: one against communism and the other against venereal disease. While venereal disease threatened the soldiers's readiness to fight in the war, the U.S. military could not properly control the soldiers's sexual behaviors.[52] To control VD among the soldiers, both the U.S. military and the Korean government regulated prostitution rather than abolishing it. As a result, Western princesses could sell sex only in designated areas, after having proved to be clean of VD. However, the effort to control VD failed because the soldiers could take sexual advantage of poor Korean women. As long as the American soldiers saw the Korean women as sexually exploitable, colonized bodies, the military's effort to control VD was useless.

During the Korean War, makeshift camptowns visibly sprang up wherever bases were located, only to be torn down as troops retreated or advanced.[53] Since troop access to civilian villages was strictly controlled during the war, poor women carrying blankets made deals outside the villages or in the mountains. They were called the "blanket squad" because they offered soldiers outdoor sex or sold sex literally for a piece of blanket which would protect them from the cold winter.[54] The presence of these women divided an ordinary village into so-called upper and down villages. An upper village was considered a dangerous space where American soldiers and sexually corrupted Korean women intermingled for conjugal pleasure, while virtuous women down the hill were protected by Korean men from wild American soldiers with high sex drives.[55] Ironically, it was the prostitutes who safeguarded the chastity of virtuous women in the down village, although they became the archetypal "fallen women." Some of the camptown prostitutes were, in fact, rape victims of American soldiers rather than having voluntarily walked into the business of camptown. In addition, the majority of Western princesses during the war were war widows. Among an estimated 300,000 to 430,000 prostitutes, 150,000 to 200,000 were widows.[56]

Camptown prostitution was usually confined around Imperial Japan's implemented public brothels and military bases in South Korea until the Korean War. It became systematized and has expanded through the country, as the U.S. armed forces have been stationed in Korea for an indefinite period after the war. After the armistice had been signed, camptowns were concentrated in small villages along the truce line. These villages had been sparsely populated prior to the war but were turned into military cities throughout the war, attracting prostitutes and the urban and rural poor. For example, Dongducheon was mostly desolate land, agricultural fields, or public graveyards in the beginning of the Korean War. In 1952, the U.S. Seventh Calvary was stationed there, turning the village into a military town. The town became one of the most notorious camptowns, having housed four different U.S. infantry divisions, which occupied thirty percent of the town. In its heydays in 1962, approximately seven thousand prostitutes worked in the town.[57] These camptowns became GI kingdoms in the 1960s through the 70s and were the backbone of the Korean economy as well as the construction of Korean America. The life of Western princesses further unfolds militarized Korean immigration to the United States through marriages between Korean women and American soldiers.

The U.S. bases have transnationally industrialized prostitution. Today, around thirty thousand American servicemen and their families are stationed in South Korea. Advanced transportation between Seoul and the rest of South Korea enables American soldiers to visit clubs and bars in Seoul for recreation over the weekend rather than looking for entertainment in the camptown. The camptown entertainment business is now filled with women from the Philippines and former Soviet Union. In addition, longtime camptowns, such as those in Itaewon in Seoul and Pyeongtaek, have become tourist spots and residential areas for foreigners.

WHERE HAS SOOKJA BEEN?: STUDYING MILITARY
PROSTITUTION AS A FEMINIST PRAXIS AGAINST
TRANSNATIONALIZED U.S. MILITARISM

I first met Sookja at the Sunlit Center in Anjungri of Pyeongtaek nearby
Camp Humphreys. She left her trace on the wall of the Center, a community center for senior women who used to work in camptown prostitution and still live around the town even after their bodies could no longer
perform sexualized labor. At the bottom of a big, colorful flower graffiti,
one can spot the name, Sookja, as if she hid from the world but wanted to
be glimpsed by someone. Sookja is a popular name among senior Korean
women. In the summer of 2013, the senior women at the Sunlit Center
performed a play, entitled *Sookja's Story*. The play interwove the stories of
two Sookjas. The two Sookjas lived distinctive lives, although both were
born into post-Korean War poverty, sent to rich families in the city as
domestic laborers, and abused by their masters. Their particular life stories merged in the Anjungri camptown, where it became difficult to dif-
ferentiate which story belonged to whom. They had to learn how to
please "Hellos"[58] and pimps. One Sookja gave up her son for adoption in
the United States, while the other Sookja was brokenhearted after her GI
lover had left for the United States without leaving any words. Both
witnessed lonely deaths of camptown prostitutes—young and old, countless Geum-i Yuns. Sookjas were once called patriots by the military
government in the 1970s because their service for American GIs was
necessary for South Korea's security. Sookjas in their old age patted each
other's back in silence, prayed to God, and sang Christian hymns together, as if reclaiming their sacred space. Sookjas joined a group of Western
princesses and feminist activists, demanding that the Korean government
compensate Western princesses for the systemic exploitation they suffered through government-installed VD clinics.

Watching the Sunlit Center women play their life stories, I felt familiar
with the stories—extraction of sexualized labor from women until their
bodies are useless, limited options for women and girls in extreme poverty, and the state's involvement in the systematic prostitution of poor
women sound strangely ordinary. Nothing unique or special is found in
the stories of the two Sookjas, who challenged me to theo-ethically reflect
on my encounter with them. Sookja has been to many places: Japan's
military comfort stations, militarized brothels in Vietnam, Subic Bay in
the Philippines, and rape camps in Bosnia, Rwanda, and Northern Iraq.
Sookja does not tell her past but unfolds "our" present stories, retrieved
from the future. If Sookja has walked around many parts of human history, can we also find her palimpsest in Christianity?

Mainstream Christianity often portrays prostitutes as a "unique"
group of wanton women who undermine sexual morality in society and
the heteropatriarchal family. Christian discourse has constantly singled

out prostitutes from the rest of society, as if only unlucky or sexually corrupt women entered prostitution. As these women are morally condemned in the Christian Church, there has existed an irreconcilable gap between Christian imagination of prostitution and its reality. Prostitution is a controversially normalized practice but has never been morally accepted. Controversial normalization means that the institution of prostitution has existed for a long time; people consider it part of human history but rarely question why it is there, while morally condemning those who sell sex.

Military prostitution to which Sookja's body witnesses should not be conflated with other forms of prostitution, although the Marxist concept of alienation of a woman's (sexualized) labor from herself (or her body and her humanity) can be used to analyze any practice of prostitution in capitalism. Instead, military prostitution is part of the war and military project that intentionally recruits female bodies for sexualized labor for (male) soldiers. By using the prostituted bodies of women, the state can ease the soldiers's anxiety and fear, control VD, and avoid its soldiers's rape of local women. As long as the patriarchal assumption that soldiers's sex drives are uncontrollable prevails in society, the state can morally justify military prostitution. In South Korea, U.S. military bases have been the stumbling block to publicly discuss prostitution — gender-based violence in the variety of forms. Furthermore, while the cultural ethos in South Korea strongly opposes prostitution, military prostitution has been tolerated in society. The presence of U.S. military prostitution only shows the extent to which Korean society is militarized.

A Christianity of liberation that has a strong tradition of God's preferential option for the poor has challenged the status quo in society and the existing power structure. As a Christian feminist ethicist whose work is rooted in liberation theology, I propose studying military prostitution as feminist praxis for God's preferential option in the context of war and to resist the U.S. empire of bases and the U.S.-led militarized global security.

As Cynthia Enloe, a feminist international relations scholar, argues, military prostitution in any city in the world holds important truth about gendered and militarized international politics. [59] This institution directly and indirectly affects countless women's lives. Men's lives are also affected by military prostitution because "so many men have had their expectations of and fantasies about women shaped by their own participation in militarized prostitution."[60] Furthermore, by studying military prostitution, we can uncover military policy makers's attempts to construct a type of masculinity that best suits their military's missions and gendered foreign policies and international alliances. Any military's policies on prostitution are related to its policies on "rape, recruitment, sexual harassment, morale, homosexuality, pornography, and marriage."[61] Subsequently, the presence of prostitution for a foreign military often captures the double moral standards of local male nationalists. These men often ignore the prostitution policies of their own country's military and resist local feminists's efforts to make "sexuality an explicit issue in the wider nationalist movement," while condemning the foreign military's use of local women's sexuality, as we saw in the case of Geum-i Yun.[62] Military prostitution unveils the raw faces of gendered, racialized, and sexualized politics on a domestic and a global level—how the politicians's decisions of war and military policies are transfused in ordinary people's lives.

The feminist knowledge earned through military prostitution must be connected to Christian discourse on war and peace. As Susan Thistlethwaite argues, the dominant Christian theologies of war and peace (for example, Just War, Pacifism, and Just Peacemaking) all justify violence against women.[63] While women's bodies literally serve as a site of battle through militarized violence, Christian discourse is far behind the reality that many female bodies endure everyday. The bodies of Sookja and Geum-i Yun testify that women's bodies are not only mutilated during wartime, but they also experience war during the so-called peacetime. This is why we need more gender- and sexuality-conscious discourse on Christian peacemaking—discourse that is strong, persistent, and strategic enough to resist militarized and normalized violence against women.

Furthermore, studying military prostitution, particularly in the Korean context, cannot be separated from studying genocide during the Korean War. As analyzed earlier, the Western princess embodies the victims of genocide committed by American soldiers during the Korean War. Furthermore, many genocide stories include rape and forced prostitution of women. Christian feminist approaches to U.S. militarism need to interrogate America's genocides across the globe (like the genocide of American Indians, Koreans, and Vietnamese) in relation to other stories of genocide (such as the Nazi genocide of Jews, Israelis's slow genocide of Palestinians, and ISIL's genocide of Yazidis). The relationship between genocide and deadly sexualized violence against women is an area of study that urgently requires both religious and feminist perspectives.

CONCLUSION

The collective body of Western princesses diversifies and demystifies the masculinist Korean War narrative and U.S.–Korean relations. Examining America's war through the eyes of Western princesses requires the new process of re-memorializing and re-interrogating U.S. overseas bases in the whispers of the silenced bodies—the bodies that were massacred, exploded by bombs, burnt by napalm, and tortured—as well as through brutal war's intergenerational and transnational haunting effects. Furthermore, the body of Western princesses bears the death mark of sovereignty that exercises killing, regulates women's lives, and most of all, survives and evolves at the cost of hypersexualized female bodies.

By studying military prostitution through feminist consciousness, we, Christians, can envision God's peace on earth more concretely, heal our past that is still bleeding with war and sexualized violence against women, embrace and understand our present moment as it is, and imagine our future free from militarized peace and security. Through the Christian feminist studies of U.S. military prostitution, may we be liberated from the fear and oppression of the mighty military power of the United States.

BIBLIOGRAPHY

Alexander, M. Jacqui. *Pedagogies of Crossing: Meditations on Feminism, Sexual Politics, Memory, and the Sacred.* Durham: Duke University Press, 2005.

Cho, Grace. *Haunting the Korean Diaspora: Shame, Secrecy, and the Forgotten War.* Minneapolis: University of Minnesota, 2008.

Enloe, Cynthia. *Maneuver: The International Politics of Militarizing Women's Lives.* Berkeley: University of California Press, 2000.

Gang, Yi-Soo. "Prohibition of Public Prostitution and Women's Movements during the American Military Occupation." In *Social Changes and History of Korea during American Military Occupation, vol. II,* 261–292. Chooncheon: Hanrim University Institute of Asian Cultural Studies, 1999.

Hong, Seong-cheol. *History of Yu-Kwak.* Seoul: Paper Road, 2007.

Jeong, Hee-jin. "Human Rights of the Women, Who Should Die in Order to Live." In *The History of Korean Women's Human Rights Activism,* edited by Korean Women's Hotline, 300–318. Seoul: Hanul, 2005.

Kim, Dong Choon. "Forgotten War, Forgotten Massacres—the Korean War (1950–1953) as Licensed Mass Killings." *Journal of Genocide Research* 6, no. 4 (2004): 523–544.

Kim, Gi-jin. *Korean War and Civilian Massacre: The First Testimony of the U.S. Secret Documents.* Seoul: Pooreun-Yeoksa, 2005.

Kim, Jodi. *Ends of Empire: Asian American Critique and the Cold War.* Minneapolis: University of Minnesota Press, 2010.

Kim, Sam-woong. "Prostitution Is Civilization—Japan's Unscrupulous Colonial Governance." *Same-i-Gipeun-Mool.* March 1998. 114–115.

LaDuke, Winona. *The Militarization of Indian Country.* East Lansing: Michigan State University Press, 2012.

Lee, Na-young. "The Construction of Camptown [*kijichon*] Prostitution and Women's Resistance." In *Women and Peace,* edited by Peace Institute of Korean Women and Peace, 170–197. Seoul: Hanul, 2010.

Moon, Katherine. *Sex among Allies: Military Prostitution in U.S.–Korean relations.* New York: Columbia University Press, 1997.

Moon, Seungsook. "Regulating Desire, Managing the Empire: U.S. Military Prostitution in South Korea, 1945–1970." In *Over There: Living with the U.S. Military Empire from World War Two to the Present,* edited by Maria Hoehn and Seungsook Moon, 39–77. Durham: Duke University Press, 2010.

Niebuhr, Reinhold. *The Irony of American History.* New York: Charles Scribner's Sons, 1952; reprinted by University of Chicago Press, 2008.

Rose, Lisle. *Roots of Tragedy: The United States and the Struggle for Asia, 1945–1953.* Westport: Greenwood Press, 1976.

Thistlethwaite, Susan. *Women's Bodies as Battlefield: Christian Theology and the Global War on Women*. New York: Palgrave Macmillan, 2015.
Yuh, Ji-yeon. *Beyond the Shadow of Camptown: Korean Military Brides in America*. New York: New York University Press, 2002.

NOTES

1. Katherine Moon, *Sex among Allies: Military Prostitution in U.S.–Korea Relations* (New York: Columbia University Press, 1997), 28.
2. Moon, *Sex among Allies*, 28.
3. Grace Cho, *Haunting the Korean Diaspora: Shame, Secrecy, and the Forgotten War* (Minneapolis: University of Minnesota, 2008), 3.
4. M. Jacqui Alexander, *Pedagogies of Crossing: Meditations on Feminism, Sexual Politics, Memory, and the Sacred* (Durham: Duke University Press, 2005), 190.
5. Alexander, *Pedagogies of Crossing*, 190.
6. Cho, *Haunting the Korean Diaspora*, 5–6.
7. Cho, *Haunting the Korean Diaspora*, 7.
8. Hee-jin Jeong, "Human Rights of the Women, Who Should Die in Order to Live," in *The History of Korean Women's Human Rights Activism*, ed. Korean Women's Hotline (Seoul: Hanul, 2005), 334–335.
9. Jeong, "Human Rights of the Women," 339.
10. Jeong, "Human Rights of the Women," 340–342.
11. Cho, *Haunting the Korean Diaspora*, 20.
12. Cho, *Haunting the Korean Diaspora*, 11.
13. Cho, *Haunting the Korean Diaspora*, 18.
14. Lisle Rose, *Roots of Tragedy: The United States and the Struggle for Asia, 1945–1953* (Westport: Greenwood Press, 1976), 98.
15. Rose, *Roots of Tragedy*, 101.
16. Na-young Lee, "The Construction of Camptown [*kijichon*] Prostitution and Women's Resistance," in *Women and Peace*, ed. Peace Institute of Korean Women and Peace (Seoul: Hanul, 2010), 176.
17. Yi-Soo Gang, "Prohibition of Public Prostitution and Women's Movements during the American Military Occupation," in *Social Changes and History of Korea during American Military Occupation, Vol. II* (Chooncheon: Hanrim University Institute of Asian Cultural Studies, 1999), 263–265.
18. Seungsook Moon, "Regulating Desire, Managing the Empire: U.S. Military Prostitution in South Korea, 1945–1970," in *Over There: Living with the U.S. Military Empire from World War Two to the Present*, ed. Maria Hoehn and Seungsook Moon (Durham: Duke University Press, 2010), 41.
19. Seong-cheol Hong, *History of Yu-Kwak* (Seoul: Paper Road, 2007), 31.
20. Hong, *History of Yu-Kwak*, 82–83.
21. Gang, "Prohibition of Public Prostitution and Women's Movement during the American Military Occupation," 267.
22. Sam-woong Kim, "Prostitution Is Civilization—Japan's Unscrupulous Colonial Governance," *Same-i-Gipeun-Mool*, March 1998, 114–115.
23. Moon, "Regulating Desire, Managing the Empire," 42.
24. Moon, "Regulating Desire, Managing the Empire," 42.
25. Gang, "Prohibition of Public Prostitution and Women's Movement during the American Military Occupation," 273.
26. Gang, "Prohibition of Public Prostitution and Women's Movement during the American Military Occupation." In 1944, ninety percent of Korean women were illiterate.

27. Gang, "Prohibition of Public Prostitution and Women's Movement during the American Military Occupation," 275.

28. Gang, "Prohibition of Public Prostitution and Women's Movement during the American Military Occupation," 276.

29. Gang, "Prohibition of Public Prostitution and Women's Movement during the American Military Occupation," 276.

30. Hong, *History of Yu-Kwak,* 164–170.

31. Gang, "Abolishment of Public Prostitution and Women's Movements during American Military Occupation," 288.

32. Jodi Kim, *Ends of Empire: Asian American Critique and the Cold War* (Minneapolis: University of Minnesota Press, 2010), 156.

33. Jodi Kim, *Ends of Empire,* 156.

34. Jodi Kim, *Ends of Empire,* 147.

35. Jodi Kim, *Ends of Empire,* 147.

36. Bruce Cumings, *Korea's Place in the Sun: A Modern History* (New York: Norton Press, 1997), 298.

37. Kim, *Ends of Empire,* 150.

38. Kim, *Ends of Empire,* 150.

39. Dong Choon Kim, "Forgotten War, Forgotten Massacres—the Korean War (1950–1953) as Licensed Mass Killings," *Journal of Genocide Research* 6, no. 4 (2004): 529.

40. Cho, *Haunting the Korean Diaspora,* 60.

41. Cho, *Haunting the Korean Diaspora,* 57.

42. Cho, *Haunting the Korean Diaspora,* 57–58.

43. Winona LaDuke, *The Militarization of Indian Country* (East Lansing: Michigan State University Press, 2012), 8.

44. Gi-jin Kim, *Korean War and Civilian Massacre: The First Testimony of the U.S. Secret Documents* (Seoul: Pooreun-Yeoksa, 2005), 151–152.

45. Gi-jin Kim, *Korean War and Civilian Massacre,* 153.

46. Kim, "Forgotten War, Forgotten Massacres—the Korean War (1950–1953) as Licensed Mass Killings," 523.

47. Kim, "Forgotten War, Forgotten Massacres," 531.

48. This view seems dominant in America during the Korean War, as Reinhold Niebuhr portrays "Oriental" as the people in slumbering culture who could be easily attracted to dynamic religion-like communism. Reinhold Niebuhr, *The Irony of American History* (New York: Charles Scribner's Sons, 1952; reprinted by University of Chicago Press, 2008), 123–126.

49. Kim, "Forgotten War, Forgotten Massacres—the Korean War (1950–1953) as Licensed Mass Killings," 531.

50. Cho, *Haunting the Korean Diaspora,* 84.

51. Moon, "Regulating Desire, Managing the Empire," 41.

52. Moon, "Regulating Desire, Managing the Empire," 43.

53. Ji-yeon Yuh, *Beyond the Shadow of Camptown: Korean Military Brides in America* (New York: New York University Press, 2002), 20.

54. Moon, *Sex among Allies,* 27.

55. Yuh, *Beyond the Shadow of Camptown,* 21.

56. Hong, *History of Yu-Kwak,* 181.

57. Hong, *History of Yu-Kwak,* 185; Moon, *Sex among Allies,* 28.

58. In *Sookja's Story,* camptown prostitutes called an American GI "Hello."

59. Cynthia Enloe, *Maneuver: The International Politics of Militarizing Women's Lives* (Berkeley: University of California Press, 2000), 51.

60. Enloe, *Maneuver,* 51.

61. Enloe, *Maneuver,* 51.

62. Enloe, *Maneuver,* 51.

63. Susan Thistlethwaite, *Women's Bodies as Battlefield: Christian Theology and the Global War on Women* (New York: Palgrave Macmillan, 2015), 9.

SIX

Blinking Red

The Escalation of a Militarized Police Force and Its Challenges to Black Communities

Pamela Lightsey

In its final report of the circumstances leading up to the fatal terrorist attack on September 11, 2001, the 9/11 Commission quotes former Director of Central Intelligence George John Tenet's reflections on notable credible evidence and the failure to have a more ready counterterrorism response: "Tenet told us that in his world, 'the system was blinking red.' By late July, Tenet said, it could not 'get any worse.'"[1] As a military veteran and mother of a son who served in Iraq, I hesitate to draw upon Tenet's response since I, admittedly, have always taken issue with the CIA's assertion that Iraq had weapons of mass destruction and the intelligence failures of the agency. Nonetheless, Tenet's words were right: In the case of 9/11, the peril to the nation was real, as were the sleeper agents living within U.S. borders.

I'm drawn to Tenet's words because in somewhat similar fashion— though I pray not as disastrous—the current transformation of police departments to quasi-military forces is indicative of *a system blinking red.* Our community intelligence reports among Black people, the current administration's executive order to rescind the Obama-era Executive Order 13688 (which required approval for acquisition of military equipment), and the continued use of excessive police force with impunity are all indicative of *a system blinking red*, telling us that the United States's project of oppression against Black people is tantamount to war and not likely to improve under 45's leadership.

This chapter will interrogate the presence of militarized police forces in Black communities. I will treat this idea of a militarized citizenship (for example, police force, citizen security) while at the same time reflecting on ways the Church is used as an instrument to wield the sword of the State vis-à-vis an organized militia. Admittedly, I am personally invested in this work.

My investment is derived from my 2014 on-the-ground experiences in Ferguson, my perspectives as a *female* military veteran, and the long-standing history of existential threats and anxieties that come with living as Black in America, especially as a Black woman. This is why, interspersed—as perhaps parenthetical reminders—throughout this chapter, I draw attention to the history of Black women's work of liberation against the increasing and frequent buildup of militarized forces against Black communities. But first, to begin this analysis and to do justice to this chapter, a reasonable but all too brief overview of policing in America is necessary.

Let us suspend for just a bit the knee-jerk tendency to think of policing as the contemporary *thin blue line*, and the local personnel as those who honorably *protect and serve*. Despite this tendency to think of *policing* as the material enforcement of law for the purposes of maintaining *pax*— specifically the peace of the city[2]—policing human bodies has entailed much more. For Africans—brought to the early American colonies as slaves—policing has been enforced through physical, legal, and theological methods. These colonizers of Africa and North America used the latter method to shore up their justification for such a brutal enterprise— to maintain a slavocracy with apodictic assurance of its beneficence. One has but to turn to the oral narratives and writings of former slaves to get a sense of the theological policing attempted by slave owners. Frederick Douglass, abolitionist and statesman who escaped slavery and during his life published several works, describes it in this way:

> It was in vain that we had been taught from the pulpit of St. Michael's, the duty of obedience to our masters; to recognize God as the author of our enslavement; to regard running away an offense, alike against God and man; to deem our enslavement a merciful and beneficial arrangement; to esteem our conditions, in this country, a paradise to that from which we had been snatched from Africa; to consider our hard hands and dark color as God's mark of displeasure, and as pointing us out as the proper subjects of slavery; that the relation of master and slave was one of reciprocal benefits; that our work was more serviceable to our masters, than our master's thinking was serviceable to us.[3]

While such fallacious argumentation did not deceive Douglass and many others, the repetitiveness by which this argument was deployed and shows up in the historical archives demonstrates that in the eyes of slaveholders this was an efficient way to keep slaves docile, deceived, and unwilling to revolt or flee, though flee they would. During the Revolutionary War, slaves escaped to the British Army, which offered freedom to slaves who joined their forces. Other slaves found relative freedom in free states[4] where slavery was illegal. Others, such as Douglass's wife, used their innate capacities to protect Black people from being captured and enslaved by early colonists.

Not much is said of Douglass's wife, Anna Murray; she was born as a free Black person who later worked with the American Anti-Slavery Society in Boston. According to her daughter, Rosetta Douglass Sprague, Anna Murray not only took care of the family in her father's absence, but she also donated a portion of her meager earnings from binding shoes to support the work of the Society.[5] She thought of herself as "one of the first agents of the Underground Railroad," ensuring the comfortable accommodations of runaway slaves headed for Canada.[6]

It was the work-capital of Anna Murray and other Black women—free and slave—that helped the movement to end slavery. This work-capital or "work as capital" has proven to be a much-needed investment that has helped secure greater freedoms for Black people throughout the history of the movement for liberation. It was their specific action(s) undertaken from a communal perspective—not the care of *a person* or *a man* but what care could be done for one of many members of *the community*. Therefore, you will find time and again—from the Underground Railway ensuring safe passage against the wiles of the patterrollers, to the current leadership of Black women wielding political and activist power—that Black women have sacrificed their time, skills, and yes, their earnings, combatting racial oppression through the mechanisms of the colonial state. Most significantly, you will find in African American history no era in the movement for liberation where the work-capital of Black women has not played a crucial role to protect the lives of Black people from the terrors of slavery and the brutality of militarized police forces.

But in the early centuries of the nation, the work-capital of Black women, the determination of slaves, and abolitionist efforts did not go unchallenged. In response, slave owners turned to legal mechanisms such as inserting into the Constitution the Fugitive Slave Clause of 1793:

> No Person held to Service or Labour in one State, under the Laws thereof, escaping into another, shall, in Consequence of any Law or Regulation therein, be discharged from such Service or Labour, but shall be delivered up on Claim of the Party to whom such Service or Labour may be due.[7]

Having established by law the requirement that runaway slaves be returned to captivity, the progenitors of the first mass incarceration of Black people in the United States turned to physical policing to put these laws into effect. This public and legalized regulation of Black bodies ushered in somewhat of an *avant la lettre* model of policing for the purpose of making oppressors feel safe and comfortable.

> With us, every citizen is concerned in the maintenance of order, and in promoting honesty and industry among those of the lowest class who are our slaves; and our habitual vigilance renders standing armies, whether of soldiers or policemen, entirely unnecessary. Small guards in our cities, and occasional patrols in the country, insure us a repose and security known nowhere else. [8]

Former governor James Hammond's argument in 1845 describes not only the "repose" enjoyed by white citizens of South Carolina but also the fear of violent retribution upon white people by Black people. At the time of Hammond's writing, it had been less than a decade since sixty white people were killed in the uprising of slaves and freemen led by Nat Turner. This revolt, along with the successful Haitian Revolution and the unsuccessful Richmond and Charleston uprisings planned by Gabriel Prosser and Denmark Vessey, respectively, would no doubt leave white people on edge. There was no way to keep human beings enslaved and support the project of colonizing the Americas without some means to maintain this inhumane institution and, at the same time, promote feelings of peace and security. What better way than primitive bands of white citizen police?

Although many historians will locate the origins of police forces in the United States to the 1838 Day Police and Night Watch of Boston, Massachusetts, there was another citizen group that predated the Boston Police. They were established as a means to maintain slavery and the "repose and security" described by Hammond. African slaves were controlled not only by slave owners but also by these bands of armed civilian and militia patrols known as patterrollers (also called paddyrollers). As a mechanism used to enforce fugitive slave laws, patterrollers were a constant source of intimidation to African slaves, a key consideration for any insurrection plans, and a resource that helped colonize the Americas. Slaves feared—and rightly so—encounters with patterrollers. In Frederick Douglass's chronicles of the days leading up to his escape, you see how mindful slaves were of these evil patrols.

> Then, too, we knew that merely reaching a free state did not free us; that, wherever caught, we could be returned to slavery . . . I knew something of theology, but nothing of geography . . . New York City was our northern limit, and to go there, and to be forever harassed with the liability of being hunted down and returned to slavery—with the certainty of being treated ten times worse than we had ever been treated before—was a prospect far from delightful, and it might well cause some hesitation about engaging in the enterprise. The case, sometimes, to our excited visions, stood thus: At every gate through which we had to pass, we saw a watchman; at every ferry, a guard; on every bridge, a sentinel; and in every wood, a patrol or slave-hunter. [9]

Douglass and others before and after him were willing to risk their lives to live in freedom. We love Harriet Tubman so much not just because she was a brilliant conductor of the Underground Railroad but because she risked her life time and time again.

Yet getting past the patterrollers was only one crossing on the road to liberation. Slave hunters and, later, Jim Crow laws would require Black people to exercise an everyday liberatory-diligence. There has been no period in time when Black bodies have not been the targets of white policing strategy (even when Black people were finally enlisted as police), but Black people would develop sophisticated systems to stand against their tyranny. At their best, these systems designed to secure the liberation of Black people have always honored the struggles of our slave ancestors and the mechanisms slave and later free Africans developed to survive.

Generations of the progeny of slaves would come to know policing as the state-sanctioned capture and torture of Black citizens. Police forces would monitor and attack Black people during the antebellum, '60s Civil Rights, and Black Power eras. Moving beyond slavery into the mid-twentieth century, etched onto the historical landscape of the United States are the many pictures of Black men and women being viciously attacked by police using dogs, high pressure water hoses, clubs, and their fists.

Police forces of the '60s Civil Rights era enjoyed such a favorable place in American hegemonic ideology that one of the reasons stated by the Board of Regents for firing Black feminist Angela Davis from her position at the University of California was her constant use of the term "pig" to refer to police. (I have a particular affinity for this period of time and the characterization of police as "pigs" because this phrase was so thoroughly utilized by my generation and the generation before.) Davis and others, especially the Black Panther Party, developed a strong, independent voice and stance as Black radical intellectuals and organic intellectuals capable of analyzing, deconstructing, and counteracting the propaganda espoused by the emerging militaristic police force. It was the independence of the radical, shotgun-wielding Black Panther Party that comforted and made Black people feel protected during this time of extensive police aggression.

Yet, for all the rigor of the Black Panthers to protect Black people, they could not protect themselves nor could they still the simmering rage of their community against white supremacy. Though it was assumed that local police in the Los Angeles area would one day go head-to-head with the Black Panthers, it was not an interaction with the Black Panthers but the police brutality of the Los Angeles Police Department upon one unarmed Black man that would lead to the historic 1965 Watts Rebellion. The well-reported comment of LAPD Chief William Parker demonstrates the level of racism at the highest levels of the police department, for it was Parker who described the riots in this way: "One person threw a rock and then, like monkeys in a zoo, others started throwing rocks."[10]

Interestingly enough, it was another LAPD officer, Daryl Gates, who would later recount the events of Watts that led to his helping to develop a cadre of elite police officers who had specialized (specialized in this case meaning military) training for handling snipers and other incidents, such as riots and protests.

> One day, with a big smile on my face, I popped in to tell my deputy chief, Ed Davis, that I thought up an acronym for my special new unit. He was still, as we all were, glued to the classic concepts of policing, which discourage the formation of military-type units. But he realized some changes would have to be made. "It's SWAT," I said. "Oh, that's pretty good. What's it stand for?" "Special Weapons Attack Teams." Davis blinked at me. "No." There was no way, he said dismissively, he would ever use that word 'attack.' I went out, crestfallen, but a moment later I was back. "Special Weapons and Tactics," I said. "Okay?" "No problem. That's fine," said Davis. And that was how SWAT was born.[11]

By 1969, Gates would not only be able to supply his officers with military weapons and training but he was also—with the help of legislation like The Omnibus Crime Control and Safe Streets Act of 1968—able to create an air of security in the city, though not the same level of repose Hammond bragged about centuries earlier. All this preparation climaxed in an epic standoff between LA's SWAT team and the Black Panthers. "On December 9th, search warrants for illegal weapons were served at the Black Panther Headquarters at 41st and Central Streets. The Black Panthers resisted and attempted to shoot it out with 40 members of the SWAT Team."[12]

Rather than being a hands-down success, because of the disproportionality of resources used by LAPD SWAT versus the Black Panthers, the raid ended up drawing massive negative public responses. Why? Imagine tons of ammunition and hundreds of police officers attempting to arrest only six Black men with far less artillery and training. Additionally, what set this event apart from other standoffs was not simply the massive amounts of ammunition used but that it was the first time a United States police unit used military resources on civilians.

> The Panthers had prepared for a confrontation with the LAPD, but what came of their initial plans was an unknowing highly equipped unit ready to construct a raid. After a four-hour stand off—Panthers vs. the newly formed SWAT UNIT—a shoot-out occurred in which Daryl Gates made a call to the Department of Defense asking for permission to use a grenade launcher.[13]

This was the making of a public relations disaster. Tensions between the police and Black citizens had been tenuous at best. Reports of police brutality long preceded this standoff. The police had established a pattern of stopping Black men for no valid reason and harassing members of the community. Even by 1969 there remained a lingering suspicion of the police after the week-long Watts Riot of 1965 "resulting in 34 deaths, 1,032 injuries and 4,000 arrests, involving 34,000 people and ending in the destruction of 1,000 buildings, totaling $40 million in damages."[14] One witness described the standoff in this way:

> The police were surrounding the Panther office. Seemed like it was a battle. They had about five or six people trapped up in the building. Shooting, you know. And whenever the Panthers run out, you know, they brought out something bigger, you know. I even seen a tank roll up the street you know with police (untranslatable).[15]

Records of the shoot-out and the accounts given by Gates show that the LAPD had been preparing themselves for Vietnam-style guerilla/irregular warfare. Support for their tactics came from as high as the Pentagon. Though grenades were never launched, this paramilitary crackdown in an urban area was shocking. Political leaders attempted to shift the blame for conditions of socioeconomic inequality to rest on the shoulders of the oppressed, those dubbed as nothing more than insurgents. Yet many Black people living across the nation understood the true causes for these uprisings: ghetto conditions with little opportunity to improve one's lot. Very few adults in my south Florida hometown watching the riots were remotely surprised then, especially those "long hot summer" riots of 1967. "See, we knew this shit was coming!" the elders proclaimed.

These highly anticipated standoffs between militarized police and Black citizens became part and parcel of an ongoing white supremacist narrative abut Black people. Urban areas were described on nightly newscasts as inhabited by criminals, menaces to society, troublemakers, lazy people unwilling to work or to care for property.

That said, riots were predictable; the police's warfare-styled response of 1969 was unpredictable. American liberalism was failing, and this show of police force demonstrated the ways in which white liberals had become ineffective at best and participatory at worst in the demonization, torture, surveillance, and destruction of Black people who dared stand up to institutional and structural racism.

There were, and remains, no shades of grey when it comes to how the nation organized—and continues to organize—as a show of force against Black people demanding the same rights and benefits as white citizens of the United States. Bobby Seale, founding chairman of the Black Panther Party, described the well-organized and equipped SWAT team and that this style of attack by local police could not be predicted.

> The massive exchange of gunfire was between a cluster of six Panther members who happened to be inside the headquarters and what would ultimately grow to be a force of 200 Los Angeles police officers, includ-

ing a newly created LAPD team that would have its first real outing on that day. Most dramatically the LAPD deployed its new SWAT (Special Weapons and Tactics, a militarized police unit) teams, a warrant, a battering ram, helicopters, a tank, trucks, dynamite, and 400 police officers to raid three L.A. Black Panther Party facilities including the Central Ave. headquarters.[16]

Let me underscore; this response on the part of *local police* was unpredictable, but it was not the first time Black people living in urban areas had been attacked—with political approval—with weapons of this style for the purposes of repressing an uprising. One has only to review the riots that took place in Detroit several years prior when, after police raided an unlicensed bar, riots ensued. Then-Governor George Romney called in the National Guard, "and Detroit turned into a war zone, suddenly populated with three thousand police officers, five hundred state troopers, two thousand members of the Michigan National Guard, and five-thousand paratroopers from the Eighty Second Airborne."[17] Police and military units perceived their work as taking war strategies to Black urban communities.

Professor of American Studies, Malcolm McLaughlin, does an excellent job describing how the trope of irregular warfare was used by mainstream media to describe urban cities largely populated by Black citizens, what were then called ghettos, where stereotypes of violence and savagery were deployed to justify heavy-handed police tactics.

> At the height of the crisis, NBC viewers tuned into *The Huntley-Brinkley Report* to hear soldiers of the eighty-second Airborne, veterans of the Vietnam War, were now venturing out, helicopters buzzing overhead into an urban "jungle" at home. Don Oliver reported the mood of the troops: "they say war is war" he explained chillingly, "and if they're called out to fight [. . .] tonight, that will be war.[18]

"War is war." Military troops given direct orders by legal authorities do not have the luxury to make distinctions about the aims of their assaults. They are given orders; they must carry out all lawfully given orders. Along with the National Guard, President Lyndon Johnson ordered in the 82nd and 101st Airborne Divisions. Their orders were to bring an end to the riots, but the entrance of military personnel working within civilian communities led Black people to conclude that local police, supported by military troops, were engaging in undeclared war upon American citizens—especially targeting members of the Black Panther Party. I think it's important to share the little known work of the group to help you understand why it was such a threat to the white supremacist project.

Founded in 1966 by Bobby Seale and Huey Newton, the Black Panther Party (BPP) worked as both a self-help and defense agency within Black communities. Elaine Brown, the only woman to lead the BPP (from August 1974 until Huey Newton's return from exile in 1977), wrote about her tenure and the BPP. "Here I was, a woman, proclaiming supreme power over the most militant organization in America. It felt natural to me."[19] To counter the extreme conditions of poverty and poor health care, the party developed breakfast and education programs for children and provided—through Black medical personnel—free minor health care services. Their radical stance against racism and the oppression of Black people was adored by communities across the country.

As a womanist theologian, I find the self-help work of the BPP[20] in many ways strikes at the core of the theological conversations among liberationists related to endeavors that counter those *powers and principalities* that inhibit the human being from surviving, thriving, and living in right relationship with God. Though not a faith organization, the BPP, their commitment to serve "the least of these," their socialist ideology of cooperative/communal ownership, their ethical posture of being prepared to die, if need be, protecting lives other than their own, their capacity to speak truth to political and economic oppressors; in short, what Newton called revolutionary intercommunalism[21] attracted many Black people to them in ways that the sermonizing of many Black preachers of that day could not. In contrast to Black preachers, the BPP conveyed a gospel that opened the eyes of the masses to the deceitful ways of our government and, yes, Black leadership that sold their souls to the political order. The premiere work of the Black Panther Party can be summed up as countering the hegemonic narrative that whiteness and all the benefits it bestowed upon its carriers are proof of a *natural order* of white superiority. In so doing, the BPP, with a particular kind of Black bravado—a bravado stunningly courageous after so many years of Jim Crow—showed that whiteness was antithetical to the project of democracy and its pundits's rhetoric of the inclusion of all people.

That said, it would not be an exaggeration to say that the Black Panther Party, in its determination to show the inherent contradictions to democracy within the American political order, was one of the most highly surveilled and attacked grassroots organizations. Under the Hoover administration, the FBI used every means possible to exploit, infiltrate, and denigrate the party's work. Though the BPP legally carried weapons, it was not the gun toting alone that Hoover found threatening, it was their remarkable ability to engender support among Black people for their care and concern for Black children. Thus, on May 15, 1969, Hoover sent a memo to all FBI field offices stating,

> The BCP (Breakfast for Children Program) has been instituted by the BPP in several cities to provide a stable breakfast for ghetto children . . . The program has met with some success and has resulted in considerable favorable publicity for the BPP . . . The resulting publicity tends to portray the BPP in a favorable light and clouds the violent nature of the group and its ultimate aim of insurrection. The BCP promotes at least tacit support for the Black Panther Party among naïve individuals . . .

and, what is more distressing, it provides the BPP with a ready audience composed of highly impressionable youths. Consequently, the
BCP represents the best and most influential activity going for the BPP,
and, as such, is potentially the greatest threat to efforts by authorities ... to neutralize the BPP and destroy what it stands for.[22]

Within the highest policing office in the government, the BPP was singled
out for attack. Therefore, in some ways, the presenting detail—that the
BPP had in their possession illegal weapons—was simply the immediate
rationale for attack. In truth, the government had been building up a plan
to destroy the BPP—and for that matter any Black-affinity group that
resisted oppression—for years. The tactics of the SWAT teams simply
carried on the legacy and ultimate aim of the patterrollers: the complete
control of Black people. Moreover, attacking the BPP was viewed by
many within the ranks as war, and to some extent they were certainly
correct; it was nothing short of war. Now for a bit of an excursive on war.

Having introduced the term war in this way may be a bit too strong of
language for some, particularly those invested in traditional just war concepts. Nonetheless, my argument is that war is, in fact, armed clashes and
militarized strategies between nations and/or *against groups*. War always
involves the use of military or militarized forces and results in destruction, the taking of prisoners, and the stealing of land. Though the basic
perspective of war for many citizens of the United States has been violent
clashes between military forces of two or more *countries,* in contemporary
times—because of irregular warfare taking place between local rebel
groups waging armed insurgency against their governments—the idea of
war is often readily understood as governments against citizens.

That said, if one is to abide only by just war tradition, the definition of
war must honor certain criteria, such as having a just cause (such as self-
defense), initiation by sovereign authorities (kings, emperors, political
leaders of nations/countries), war being an act of last resort, and the
probability of success. However, our history has shown that America has
not always kept to this tradition. The war in Iraq was launched under the
Bush doctrine of "preemptive strike" and continued as a response to al-
Qaeda (a group, not a country). Here, on this continent, the land of Native Americans was not given but taken by early colonizers during what
is commonly known as the American Indian Wars.

Any subversive organization or individual unwilling to be an obse-
quious servant of the supremacist colonial order has repeatedly been
subject to an American campaign of attack. In fact, after the attacks
against the BPP, politicians began to phrase their initiatives that were
nothing less than attacks against Black and Brown people by using the
code language of "the war on . . ." and using SWAT teams as resources to
implement their doctrine. If SWAT teams and legislation were the only
resources used, the repressive tactics would have failed.

Stunningly, as time moved on, what made these "war on . . ." initiatives more harmful to Black communities were the ways in which the self-anointed leadership of Black faith communities used their priestly roles to support the influx of policing in Black communities. For example, nearing the close of the twentieth century, at a time of almost deafening silence of civil rights activism, thirty-nine African American pastors and bishops drafted and sent to the Congressional Black Caucus a letter of support for the 1994 crime bill. In this letter, every one of its male signatories concurred with the belief in "putting 100,000 well-trained police officers on the streets of our most violence-plagued communities and urban areas."[23] It was as if they saw no problem with supporting a piece of legislation containing provisions for the death penalty, longer sentencing (the three-strikes element), and increased incarceration of Black citizens. Being tough on crime usually means being tough on Black communities.

The dangers of unintentionally harming your own people is the very reason why faith leaders ought always be concerned about the possibility that they may be used—willingly or unaware—as swords of the state to naïvely carry out the wishes of a despotic political order. It was, after all, white clergymen who issued the "Appeal for Law and Order and Common Sense," an open letter to Alabamians about the impending desegregation of schools. The letter was filled with deference to laws and an appeal that the citizens of the state not resort to violence to convey their racist convictions. The later letter to Rev. Dr. Martin Luther King, Jr. includes commendations to the local police and calls the protests "unwise and untimely."[24] In order to avoid being party to injustice, it seems rather important that clergy regard the work of helping to usher in justice for the transformation of the world into what Dr. King, Jr. called the Beloved Kingdom as paramount. As Ambrose of Milan said, "The scope of justice is apparent. There is no place, no person, no time to which it is irrelevant."[25]

I am not trying to suggest that policing, in and of itself, is a harmful order. Rather, I am arguing that policing can be corrupt, anti-peace, and in lockstep with the kind of military buildup seen around the globe. I am also arguing, as a Black woman, that policing in communities of color is failing and that it is failing because the methods used are far too often in service to an irrational *fear* of nonwhite people and xenophobia. "I feared for my life" is the go-to justification for lethal responses to Black people identified as threats to what I see as this ongoing Hammondian ideal of white "repose and security."

But we are no longer in times of righteous slave uprisings. The patter-rollers have been replaced by militarized police forces. During these times of uprisings, National Guards are ordered to stand alongside SWAT units in Black communities. Over the last decade, this disposition of irrational fear by far too many Americans of Anglo-European descent has increasingly tended to look like they have become dangerously *un-*

glued. We are seeing the warning signs—the blinking red lights. This "I feared for my life" of those who do not fit into the cliché of the melting pot can lead to malevolent security sheltered under a presumption of peace-making practices, either at the hands of police or pseudo-police (here I am thinking of the dangerous practice of calling 911 to report perfectly legal behavior by Black citizens). Conquest and control—traits of colonialism—is becoming the order of the day for policing in local Black and Brown communities.

For many activists, the events that took place in Ferguson, Missouri, are an excellent example of this irrational fear leading to bad police practices operating within a legislative system that often undergirds such malevolent behavior.[26] Not only did the police use their authority in ways that ignored the civil rights of local citizens, when these citizens rose up in protest, state authorities—guided by irrational fear and institutional racism—attempted to end those protests through use of National Guards and militarized policing tactics. As shown earlier in this chapter, this use of military and SWAT forces can be dated back to the riots of the late 1960s and 1970s, but it must also take into account the 1990 National Defense Authorization Act (aka the 1208 Program) used in concert with the war on drugs, the agenda set forth by the 9/11 Commission, and the increased fear of domestic terrorism subsequent to the events of September 11, 2001.

> We learned about an enemy who is sophisticated, patient, disciplined, and lethal . . . We learned that the institutions charged with protecting our borders, civil aviation, and national security did not understand how grave this threat could be, and did not adjust their policies, plans, and practices to deter or defeat it . . . We need to design a *balanced strategy* [italics mine] for the long haul, to attack terrorists and prevent their ranks from swelling while at the same time protecting our country against future attacks. We have been forced to think about the way our government is organized. The massive departments and agencies that prevailed in the great struggles of the twentieth century must work together in new ways, so that all the instruments of national power can be combined.[27]

After the terrorist attacks that destroyed the twin towers of the World Trade Center—resulting in the deaths of nearly three thousand people—*fear* of the "other" escalated in the American psyche. On a far greater level than the earlier militarization of SWAT teams, local police were able to increase their stash of military equipment through grants given by the Department of Defense's 1033 Program. The *balanced strategy* encouraged by the 9/11 Commission allowed over $4 billion of military equipment to find its way into the hands of local law enforcement agencies,[28] especially reinforcing the arsenals of local SWAT forces for what were to be counternarcotics and counterterrorism operations.

There was no identifiable terrorism taking place in Ferguson except for those actions by police against private citizens. A Department of Justice report, completed months after the killing of Michael Brown, found that Ferguson police used racial profiling and other unjust practices to target Black residents. These were violations of the United States Constitution (the 14th Amendment), the very document police swear to uphold. During the weeks and months after Brown was killed, many activists on the ground in Ferguson—myself included—watched the increasing use of military (not *military-style*) equipment being used to control protestors. Police in body armor, combat-wear, BearCat-like[29] armored vehicles, tear gas launchers, and assault rifles stationed themselves on West Florissant Avenue, often rushing—unprovoked—towards the marching protestors and arresting individuals for unknown reasons. The words I place on this paper will not do justice to what I saw with my own eyes and the strong air of disdain (and at times hostility) within the air those nights; a disdain towards the police that had centuries to simmer and build; the disdain of a people who have been the objects of brutal attack by patterrollers, bondsmen, and police bands.

Amidst the pain of seeing over and over again recordings of Black people being killed by police, Black women are responding with courage, media and tech savvy. The leadership of Black women in this *leader-full* movement for Black lives has proven a key element in the pushback against the presence of militarized police forces in civilian neighborhoods. Initiatives such as the hashtag #SayHerName campaign brought attention to the use of excessive and deadly police force against Black women. In addition, it demonstrated how these images of a militarized police force advance patriarchy, violence, and therefore are ultimately a detriment to women *and* men. The movement also opened up space to think globally about the many women harmed by military actions, especially noncombatants.

Hashtag activism was not the only strategy used by young female activists. This generation of justice workers are tech savvy and use social media and design websites as resources in their work. I think of www.campaignzero.org, which is a website that provides strategies for ending police violence; specifically, the demilitarization of police departments. This platform, as well as other platforms of the movement, is maintained and/or created by Black feminists and womanists. It provides resources to have informed conversations and highlights otherwise unknown data.

While I could write more about the mechanism young activists are deploying to combat the militarization of police forces, I want to wrap up this chapter with a few words about what I feel is the most significant area of work that feminists and womanists must attend to if we are to have any gains against the militarization of policing happening across the country: putting our efforts into helping disenfranchised persons exercise their right to vote.

If I had another chapter to write, it would concentrate on gentrification, gerrymandering, and the conservative quest to write the laws of our nation to disadvantage persons of color, Muslims, and immigrants. This quest lends to the hyperactive policing of communities of color and concomitant legislation to bring it to fruition. In this way, as we are at the cusp of America becoming a majority minority nation, and we are at the same time seeing more and more measures taken to deny Black and Brown people the right to vote. Militarized policing is an extension of the practices of colonialism and control. It impacts the voting process in that arrests may lead not only to incarceration but loss of one's voting rights. It impacts women who suffer disproportionately from highly patriarchal political administrations such as we have under the current presidential administration.

Finally, as a veteran and the mother of a son who served in Iraq and was there on the night known as "Shock and Awe," I urge we who call ourselves feminists and womanists to know what is also at stake in the expansion of U.S. militarization through policing: the glorification and proliferation of weapons and power. The fight against legislating any reasonable gun control. We are, to use Tenet's words, *blinking red*. However, we can turn this around.

It is my hope that the reader will understand that the history and analysis that I have offered in this chapter is owned by humanity. Thus, we must all of us own the responsibility to resist tyranny and to help create communities, indeed a world, where might is not tantamount to power and the phrase "to protect and serve" is realized as "to respect and do justice."

BIBLIOGRAPHY

Ambrose of Milan. "The Duties of Clergy." In *From Irenaeus to Grotius,* edited by Oliver O'Donovan and Joan O'Donovan, 66–88. Grand Rapids: Eerdmans, 1999.
"Bobby Seale's public Facebook Page." March 29, 2015. www.facebook.com/bobby.seale1.
Brown, Elaine. *A Taste of Power: A Black Woman's Story.* New York: First Anchor Books, 1993.
Carlson, Jennifer. *Citizen Protectors: The Everyday Politics of Guns in an Age of Decline.* Oxford: Oxford University Press, 2015.
"The Constitution of the United States: A Transcription." National Archives. 2015. www.archives.gov/founding-docs/constitution-transcript. Accessed November 4, 2015).
Douglass, Frederick. *My Bondage and My Freedom.* New York: Miller, Orton and Mulligan, 1855.
Gates, Daryl. *Chief: My Life in the LAPD.* New York: Bantum,1992.
Hammond, James Henry. "Gov. Hammond's Letters on Southern Slavery: Addressed to Thomas Clarkson, the English Abolitionist." 1845. The British Library.

www.archive.org/stream/lettersonsouther00hamm/lettersonsouther00hamm_djvu.txt.

Harvey, Thomas, et al. "ArchCity Defenders Municipal Courts White Paper." August 22, 2014. www.archive.org/details/pdfy-iyuTY46j7R_fAvpK.

Hoover, J. Edgar. "Hoover Memo on Black Panthers' Breakfast for Children." May 15, 1969. www.genius.com/Federal-bureau-of-investigation-hoover-memo-on-black-panthers-breakfast-for-children-program-annotated.

King Jr., Martin Luther. "Letter From a Birmingham Jail." April 16, 1963. Excerpt. Clergymen. "Letter to Martin Luther King." April 12, 1963. www.morningsidecenter.org/sites/default/files/files/Excerpts%20Clergymen%20%26%20King%20letters.pdf.

"LAPD Raid on the Black Panther's LA Headquarters, 1969." YouTube. March 2, 2015. www.youtube.com/watch?time_continue=1&v=xwQI79lYsTI.

"Los Angeles Police Chief, William Henry Parker 3d." *The New York Times*. August 14, 1965.

McLaughlin, Malcolm. *The Long Hot Summer of 1967: Urban Rebellion in America*. New York: Palgrave MacMillan, 2014.

National Commission on Terrorist Attacks Upon the United States. "The 9/11 Commission Report." New York: W.W. Norton & Company, 2004.

"Netflix Bringing 1969 LAPD Raid on Black Panthers to Screen." *Ebony*. March 16, 2017. www.ebony.com/entertainment/netflix-black-panther-lapd-raid. Accessed February 2018.

Sprague, Rosetta Douglass. "Anna Murray Douglass: My Mother as I Recall Her." Library of Congress. May 10, 1900. www.loc.gov/item/mfd.02007/.

"Statement By African-American Religious Leaders." Office of the Press Secretary, The White House. August 16, 1994. www.clintonwhitehouse6.archives.gov/1994/08/1994–08–16-african-american-religious-leaders-support-crime-bill.html.

"SWAT: Special Weapons and Tactics." LAPD Online. www.lapdonline.org/inside_the_lapd/content_basic_view/848.

"Watts Riot." History. www.history.com/topics/watts-riots.

Wofford, Taylor. "How America's Police Became an Army: The 1033 Program." *Newsweek*. August 13, 2014. www.newsweek.com/how-americas-police-became-army-1033-program-264537.

NOTES

1. National Commission on Terrorist Attacks Upon the United States. "The 9/11 Commission Report: Final Report of the National Commission on Terrorist Attacks Upon the United States," authorized edition (New York: W. W. Norton & Company, 2004).

2. Here I am admittedly influenced by the writings of St. Augustine's *The City of God*.

3. Frederick Douglass, *My Bondage and My Freedom* (New York: Miller, Orton & Mulligan, 1855).

4. Mostly northern and midwestern states along with Kansas and California. A good source that lists the number of slaves per state is the 1860 Census. These states that had far less agricultural production and, some would deduce, less need for the type of fieldwork demanded by the southern, largely rural states.

5. Rosetta Douglass Sprague, "Anna Murray Douglass: My Mother As I Recall Her," May 10, 1900, Library of Congress, Washington, DC, www.loc.gov/item/mfd.02007/ (accessed September 3, 2018).

6. Douglass Sprague, "Anna Murray Douglass."

7. "The Constitution of the United States: A Transcription," National Archives, 2015, www.archives.gov/founding-docs/constitution-transcript (accessed November 4, 2015).

8. James Henry Hammond, "Gov. Hammond's Letters on Southern Slavery: Addressed to Thomas Clarkson, the English Abolitionist," 1845, The British Library, www.archive.org/stream/lettersonsouther00hamm/lettersonsouther00hamm_djvu.txt.

9. Douglass, "My Mother As I Recall Her," 282.

10. "Los Angeles Police Chief William Henry Parker 3d," *The New York Times*, August 14, 1965.

11. Daryl Gates, *Chief: My Life in the L.A.P.D* (New York: Bantam, 1993).

12. "S.W.A.T.-Los Angeles Police Department," www.lapdonline.org/inside_the_lapd/content_basic_view/848 (accessed September 3, 2018).

13. "Netflix Bringing 1969 LAPD Raid on Black Panthers to Screen," *Ebony*, March 16, 2017, www.ebony.com/entertainment-culture/netflix-black-panther-lapd-raid (accessed September 2, 2018).

14. "Watts Riot Begins - Aug 11, 1965," History, www.history.com/this-day-in-history/watts-riot-begins (accessed September 2, 2018).

15. "LAPD Raid on the Black Panthers' LA Headquarters, 1969," www.youtube.com/watch?v=xw!1791YsTI (accessed September 2, 2018).

16. "Bobby Seale's Public Facebook Page," March 29, 2015, www.facebook.com/bobby.seale1 (accessed September 2, 2018).

17. Jennifer Carlson, *Citizen-Protectors: The Everyday Politics of Guns in an Age of Decline* (Oxford: Oxford University Press, 2015).

18. Malcolm McLaughlin, *The Long, Hot Summer of 1967: Urban Rebellion in America* (New York: Palgrave Macmillan, 2014).

19. Elaine Brown, *A Taste of Power: A Black Woman's Story* (New York: Anchor Books, 1993).

20. I am not suggesting that the entire activities of the Black Panther Party were helpful for Black people—and certainly not for Black women. There were stories of sexism and abuse of women (especially the beating of Regina Davis) within the ranks abound.

21. This term was a commonly known ideological term used by Huey Newton in several of his speeches.

22. Hoover, J. Edgar, "Hoover Memo on Black Panthers' Breakfast for Children," May 15, 1969, www.genius.com/Federal-bureau-of-investigation-hoover-memo-on-black-panthers-breakfast-for-children-program-annotated (accessed September 2, 2018).

23. "Statement By African-American Religious Leaders," Office of the Press Secretary, The White House, August 16, 1994, www.clintonwhitehouse6.archives.gov/1994/08/1994-08-16-african-american-religious-leaders-support-crime-bill.html.

24. See both the clergy letter to Dr. King, Jr. and his letter written from jail at www.morningsidecenter.org/sites/default/files/files/Excerpts%20Clergymen%20%26%20King%20letters.pdf.

25. Ambrose of Milan, "The Duties of Clergy," in *From Irenaeus to Grotius,* ed. Oliver O'Donovan and Joan O'Donovan (Grand Rapids: Eerdmans, 1999).

26. Thomas Harvey, et al., "ArchCity Defenders: Municipal Courts White Paper," August 2014, www.archive.org/details/pdfy-iyuTY46j7R_fAvpK (accessed March 16, 2018).

27. National Commission on Terrorist Attacks Upon the United States, "The 9/11 Commission Report," xvi.

28. Taylor Woodford, "How America's Police Became an Army: The 1033 Program," *Newsweek*, August 13, 2014, www.newsweek.com/how-americas-police-became-army-1033-program-264537 (accessed August 13, 2014).

29. I list it in this way because local police denied using actual BearCat armored vehicles.

SEVEN

The Muslim Ban and the (Un)Safe America

Nami Kim

THE MUSLIM BAN

Amid[1] intensifying military tension between the United States and North Korea over North Korean missile launches, as well as a worsening "war of words" between Donald J. Trump and Kim Jong Un, the Trump administration banned U.S. citizens from traveling to North Korea in September 2017.[2] What followed shortly after this travel ban was the third edition of Executive Order no. 13769, also known as the Muslim Ban. The first Muslim Ban issued by the Trump administration in January 2017 listed seven Muslim-majority countries (Iran, Iraq, Libya, Somalia, Sudan, Syria, and Yemen), whereas its third edition added Venezuela and North Korea to five Muslim-majority countries (Iran, Libya, Somalia, Syria, and Yemen) of which nationals are not allowed to enter the United States with a few exceptions.[3]

Like his presidential election slogan, "Make America Great Again," Trump's executive order is pitched as a directive that will "make America safe." In his tweet regarding the third edition of the Muslim Ban, Trump promoted his executive order as a necessary measure to keep "America" safe. "Making America Safe is my number one priority. We will not admit those into our country we cannot safely vet," he tweeted in September 2017.[4] Solicitor General Noel Francisco was reported to have also argued in court papers that the ban was necessary "in order to protect national security."[5] Whose America is Trump referring to and whose safety is he concerned about, if safety is indeed his agenda?

141

The restrictions on foreign nationals's entry to the United States are not without precedents.[6] As such, Executive Order no. 13769, entitled "Protecting the Nation from Foreign Terrorist Entry into the United States," is a symptom of a deeply entrenched racism against selected "others" as "dangerous foreigners," "security threats," "perpetual enemies," and/or "terrorists," though the perception of who belongs to these categories has shifted in accordance with U.S. domestic and foreign policy changes throughout U.S. history. Such shifts have in turn created what political philosopher Falguni Sheth calls the outcast population in the United States — those who are not protected by constitutional law and thereby lose the protection of their human rights.[7] In the current global geopolitical context, the outcast population are Muslims.[8]

This chapter aims to critically examine the ways in which the notion of violence against women, as well as the idea of the oppression of people due to race, gender, and sexuality, are deployed to justify Executive Order no. 13769. In such deployment, Muslims (read: Muslim men) are singled out as perpetrators of violence who are deemed to imperil America's safety. A critical examination of the Muslim Ban is necessary for two interrelated reasons. First, it helps us to understand the impact on Muslims whose entries to the United States are barred as well as Muslims who are residing in the United States. Moreover, it discloses the multiple layers of problems that are prevalent in a country that has *not* been a safe place for women, especially women of color, sexual and gender minorities, racialized immigrants, and Indigenous people. In this sense, this chapter is concerned with what the Muslim Ban does *not* say as much as with what it says. Secondly, such critical examination of the Muslim Ban can serve as a caution for feminists, especially those of us who are based in the United States, not to deploy the rhetoric of "violence against women" as a device that underpins the U.S. militarist imperial agenda by positioning the West/America as the frontrunner of antiviolence against women in contrast to the rest of the world as seriously marked by gender-based violence, which has been used as justification of U.S. military intervention. Although quite a few feminists have already criticized the ongoing operation of colonialist binary logic in (imperial) feminist projects, it seems necessary to reiterate the importance of avoiding such binary logic when we seek to eliminate violent acts and practices against women that are rife globally.

By scrutinizing the ways in which the Muslim Ban is justified primarily in relation to the notion of violence against women, I hope to provide a critical intervention in the normative understanding of security as the condition of being free from the danger posed by "unknown others" or "foreign enemies" in the context of the United States, which has become a counterterrorist security state in its continuing fight against "terror" inside and outside of its declared borders. First, however, I will briefly address the lingering question of the inclusion of North Korea in the Muslim Ban.

DOES THE INCLUSION OF NORTH KOREA IN THE MUSLIM BAN MAKE A DIFFERENCE?

"Are you *originally* from South Korea or North Korea?" I am often asked this question when people find out that I am an ethnic Korean. When I reluctantly respond, the reactions I receive are almost always identical: "I knew it. I knew you were from South Korea. South Korea is different from North Korea." I try not to lose my temper whenever I am asked that question and hear similar responses. Even with the history of U.S. military involvement in the Korean War and the dubbing of North Korea as one of the three axis of evil by former U.S. President George W. Bush, people do not seem to know that only a very small number of North Koreans have traveled to the United States, not to mention that no one has ever emigrated or can emigrate directly to the United States from North Korea. The travel restrictions on North Korea existed long before the Muslim Ban issued by the current administration. Thus, when North Korea was added to the third edition of the Muslim Ban, some experts voiced that adding North Korea to the existing list of banned Muslim-majority countries was nothing more than symbolic.[9]

What I find troubling in people's seemingly delighted reaction to, along with their sighs of relief about, my country of origin is the implicit Orientalist rendering of North Korea. Although ethnic Koreans from both Koreas, and any other "Asians," can be subjected to Orientalism, the ways in which North Korea and North Koreans have been portrayed by the mainstream U.S. media reflect the ongoing pernicious Orientalist gaze. Some of the popular images of North Korea in the U.S. media have included serious violations of human rights, lack of freedom, starvation, persecution of political prisoners and Christians, bellicose manufacturing of nuclear weapons, and so on; accordingly, North Koreans have been depicted primarily as deprived, repressed, starved, controlled, and brainwashed under three generations of communist dictatorship. What is missing in this representation is a nuanced, contextualized analysis of North Korea, of which history and the current situation cannot be comprehended apart from U.S. military intervention during the Korean War and the following U.S. propaganda against North Korea during the Cold War era. Instead, the list of the characteristics associated with the "Oriental rogue country" goes on—uncivilized, barbaric, undemocratic, authoritarian, incapable of controlling nuclear weapons, impulsive, irrational—as opposed to the civilized, democratic, capable of dealing with lethal weapons, reflective, rational West/United States. Such Orientalist portraits of North Korea/Koreans were also captured in Trump's tweet regarding the Muslim Ban on North Korea when he tweeted, "Kim Jong Un of North Korea is obviously a madman who doesn't mind starving or killing his people."[10] This tweet implies that unlike Kim, who is called a "madman," Trump *does* mind the starving or killing of "his" people. While he is critical of Kim Jong Un as a cruel, cold-hearted authoritarian, he himself is oblivious of the level and degree of poverty, incarceration, surveillance, and state violence that people of color, sexual minorities, gender nonconforming people, racialized (im)migrants, and Indigenous people experience in the United States. It is evident that these marginalized groups are not counted as "American," and therefore, their "safety" does not matter to him. But Trump's tweet is not unique in the sense that his view of North Korea/Koreans is widely shared by the U.S. media, the public, and so-called liberals, even if they are critical of Trump.

Because of such Orientalist renderings of North Korea, when North Korea was added to the Muslim Ban's third edition, those who know the racist (im)migration history in the United States said that not only "Koreans" but also all "Asians" [read: those who look "(East) Asian"] will be seriously scrutinized, if not completely barred, when they attempt to cross the U.S. borders. This is not an absurd scenario. Although I knew in theory that being a permanent U.S. resident does not guarantee one's "permanent" residency in the United States, it felt different under this administration's ruthless anti-immigrant policies and practices. As far as I can recall, it was the first time that the institution where I work advised non-U.S. citizen faculty to carry an employment verification letter issued by the college when they travel abroad. I carried the letter with me when I traveled abroad in summer 2017. U.S. border crossing has always been an anxiety-producing process even though I am a "permanent U.S. resident." As this madness of border crossing has been exacerbated under the Muslim Ban and other border controls,[11] I cannot imagine the anxiety, dread, distress, and ordeals that people who look "suspicious," are undocumented, or hold temporary visas would have to endure when they cross or attempt to cross the borders to enter the United States—a "home" for many of these people.

Whatever the "real" intention behind the inclusion of North Korea in the Muslim Ban and its effects may be, the inclusion of North Korea is not going to change the fact that the executive order issued by Trump is indeed a Muslim Ban. It is possible that North Korea might be removed from the banned countries sooner than expected due to the recent amicable political development shown in the Singapore Summit between Trump and Kim. Yet North Korea's stay in the list may be long if anything goes wrong between North Korea and the United States. Even if that is to be the case, however, it won't affect North Koreans in general, since only a small number of North Koreans have visited the United States. This only shows that adding North Korea, a non Muslim-majority country, to the third edition of the Muslim Ban serves to mitigate or divert the criticism that the ban is undeniably targeting Muslims.

WHAT DOES THE MUSLIM BAN HAVE TO DO WITH VIOLENCE AGAINST WOMEN?

When Trump signed an executive order that bans all visas from seven Muslim-majority countries for ninety days in January 2017, concerned people expressed outrage against this order and protested at the airports where people immediately affected by this order were detained. Some critics have voiced that a ban that restricts travel based on nationality is in and of itself unlawful and unconstitutional.[12] Although it was the previous administration that first listed the seven Muslim-majority countries from which travelers were imposed with stricter U.S. entry requirements, this new executive order sought to suspend all visas to nationals from those countries under the banner of "protecting Americans" and "America's security." This order is a manifestation of what Trump called for, namely a "total and complete shutdown of Muslims entering the United States,"[13] on his campaign trail.

Aside from debating whether this executive order is unlawful or not, what I want to call attention to is the problematic ways in which the Muslim Ban is rationalized, particularly in relation to the notion of violence against women as well as the idea of the oppression of members of certain races, genders, or sexual orientations.

Take a look at an excerpt from Section 1 in "Protecting the Nation from Terrorist Attacks by Foreign Nationals."

> In order to protect Americans, we must ensure that those admitted to this country do not bear hostile attitudes toward our country and its founding principles. We cannot, and should not, admit into our country those who do not support the U.S. Constitution, or those who would place violent religious edicts over American law. In addition, the United States should not admit those who engage in acts of bigotry and hatred (including "honor" killings, other forms of violence against women, or the persecution of those who practice other religions) or those who would oppress members of one race, one gender, or sexual orientation.[14]

As I will discuss further below, one of the ways in which the notion of violence against women is deployed as a rhetorical device to justify the Muslim Ban is through the "culturalization" of violence against women, which further produces two serious effects: first, it disciplines and polices Muslim communities in the Ubited States, and second, it justifies the U.S. war on terror as the righteous duty of the United States. Another way of justifying the Muslim Ban is through the erasure of multiple forms of violence against marginalized and vulnerable populations in the United

States. One of the problems with this erasure is that it continues to render the lives of women, especially women of color, and other vulnerable populations unsafe and unprotected because it makes invisible various types of violence against them in the United States. In contrast to this, violence committed ostensibly by "others" becomes "hyper-visual." Another problem with this erasure is the overlooking of the vulnerabilities of refugee and migrant women who are directly affected by the Muslim Ban, which I will discuss later.

The Culturalization of Violence against Women

In its deployment of the idea of "violence against women" to warrant the banning of entry from seven Muslim-majority countries, the Muslim Ban calls out a particular form of violence called "honor killings." It, however, does not define what "other forms of violence against women" are. As cultural anthropologist Lila Abu-Lughod argues, the category of "honor crime" stigmatizes the Muslim world and does not rightly serve women either.[15] Abu-Lughod continues that the problem with that category is that it stigmatizes "not particular acts of violence but entire cultures or communities."[16] In a similar vein, the way in which "honor killings" are singled out in the Muslim Ban can be considered what Sherene Razack calls the "culturalization" of violence against women.

In the culturalization of such violence, culture becomes "the sole source of patriarchal violence" while the multiple factors that cause and feed violence against women are obscured.[17] To put it differently, violence against women is culturalized through "an exclusive focus on culture, understood as frozen in time and separate from systems of domination."[18] Furthermore, the culturalization of violence against women attributes violence to Muslim men, implying that Muslim men commit acts of violence against women and that such acts are sanctioned by Islam. Rendering violence as a defining characteristic of Muslims serves to generate fear of the threat that (unidentified) Muslim men allegedly pose to the United States.[19] In other words, (unidentified) Muslim men are viewed as dangerous because of their ostensibly violent, misogynist acts, first against Muslim women, and then against "American" women if they are admitted to the United States. What is implied in this scheme is that the United States will be safe as long as Muslim men, whose violent acts are seen as being sanctioned by their religion, don't enter; without Muslim men, "American" women will be safe in theUnited States. Such a depiction of Muslim men and Islam in relation to violence against women only intensifies gendered Islamophobia in ways that Muslim men are represented as perpetrators of violence both against "Muslim women" and "American women." Muslim men's deplorable actions are seen as being permitted by Islam, whereas Muslim women are portrayed as silent victims of Muslim male violence, Muslim culture, and Islam. The ways in which gendered Islamophobia works is complicated in that while Muslim women are depicted primarily as tormented victims of Muslim male violence, they are also described as "murderous mothers" who "bring up terrorists," or "nameless veiled women" who completely lack agency.[20] No matter how they are depicted, these unidentified Muslim men and women always remain as "others" who are either to be "saved" or to be "defeated."

Islamophobia manifested through the stigmatization of Muslim men as innately abusive and sexist, and of Islam as unapologetically patriarchal, also reinforces what Sarah Farris calls the "racialization of sexism" that foregrounds the ways in which racism operates "through the portrayal of sexism and patriarchy as the exclusive domains of the (non-western and Muslim) Other."[21] The logical conclusion of such racism is that Muslim men who engage in violent, sexist practices that are rooted in an inherently patriarchal culture should not be allowed to enter the United States., or should be placed under constant surveillance if they are already in the United States, because they will make America unsafe. As Razack argues, if the problem is viewed as "cultural in origin," the "right" legal response can only be through border control and criminalizing,[22] so that anyone who belongs to such a "culture," including Muslim women who are alleged victims of Muslim male violence, should be banned from entering theUnited States and subject to the same surveillance. The deployment of the culturalization of violence against women to justify the Muslim Ban further produces two interrelated effects.

Disciplining and Criminalizing Muslim Communities in the United States

The framing of Muslim men's violence against women as originating from their culture not only justifies the prohibiting of Muslims from entering the United States but also serves to discipline Muslim communities within the United States through "the extraordinary measures of violence and surveillance required to discipline."[23] The culturalization of violence against women serves as an effective device in domestic profiling, policing, and criminalizing U.S. Muslims and Muslim organizations without legal repercussions because all of these are done in the name of national security and the protection of Americans. However, this conceals the violence faced by U.S. Muslim communities. U.S. Muslims and Muslim organizations are excluded from state protection as outcasts, are subject to racist violence and discrimination, are profiled as being engaged in or in support of terrorism, and therefore are criminalized as threats to the larger society. Such disciplining and criminalizing take place through the operation of what Dean Spade calls two different yet related modes of power, "disciplinary" and "population-management." The disciplinary mode of power operates in ways that divide people as either "moderate" or "extreme" and pits "tolerable" moderates who are "acceptable" and "deserving" against "unacceptable" and "undeserving" extremists who are a major threat to the United States. However, the idea of the "deserving" or "undeserving" subject that is found in the disciplinary mode of power no longer works when the entire Muslim population inside the United States is "managed" as a threat group. Once a population group is designated as an "outcast" population, the line between deserving and undeserving becomes effaced. As Spade argues, for instance, the new framing of immigration policy-related matters as "terrorism prevention" has justified legal and policy changes that brought about the locking up of immigrants.[24] What Spade calls the "population-management" mode of power has also been operating in immigration law and policy among many other laws and policies, such as the Secure Communities Program, a deportation program operated through collaboration of local, state, and federal agencies.[25] As Soo Ah Kwon points out, the increase in deportation and detention of Arab, Arab American, Muslim, and South Asian immigrants as part of the U.S. war on terror shows that deportation is a system of removal aimed at unwanted immigration populations.[26] The Muslim Ban can be viewed as an extension of such law.

As Falguni Sheth has argued, sovereign authorities have always made an "exception"—an outcast group whose rights are not protected by constitutional law.[27] While they are excluded from law's protection, as Lisa Marie Cacho argues, they are "not excluded from law's discipline, punishment, and regulation."[28] U.S. Muslim communities are then policed and are often criminalized no matter how "deserving" or "good" individual Muslims are because they, as a collective, are regarded as potential threats to the United States. Muslims outside the United States are also characterized as perpetrators of violence—terrorists who are deemed to be the "perpetual enemy" who need to be defeated at all costs or prevented from entering the United States. What transnational feminist scholar Chandra Mohanty states rings true: "While the U.S. imperial project calls for civilizing brown and black (and now Arab) men and rescuing their women outside its borders, the very same state engages in killing, imprisoning, and criminalizing black and brown and now Muslim and Arab peoples within its own borders."[29]

Justifying the U.S. War on Terror as the
Righteous Duty of the United States

The second effect produced by the justification of the Muslim Ban through the culturalization of violence against women is that it continues to reinforce the U.S. war on terror as the righteous duty of the "civilized" United States to "liberate" Muslim women who allegedly suffer at the hands of their violent men. The Muslim Ban can be viewed as an inversion of the United States's "civilizing" mission abroad. In the age of the

U.S. global war on terror, the Muslim Ban exemplifies how imperial war "'over there' reverberates 'over here.'"[30] If the United States's outgoing "civilizing" military operation has been justified as a mission of rescuing Muslim women from their allegedly aggressive Muslim men, the Muslim Ban is an inverted operation that prevents Muslims who are viewed as committing vicious acts from entering the "civilized" territory for the protection of its own people [read: select Americans]. Both "missions" are operated based on the same logic; that is, the dangerous, unruly "other" man and his victimized woman need to be governed by the "civilized" West and kept in their own terrain. They cannot and should not cross the borders beyond their own territories, even though the United States can enter there any time. Furthermore, the justification of the Muslim Ban through the culturalization of violence against women either conceals or minimizes violent acts committed by the U.S. military and/or its allies against people in "enemy" territories, such as drone attacks against civilians, especially children, as unfortunate but unavoidable in order to eradicate terrorism. Consequently, "terrorism" continues to be associated with violent attacks from "external" or "outside" forces, although, as Angela Y. Davis contends, it is a "domestic phenomenon" that has very much shaped U.S. history.[31]

The Erasure of Multiple Forms of Violence against
Vulnerable Populations in the United States

In addition to deploying the rhetorical device of violence against women and of the oppression of members of one race, one gender, or sexual orientation, the Muslim Ban's purported goal of "protecting Americans" is also rationalized through the erasure of multiple forms of violence against the vulnerable populations who do not receive protection from the state. Such erasure makes both the severity and impacts of violence invisible and nonexistent in the U.S. context. The other side of such erasure is "gender and sexual exceptionalisms" of the United States—the United States as a nation-state where women's rights are intact and sexual minorities are safe, as opposed to the Muslim-majority countries that are ostensibly not safe.[32] As much as "women's rights" has been invoked by colonial-imperialist logic to defend Western militarist imperial expansion, "gay rights" is also summoned as a marker of civilization and democracy. This logic allows the nation-states that do not advocate "women's rights" and/or "gay rights" to be deemed backward and undemocratic, and thus validates the United States's criticism of the Muslim-majority countries as oppressors and violators of human rights.[33] Consequently, while the United States claims to be a "gay-friendly," "gay-safe" haven that does not oppress sexual minorities, Muslim-majority countries are branded as sites of intolerance, backwardness, and tyranny. The danger of promoting U.S. gender and sexual exceptionalisms is that they will not only warrant U.S. military interventions in any place where U.S. interests lie but also conceal ongoing onslaughts against women of color, sexual minorities, and gender nonconforming people in the United States. Thus, violence against them becomes an individual, private, and often insignificant matter. In the Muslim Ban, sexism, misogyny, homophobia, transphobia, sexual violence, and gender inequality prevailing in the United States are all erased, while violent or oppressive acts allegedly committed by "others" are underscored and hyper-visualized.

Making the Lives of Women and Other Vulnerable People Unsafe and Unprotected

One of the pernicious problems with the erasure of multiple forms of violence against marginalized populations in the United States is that it continues to endanger the lives of women of color and other vulnerable populations because it makes absent different types of violence committed against them.[34] This problem is related to the question of for whom is America safe and whose lives are worthy of state protection. As Beth Richie demonstrates in her book *Arrested Justice*, not only has violence against Black women, especially underprivileged Black women, increased, but the response of the state also often puts them into a more dangerous situation, as the state further violates and criminalizes them instead of "protecting" them.[35]

According to Richie, the mainstream feminist anti-violence movement that focuses primarily on gender dynamics has made great strides in the United States, but it has benefited mostly middle-class white women while leaving out women of color who experience multiplicative forms of violence.[36] She argues that the ways in which women of color, particularly underprivileged Black women, experience violence is not limited to gender-based violence in the private sphere. Critiquing the feminist anti-violence movement for having become mainstream by working closely with the state, Richie argues that it is problematic to construe violence against women only in terms of gender dynamics in the private realm without making connections among different forms of violence that women experience—state violence, police violence, economic violence, sexual violence, physical violence, emotional violence. They are not "safe" in "America," nor are they "protected" by the state. Police brutality, police profiling, criminalization, and the imprisoning of people, especially people who do not fit the category of the "deserving victim" due to their race, gender, sexuality, nationality, religion, are persistent.

While issuing the Muslim Ban, the Trump administration has prepared to cut domestic funding for programs that seek to support women who are victim-survivors of violence, which will further make America unsafe for women who suffer from violence. In December 2017, Trump signed a tax bill that takes away benefits that support women who need them the most.[37] The current administration's "global gag rule" will also further devastate women's lives globally, as women will not receive services needed for their health and survival. In fact, the current administration has jeopardized various efforts to eradicate violence against women and the oppression of sexual and gender minorities. More money is being spent on expanding the military-industrial complex, building prisons, patrolling borders, and policing, instead of providing resources necessary for people's survival, such as good quality health care, safe and affordable housing, public transportation, living-wage employment, and education.

Thus, when violence against women and the oppression of minorities due to race, gender, or sexuality are pitched as reasons to block allegedly violent Muslim men as well as their supposed female "victims" from entering the United States, it is deeply troubling because, in fact, the majority of women's lives are already unsafe and unprotected in the United States. Such justification of the Muslim Ban is self-contradictory, hypocritical, insidious, fraudulent, and disingenuous. It reveals this administration's little-to-no understanding of the gravity of violence against women committed by "American" people and "American" institutions on "American" soil. Perpetrators of violence and oppression are relegated only to imaginary predators from outside, that is, "violent Muslim men," thus perpetuating Islamophobia as anti-Muslim racism and a hatred of Islam. While erasing state violence against women of color, sexual minorities, gender nonconforming people, Indigenous people, and racialized immigrants, the United States emerges like a strong patriarchal protector that alleges it will "protect" women, children, and other vulnerable people from the dangers posed by "outside" intruders and predators. Positioning itself as the powerful "protector" is not only for the purpose of establishing the United States as a hegemonic power in relation to other countries but also for legitimizing itself as a "security state" in the domestic context.[38] The security state is the protector, and the citizens are the protected, resembling the patriarchal household in which such roles and the relationship of the protector and the protected have been "naturalized."[39] However, as the patriarchal household is often not a safe place for women and children, the patriarchal state is precisely the space where women, children, and other vulnerable subjects are not secure in their safety. Instead, it is a space where vulnerable populations have to endure various forms of violence committed by the alleged protector. State violence becomes more rampant, yet it is viewed as a "normal" aspect of domestic life. As Grace Kyungwon Hong and other women of color feminists have shown, the state is "a site of violence, not resolution."[40] As Mimi Kim points out, some anti-violence activists and organizations further challenge the notion of state as "a viable partner in the struggle against violence against women and children" and "the primacy of individual safety" for the oppressed because it is "a myth or luxury afforded to the privileged few."[41] This indicates that safety for women and other vulnerable populations cannot be achieved through policing or militarizing. As Kim compellingly points out, "reliance on the state to protect women from the patriarchal violence of 'dangerous' men can be compared to U.S. military policy that uses invasion and occupation to protect the rights of women in Afghanistan and Iraq against the tyranny of Islamic patriarchy."[42] As feminists who are critical of the mainstream antiviolence movement's reliance on the criminal legal system have cautioned, it is problematic to rely on a system that suggests "unquestioned support of policing and militarization as a solution to gender oppression and gender-based violence."[43]

Overlooking the Vulnerabilities of Refugee and Migrant Women

Another related problem with erasing multiple forms of violence against marginalized populations in the United States is that it completely overlooks the vulnerabilities of women who belong to "refugee and migrant communities." The Muslim Ban affects refugees who arrived in the United States, of which almost half were nationals of one of the affected countries, and those whose admission is indefinitely suspended.[44] This is disconcerting because the majority of the refugees are in fact women and children. I will elaborate on this point by looking at the notion of violence against women defined by the United Nations. It should be mentioned, however, that while the UN's definition of violence against women has been expanded, it is not without its limits and western biases, especially with regard to "honor killings." Since 2010, the UN has included "honor killings"[45] as one of the forms of violence against women alongside the more commonly named "domestic violence," which is, again, problematic, as Lila Abu-Lughod has argued. The reason I look at the UN's definition of violence against women, despite its limit, is to point out the Muslim Ban's duplicity.

According to the Declaration on the Elimination of Violence Against Women (DEVAW), adopted by the United Nations General Assembly in 1993, violence against women is defined as "any act of gender based violence that results in, or is likely to result in, physical, sexual, or psychological harm or suffering to women, including threats of such acts, coercion or arbitrary deprivation of liberty, whether occurring in public or private life."[46] The definition of DEVAW was further expanded in the Beijing Platform for Action, adopted in 1995, to include the following:

> violations of the rights of women in situations of armed conflict, including systematic rape, sexual slavery and forced pregnancy; forced sterilization, forced abortion, coerced or forced use of contraceptives; prenatal sex selection; and, female infanticide . . . the particular vulnerabilities of women belonging to minorities; the elderly and the dis-

placed; indigenous, refugee and migrant communities; women living in impoverished rural or remote areas, or in detention.[47]

As such, the 1995 Beijing Platform for Action includes the vulnerabilities of women who belong to "refugee and migrant communities." In light of this expanded definition of violence against women, it is evident that the Muslim Ban does not acknowledge the particular vulnerabilities of women refugees and migrants as violence against women. While the Muslim Ban plainly uses "violence against women" as a reason to ban Muslims from entering the United States, it only reveals its hypocrisy as it indefinitely halted a program that allows the resettled refugees to bring over spouses and children.[48] Furthermore, it does not admit refugees, of which the majority are women and children. For instance, three quarters of Syrian refugees fleeing from war and genocide are women and children,[49] yet their admission was indefinitely suspended by the Muslim Ban. It is, then, the current administration that is in fact engaging in "acts of bigotry and hatred" against women and children in general, particularly those who are part of refugee communities. It is revealing that only certain types of violence, such as "honor killings," are underscored, but not the vulnerabilities that women, especially women in the refugee and migrant communities, undergo in the context of war, militarized violence, forced migration, impoverishment, and famine.

RETHINKING "SECURITY" AND "PROTECTION"

The series of executive orders that ban Muslims from entering the United States have been made under the banner of the "protection of Americans" and the "security of America" by using the rhetoric of violence against women and the oppression of people based on race, gender, or sexual orientation. In the Muslim Ban, the security of the state hinges on the successful prevention of the entry of Muslim men whose aggressive acts and practices are rooted in their culture/religion: Islam. By linking violence against women to ostensibly harmful Muslim practices, Muslim men and Islam become the top threat to national security. Muslims are viewed only as a hazard to "security," while their own safety has been overlooked. Those who need protection are not protected by the state, whereas unsolicited paternalism is used in order to pretend that the government's priority is to protect its citizens from dangers posed by those who are perceived to be violent and ruthless "outsiders." As Inderpal Grewal argues, security has become "the rationale for militarized cultures of surveillance and protection that lead to insecurities, threats and fears, which work at material, affective and embodied levels."[50]

Feminist scholars have argued that "security" should be defined in "multidimensional or multilevel terms" that are related to issues that range from domestic violence, sexual violence, gender inequality, poverty, racial discrimination, and ecological destruction.[51] "Security" should not be about pointing at unidentified foreigners or outsiders as a "threat," when in fact vulnerable populations have not been "safe" nor protected in a highly militarized, racist, ableist, homophobic, transphobic, Islamophobic, and misogynistic nation-state. The security of the society cannot be maintained by surveillance, policing, incarceration, and state violence. As Angela Davis argues, we need to imagine a different kind of security that is not based on "policing and incarceration."[52] Perhaps, instead of working to maintain "security" or using the framework of (in)security,[53] we need to reimagine an entirely different kind of social structure that is "not premised on violence or the threat of violence," but that is based on "a collective commitment to guaranteeing the survival and care of all peoples."[54] The idea of a "secure" society should be altered to indicate the social condition in which people can live without fear of their lives being impinged by various forms of injustice. Society's primary concern should be about the everyday struggles of ordinary people, particularly women of color and other minorities, calling attention to an "interrelationship of violence at all levels of society."[55] Rethinking security and protection should also challenge the normalized notion that militarization, border control, the proliferation of prisons, surveillance, and police profiling are about keeping the nation secure and safe, by asking who benefits from such "security." It is impossible to eliminate the multiple forms of violence that women and other vulnerable people experience without radically transforming the social, political, economic, cultural, and militarized contexts that generate and sustain them. Without such radical transformation, America will continue to be an unsafe place for women of color and other marginalized people. Banning people's entry to the United States based on race, religion, and national origin is certainly not a solution but a testament to the already unsafe America.

BIBLIOGRAPHY

Abu-Lughod, Lila. *Do Muslim Women Need Saving?* Cambridge: Harvard University, 2015.

Beydoun, Khaled A. *American Islamophobia: Understanding the Roots and Rise of Fear.* Berkeley: University of California Press, 2018. Kindle.

Bier, David J. "Trump's Immigration Ban is Illegal." *The New York Times.* January 27, 2017. www.nytimes.com/2017/01/27/opinion/trumps-immigration-ban-is-illegal.html.

Brennan, David. "U.S. in Top 10 Most Dangerous Countries for Women." *Newsweek.* June 26, 2018. www.newsweek.com/us-top-10-most-dangerous-countries-women-report-995229.

Cacho, Lisa Marie. *Social Death: Racialized Rightlessness and the Criminalization of the Unprotected (Nation of Nations).* New York: New York University Press, 2012. Kindle.

Davis, Angela Y. *Freedom Is a Constant Struggle: Ferguson, Palestine, and the Foundations of a Movement.* Chicago: Haymarket Books, 2016. Kindle.

Deer, Sarah. *The Beginning and End of Rape: Confronting Sexual Violence in Native America*. Minneapolis: University of Minnesota Press, 2015. Kindle.

"Defining Gender-Based Violence: Gender-based violence (GBV) or violence against women VAW)?" Strengthening Health System Responses to Gender-based Violence in Eastern Europe and Central Asia: A resource package. www.health-genderviolence.org/training-programme-for-health-care-providers/facts-on-gbv/defining-gender-based-violence/21.

De León, Jason. *The Land of Open Graves: Living and Dying on the Migrant Trail*. Berkeley: University of California Press, 2015.

de Vogue, Ariane. "Supreme Court lets full Trump travel ban take effect." CNN. December 5, 2017. www.cnn.com/2017/12/04/politics/supreme-court-travel-ban/index.html.

"Executive Order: Protecting the Nation from Terrorist Attacks by Foreign Nationals." *The Washington Post*. www.apps.washingtonpost.com/g/documents/world/read-the-draft-of-the-executive-order-on-immigration-and-refugees/2289/.

Faludi, Susan. "The Patriarchs Are Falling. The Patriarchy Is Stronger Than Ever." *The New York Times*. December 28, 2017. www.nytimes.com/2017/12/28/opinion/sunday/patriarchy-feminism-metoo.html.

Farris, Sara R. *In the Name of Women's Rights: The Rise of Femonationalism*. Durham: Duke University Press, 2017. Kindle.

"Feminist Perspectives on Peace and Security." Gunda and Werner Institute: Feminism and Gender Democracy. www.gwi-boell.de/en/2010/07/30/feminist-perspectives-peace-and-security.

"Fourth World Conference on Women." United Nations Entity for Gender Equality and the Empowerment of Women. www.un.org/womenwatch/daw/beijing/platform/.

Grewal, Inderpal. *Saving the Security State: Exceptional Citizens in Twenty-First-Century America*. Durham: Duke University Press, 2017. Kindle.

Hammer, Juliane. "Center Stage: Gendered Islamophobia and Muslim Women." In *Islamophobia in America: The Anatomy of Intolerance*, edited by Carl W. Ernst. New York: Palgrave Macmillan, 2013.

Hong, Grace Kyungwon. *The Ruptures of American Capital: Women of Color Feminism and the Culture of Immigrant Labor*. Minneapolis: University of Minnesota Press, 2006.

"Impunity for domestic violence, 'honour killings' cannot continue—UN official." UN News Center. March 4, 2010. www.un.org/apps/news/story.asp?NewsID=33971#.Wl95fVQ-fOR.

Johnson, Jenna. "Trump calls for 'total and complete shutdown of Muslims entering the United States.'" *The Washington Post*. December 7, 2015. www.washingtonpost.com/news/post-politics/wp/2015/12/07/donald-trump-calls-for-total-and-complete-shutdown-of-muslims-entering-the-united-states.

Jordan, Miriam. "Appeals Court Partly Reinstate Trump's New Travel Ban." *The New York Times*. November 13, 2017. www.nytimes.com/2017/11/13/us/travel-ban-reinstated-appeal.html.

Kim, Mimi. "Alternative Interventions to Intimate Violence: Defining Political and Pragmatic Challenges." In *Restorative Justice and Violence Against Women*, edited by James Ptacek. Oxford: Oxford University, 2009.

Kim, Nami. *The Gendered Politics of the Korean Protestant Right: Hegemonic Masculinity*. New York: Palgrave Macmillan, 2016.

King, Danae. "US on track to let in fewest refugees since 1980." *The Columbus Dispatch*. March 26, 2018. www.dispatch.com/news/20180326/us-on-track-to-let-in-fewest-refugees-since-1980.

Kwon, Soo Ah. "Deporting Cambodian Refugees: Youth Activism, State Reform, and Imperial Statecraft." In *Ethnographies of U.S. Empire*, edited by Carole McGranahan and John F. Collins. Durham: Duke University Press, 2018. Kindle.

Love, Eric. *Islamophobia and Racism in America*. New York: NYU Press, 2017. Kindle.

Luse, Keith. "The Trouble with the New US North Korea Travel Ban." *The Diplomat.* October 11, 2017. www.thediplomat.com/2017/10/the-trouble-with-the-new-us-north-korea-travel-ban/.

Mohanty, Chandra Talpade. "US Empire and the Project of Women's Studies: Stories of citizenship, complicity and dissent." *Gender, Place and Culture* 13, no. 1 (February 2006): 7–20.

Naber, Nadine, Eman Desouky, and Lina Baroudi. "The Forgotten '-ism': An Arab American Women's Perspective on Zionism, Racism, and Sexism." In *Color of Violence: The Incite! Anthology,* edited by Incite! Women of Color Against Violence, 104–106. Cambridge: South End Press, 2006.

———. "Diasporas of Empire: Arab Americans and the Reverberations of War." In *At the Limits of Justice: Women of Colour on Terror,* edited by Suvendrini Perera and Sherene H. Razack. Toronto: University of Toronto Press, 2014.

Neocleous, Mark. *Critique of Security.* Montreal: McGill-Queen's University Press, 2008.

"North Korea Tourism: US Travel Ban Takes Effect." BBC. September 1, 2017. www.bbc.com/news/world-asia-41120738.

Puar, Jasbir. "Rethinking Homonationalism." *International Journal of Middle East Studies* 45, Issue 2 (2013): 336–339.

———. *Terrorist Assemblages: Homonationalism in Queer Times.* Durham: Duke University Press, 2007.

Rauhala, Emily. "Almost no North Koreans travel to the U.S., so why ban them?" *The Washington Post.* September 25, 2017. www.washingtonpost.com/world/almost-no-north-koreans-travel-to-the-us-so-why-ban-them/2017/09/25/822ac340-a19c-11e7–8c37-e1d99ad6aa22_story.html.

Razack, Sherene H. "Imperilled Muslim Women, Dangerous Muslim Men and Civilised Europeans: Legal and Social Responses to Forced Marriage." *Feminist Legal Studies* 12, no. 2 (October 2004): 129–174.

Richie, Beth E. *Arrested Justice: Black Women, Violence, and America's Prison Nation.* New York: New York University Press, 2012. Kindle.

Ritchie, Andrea. *Invisible No More: Police Violence Against Black Women and Women of Color.* Boston: Beacon Press, 2017. Kindle.

Sheth, Falguni A. *Toward a Political Philosophy of Race.* Albany: State University of New York, 2009.

"Secure Communities: A Fact Sheet." American Immigration Council. November 29, 2011. www.americanimmigrationcouncil.org/research/secure-communities-fact-sheet.

Sjoberg, Laura, ed. *Gender and International Security: Feminist Perspectives.* New York: Routledge, 2010.

Spade, Dean. *Normal Life: Administrative Violence, Critical Trans Politics, and the Limits of Law.* Brooklyn: South End Press, 2011.

Trump, Donald J. Twitter Post. September 24, 2017, 4:49 PM. www.twitter.com/realdonaldtrump/status/912101775221706752.

———. Twitter Post. September 22, 2017, 3:28 AM. www.twitter.com/realdonaldtrump/status/911175246853664768.

Valverde, Miriam. "Most Syrian refugees are women and children, as Keith Ellison said." Politifact. February 2, 2017. www.politifact.com/truth-o-meter/statements/2017/feb/02/keith-ellison/rep-keith-ellison-correct-demographic-overview-syr/.

"Violence against women: Definition and the scope of the problem." World Health Organization. July 1997. www.who.int/gender/violence/v4.pdf.

Wadley, Jonathan D. "Gendering the State: Performativity and Protection in International Security." In *Gender and International Security: Feminist Perspectives,* edited by Laura Sjoberg. Abingdon: Routledge, 2010.

Williams, Duncan, and Gideon Yaffe. "Trump's administration says the travel ban isn't like Japanese internment. It is." *The Washington Post.* May 16, 2017.

www.washingtonpost.com/posteverything/wp/2017/05/16/trumps-administration-says-the-travel-ban-isnt-like-japanese-internment-it-is.

NOTES

1. This chapter is an expanded and revised version of my blog piece, "The Travel Ban and Violence Against Women," Feminist Studies in Religion, Inc., February 22, 2017.

2. Annually, about up to one thousand U.S. citizens travel to North Korea. See "North Korea Tourism: US Travel Ban Takes Effect," *BBC*, September 1, 2017, www.bbc.com/news/world-asia-41120738 (accessed September 5, 2017).

3. I call the Executive Order 13769 a "Muslim Ban" rather than a "Travel Ban" due to its explicit target of Muslims. On June 26, 2018, the Supreme Court upheld Trump's third edition of the "Travel Ban," saying that it is not a "Muslim Ban." Chad was originally on the list in the third edition of the Muslim Ban, but it was removed.

4. Donald J. Trump, Twitter Post, September 24, 2017, 4:49 PM, www.twitter.com/realdonaldtrump/status/912101775221706752.

5. Ariane de Vogue, "Supreme Court lets full Trump travel ban take effect," CNN, December 5, 2017, www.cnn.com/2017/12/04/politics/supreme-court-travel-ban/index.html (accessed December 20, 2017).

6. The Chinese Exclusion Act of 1882 prohibited immigration of Chinese laborers. In his book *American Islamophobia*, Khaled A. Beydoun argues that Trump's Muslim Ban was driven by the same discourse and stereotypes that banned Muslim immigrants from becoming naturalized U.S. citizens from 1790 (the Naturalization Act of 1790) to 1944. See *American Islamophobia: Understanding the Roots and Rise of Fear* (Berkeley: University of California Press, 2018); See also, Duncan Williams and Gideon Yaffe, "Trump's administration says the travel ban isn't like Japanese internment. It is," *The Washington Post*, May 16, 2017, www.washingtonpost.com/posteverything/wp/2017/05/16/trumps-administration-says-the-travel-ban-isnt-like-japanese-internment-it-is (accessed July 21, 2018).

7. Falguni A. Sheth, *Toward a Political Philosophy of Race* (Albany: State University of New York, 2009), 171.

8. For the term "Muslim" as a racial category, see Eric Love's *Islamophobia and Racism in America* (New York: New York University Press, 2017); See also, Beydoun's *American Islamophobia*.

9. Emily Rauhala, "Almost no North Koreans travel to the United States, so why ban them?" *The Washington Post*, September 25, 2017, www.washingtonpost.com/world/almost-no-north-koreans-travel-to-the-us-why-ban-them/2017/09/25/822ac340-a19c-11e7–8c37-e1d99ad6aa22_story.html (accessed September 28, 2017). There are so-called defectors from North Korea, who have settled in the United States as they entered the United States via another country, and their settlement is not through "immigration." From a different angle, others say that it cannot be merely symbolic due to the loss of opportunities for the interaction between Americans and North Koreans that can potentially contribute to ease the hostile relationship between the United States and North Korea. See Keith Luse, "The Trouble with the New US North Korea Travel Ban," *The Diplomat*, October 11, 2017, www.thediplomat.com/2017/10/the-trouble-with-the-new-us-north-korea-travel-ban/ (accessed October 15, 2017).

10. Donald J. Trump, Twitter Post, September 22, 2017, 3:28 AM, www.twitter.com/realdonaldtrump/status/ 911175246853664768. I hope the reader would not misconstrue my point about the Orientalist gaze of North Korea/Koreans as an attempt to "defend" or "support" the North Korean regime.

11. For the heart-wrenching stories of the suffering and deaths of undocumented migrants who attempt to cross the border from Mexico to the United States, see Jason De León, *The Land of Open Graves: Living and Dying on the Migrant Trail*, (Berkeley: University of California Press, 2015).

12. David J. Bier, "Trump's Immigration Ban is Illegal," *The New York Times*, January 27, 2017, www.nytimes.com/2017/01/27/opinion/trumps-immigration-ban-is-illegal.html (accessed February 1, 2017).

13. Jenna Johnson, "Trump calls for 'total and complete shutdown of Muslims entering the United States,'" *The Washington Post*, December 7, 2015, www.washingtonpost.com/news/post-politics/wp/2015/12/07/donald-trump-calls-for-total-and-complete-shutdown-of-muslims-entering-the-united-states/ (accessed December 10, 2015).

14. "Executive Order: Protecting the Nation from Terrorist Attacks by Foreign Nationals," *The Washington Post*, www.apps.washingtonpost.com/g/documents/world/read-the-draft-of-the-executive-order-on-immigration-and-refugees/2289/ (accessed January 22, 2017).

15. Lila Abu-Lughod, "Seductions of the Honor Crime," in *Do Muslim Women Need Saving?* (Cambridge: Harvard University, 2015), 113.

16. Abu-Lughod, "Seductions of the Honor Crime," 114. She lists four problems with using the category of "honor crime." See 115–116.

17. Sherene H. Razack, "Imperilled Muslim Women, Dangerous Muslim Men and Civilised Europeans: Legal and Social Responses to Forced Marriage," *Feminist Legal Studies* vol. 12, no. 2 (October 2004): 132.

18. Razack, "Imperilled Muslim Women, Dangerous Muslim Men and Civilised Europeans," 131.

19. Razack, "Imperilled Muslim Women," 131.

20. See Nadine Naber, Eman Desouky, and Lina Baroudi, "The Forgotten '-ism': An Arab American Women's Perspective on Zionism, Racism, and Sexism," in *Color of Violence: The Incite! Anthology*, ed. Incite! Women of Color Against Violence (Cambridge: South End Press, 2006), 104–106.

21. Sara R. Farris, *In the Name of Women's Rights: The Rise of Femonationalism* (Durham: Duke University Press, 2017), 74. Racism against Muslims is also "sexed" to the extent that the portraits of Muslim men are based on sexual metaphors and stereotypes, such as "sexual threat" and "sexual predator" (74–75). Farris calls this "sexualization of racism."

22. Razack, "Imperilled Muslim Women, Dangerous Muslim Men and Civilised Europeans," 160.

23. Razack, "Imperilled Muslim Women, Dangerous Muslim Men and Civilised Europeans," 130.

24. Dean Spade, *Normal Life: Administrative Violence, Critical Trans Politics, and the Limits of Law* (Brooklyn: South End Press, 2011), 57. Regarding the "terrorism prevention" measures used by the U.S. government and its devastating effects on the Muslim communities in the United States, see Beydoun's *American Islamophobia*. Eric Love says that Muslim Americans are responsible for less than one percent of violent deaths in the United States more than a decade since 9/11. See Love, *Islamophobia and Racism in America*, 2100–2103.

25. The Secure Communities Program is an example of such laws and polices. It was launched in March 2008. See www.americanimmigrationcouncil.org/research/secure-communities-fact-sheet. See also, Spade, *Normal Life*, 57, 63.

26. Soo Ah Kwon, "Deporting Cambodian Refugees: Youth Activism, State Reform, and Imperial Statecraft," in *Ethnographies of U.S. Empire*, ed. Carole McGranahan and John F. Collins (Durham: Duke University Press, 2018), ch. 4.

27. See Sheth, *Toward a Political Philosophy of Race*.

28. Lisa Marie Cacho, *Social Death: Racialized Rightlessness and the Criminalization of the Unprotected (Nation of Nations)* (New York: New York University Press, 2012), 5.

29. Chandra Talpade Mohanty, "US Empire and the Project of Women's Studies: Stories of citizenship, complicity and dissent," *Gender, Place and Culture* 13, no. 1 (February 2006): 11.

30. Nadine Naber, "Diasporas of Empire: Arab Americans and the Reverberations of War," in *At the Limits of Justice: Women of Colour on Terror*, ed. Suvendrini Perera and Sherene H. Razack (Toronto: University of Toronto Press, 2014), 210.

31. Angela Y. Davis, *Freedom Is a Constant Struggle: Ferguson, Palestine, and the Foundations of a Movement* (Chicago: Haymarket Books, 2015), 75.

32. Jasbir Puar, *Terrorist Assemblages: Homonationalism in Queer Times* (Durham: Duke University Press, 2007), 39–41.

33. See Nami Kim, *The Gendered Politics of the Korean Protestant Right: Hegemonic Masculinity* (New York: Palgrave Macmillan, 2016); See also Jasbir Puar, "Rethinking Homonationalism," *International Journal of Middle East Studies* 45, Issue 2 (2013): 336–339.

34. See Andrea Ritchie's *Invisible No More: Police Violence Against Black Women and Women of Color* (Boston: Beacon Press, 2017).

35. Beth E. Richie, *Arrested Justice: Black Women, Violence, and America's Prison Nation* (New York: New York University Press, 2012).

36. Richie, *Arrested Justice*.

37. See "Patriarchs, patriarchy. . ." *The New York Times*, December 28, 2017, www.nytimes.com/2017/12/28/opinion/sunday/patriarchy-feminism-metoo.html (accessed December 30, 2017); "U.S. in Top 10 Most Dangerous Countries for Women," *Newsweek*, June 26, 2018, www.newsweek.com/us-top-10-most-dangerous-countries-women-report-995229 (accessed June 28, 2018).

38. See Jonathan D. Wadley, "Gendering the State: Performativity and Protection in International Security," in *Gender and International Security: Feminist Perspectives*, ed. Laura Sjoberg (Abingdon: Routledge, 2010).

39. Iris Young cited in Wadley, "Gendering the State," 51. By pointing out the tribal provisions of the 2013 VAWA as "patronizing and paternalistic," Sarah Deer, for instance, claims that by definition any federal legislation "institutionalizes and endorses the United States as a protector of women—and this is a cession that some are not willing to make." See Sarah Deer, *The Beginning and End of Rape: Confronting Sexual Violence in Native America* (Minneapolis: University of Minnesota Press), ch. 7.

40. Grace Kyungwon Hong, *The Ruptures of American Capital: Women of Color Feminism and the Culture of Immigrant Labor* (Minneapolis: University of Minnesota Press, 2006), xiv.

41. Mimi Kim, "Alternative Interventions to Intimate Violence: Defining Political and Pragmatic Challenges," in *Restorative Justice and Violence Against Women*, ed. James Ptacek (Oxford: Oxford University, 2009), 205.

42. Kim, "Alternative Interventions to Intimate Violence," 205.

43. Kim, "Alternative Interventions to Intimate Violence," 204.

44. Miriam Jordan, "Appeals Court Partly Reinstate Trump's New Travel Ban," *The New York Times*, November 13, 2017, www.nytimes.com/2017/11/13/us/travel-ban-reinstated-appeal.html (accessed November 15, 2017); See also Danae King, "US on track to let in fewest refugees since 1980," *The Columbus Dispatch*, March 26, 2018, www.dispatch.com/news/20180326/us-on-track-to-let-in-fewest-refugees-since-1980 (accessed March 26, 2018).

45. "Impunity for domestic violence, 'honour killings' cannot continue—UN official," UN News Center, www.un.org/apps/news/story.asp?NewsID=33971#.Wl95fVQfOR (accessed February 9, 2017).

46. "Violence against women: Definition and the scope of the problem," World Health Organization, July 1997, www.who.int/gender/violence/v4.pdf (accessed February 9, 2017).

47. "Defining Gender-Based Violence: Gender-based violence (GBV) or violence against women VAW)?" Strengthening Health System Responses to Gender-based Violence in Eastern Europe and Central Asia: A resource package, www.health-gen-

derviolence.org/training-programme-for-health-care-providers/facts-on-gbv/defining-gender-based-violence/21 (accessed February 10, 2017); See "Fourth World Conference on Women," United Nations Entity for Gender Equality and the Empowerment of Women, www.un.org/womenwatch/daw/beijing/platform/ (accessed February 10, 2017).

48. See King, "Appeals Court Partly Reinstate Trump's New Travel Ban," www.dispatch.com/news/20180326/us-on-track-to-let-in-fewest-refugees-since-1980 (accessed March 26, 2018).

49. Miriam Valverde, "Most Syrian refugees are women and children, as Keith Ellison said," Politifact, February 2, 2017, www.politifact.com/truth-o-meter/statements/2017/feb/02/keith-ellison/rep-keith-ellison-correct-demographic-overview-syr/ (accessed February 5, 2017).

50. Inderpal Grewal, *Saving the Security State: Exceptional Citizens in Twenty-First-Century America* (Durham: Duke University Press, 2017).

51. *Gender and International Security: Feminist Perspectives*, ed. Laura Sjoberg (Abingdon: Routledge, 2010), 4.

52. Davis, *Freedom Is a Constant Struggle*, 48–50.

53. For a critique of "security," see Mark Neocleous's *Critique of Security* (Montreal: McGill-Queen's University Press, 2008).

54. Critical Resistance and INCITE!, "Statement on Gender-Based Violence." Quoted in Ritchie, *Invisible No More*, 241.

55. "Feminist Perspectives on Peace and Security," Gunda and Werner Institute: Feminism and Gender Democracy, www.gwi-boell.de/en/2010/07/30/feminist-perspectives-peace-and-security (accessed March 20, 2018).

EIGHT

Feminist Strategies for Outsider-Insiders

Our Year Teaching Navy Chaplains

Kate Ott and Kristen J. Leslie

The three-day training on the Navy base was getting started and as happened at previous trainings, the commanding officer of the base greeted the group of one hundred Navy, Marine, and Coast Guard chaplains and religious program specialists (RPS)[1] with enthusiasm.[2] Deemed subject matter experts (SMEs), our team of Kristen J. Leslie, PhD, Kate Ott, PhD, Captain Kyle Fauntleroy (retired Navy chaplain), and Jane Fredricksen (Executive Director of The FaithTrust Institute) had been awarded a year-long thirteen-base Navy Chaplain Corps contract to train one thousand chaplains and RPS (making up the Religious Ministry Teams or RMTs) for their annual Professional Development Training Course, Fiscal Year 2018 (PDTC FY18). The base commander greeted the religious ministry teams, thanking them for the important work they do in helping Sailors, Marines, and Coast Guardians meet their broader missional goals. In an unflinching manner, he asserted, "Our mission is to kill people and blow things up. If we are going to do this, we need chaplains." Unsettling as that was to hear, we—Kate and Kristen—recognized that as civilians, women, progressives, and feminists, our theological, ethical, and pastoral commitments made us outsiders to this environment. Over a twelve-month period, we learned that being welcomed inside the gates into an outsider-insider position presented challenges and opportunities that taught us much about feminist strategies for engaging the military.

As feminist theologians engaged in a contract position, our outsider-insider position required we visit thirteen different Navy or Marine bases and one Army base. While teaching, we were required to follow all base protocols and security measures. Our outsider-insider status routinely highlighted gender differences in values, ways of living, learning styles, and theological approaches that, as feminists in progressive Protestant seminary contexts, we rarely negotiate. The gender differences were due in part to our white cis female identity, though the starkest differences were based on constructions of social relations that relied upon binary and complimentary constructions of sex and gender reinforced both by militarism and particular Christian theological commitments to which we do not ascribe as feminist theologians.

Our case study and critical reflection will highlight a variety of strategies necessary for feminist praxis against U.S. militarism when serving in the role of feminist outsider-insider. We briefly describe our methodological understanding of feminist analysis and its relationship to militarism and religion. We then outline the role of religious ministry teams and Navy chaplaincy to provide case study context for the reader. After presenting our case study as instructors for the PDTC FY18, we conclude with three concrete feminist strategies for working as outsider-insiders in the U.S. military.

FEMINISM, MILITARISM, AND RELIGION

Occupying an outsider-insider status afforded us a unique vantage point by which to consider feminist praxis against U.S. militarism. Some might say that any insider relationship exempts one from praxis against U.S. militarism. Indeed, our status was compromised in distinct ways. Yet our relationship also afforded us access to knowledge, leadership, and teaching, all of which provide different levels of influence. Thus, we suggest that different tools are needed to engage feminist praxis as outsider-insiders. Vigilance to co-optation is required but does not preclude transformational opportunities. Within the U.S. context, we are all implicated to varying degrees in a supportive relationship with the U.S. military.[3] Our participation as contractors with the Navy Chaplain Corps made these relationships explicit and tangible.

We employ a feminist analysis in examining our experience as outsiders inside the military context to elucidate strategies to disrupt gender oppression, which in turn often highlights the reliance of militarism on certain gender assumptions. Feminist analysis means we "explore gender as a category of analysis to speak about men, women, masculinity, and femininity not as attributes but as social relations of power that can differ in specific contexts."[4] That is to say, we do not approach gender as a description of the differences between women and men that considers gender to be stable or natural. Neither do we see gender as a standpoint or lens through which the world is constructed separate from an understanding of sex as a natural or immutable category. For us, both gender and sex are given meaning by the cultural and historical context and thus reflect social relations of power. Feminist praxis requires a social analysis of power and action toward remedying power differentials based on constructions of gender and sex differences as they intersect with other forms of identity and access.

Feminist praxis against U.S. militarism suggests an understanding of militarism that is not synonymous with the individuals or the institution of the military. Rather, militarism is an ideology that shapes and defines institutions and individuals that in turn either reinforce the ideology or disrupt it through various policies and practices.[5] The ideology of militarism incorporates distinct gender assumptions related to the naturalness of sex and gender differences, which affects women differently than men.

Hierarchy and violence (or use of force) are core military values or beliefs upon which militarism is formed. Hierarchy and violence are justified and explained through core gendered assumptions such as boys are predisposed to violence and thus better at war-making; men are more rational and physically stronger than women making men the protector of women; and finally, feminine qualities of nurture and care compromise swift and necessarily brutal decision-making in times of conflict. Militarism is dependent on defining social relations of power in dominant paradigms of male over female, man over woman, masculine over feminine.[6]

In addition to a gender critique, feminist praxis against U.S. militarism considers the impact of U.S. hegemony and empire building across the globe, the roots of capitalism, and U.S. war-making in addition to the role of Christianity in the last half century. This approach fits within a method of "critique." Shelly Rambo suggests there are three predominant theological approaches to the study of theology and U.S. militarism.[7] The first, critique, focuses on the military-industrial complex and modern effects of empire building. The second approach, stance, centers around issues of "going to war" and one's theological position vis-à-vis that war, such as pacifism or just war. Rambo defines the third approach as care. Theological approaches that preface care concentrate on the various collateral damages of war and militarism, including issues of PTSD, veteran reintegration, current military personnel struggles with multiple deployments, and so on. The care approach attends to much of the forgotten harm sustained by the U.S. individuals most directly impacted by U.S. militarism. Many theologians who are writing about issues of moral injury are bringing together the "critique" and "care" approaches. We find the intersection of these helpful in our own analysis.

From the founding of the United States, religion—Christianity in particular—has played an auspicious role in the development of U.S. militarism, as the First Amendment in the U.S. Constitution both resists government establishment of religion and provides for the free exercise of religion by citizens, including military personnel. The Constitution has additional problematic establishment issues related to gender and race which historically become entangled in the ideology of U.S. militarism.[8] In this chapter, we will focus on this confluence within the U.S. Navy Chaplain Corps. Military chaplaincy is a distinct location for the deployment of religion within militarism implicating gender in specific ways.

RELIGION IN A MILITARY CHAPLAINCY CONTEXT: THE TWO-COLLAR DILEMMA

Military chaplains are charged with attending to the religious, spiritual, and moral commitments of military members and their families. To understand what this means, it is important to understand the multiple ways chaplains live out their religious charges. Religion is first an institutionalized political force that reflects the larger American commitment to freedom of expression as promised by the First Amendment. Chaplains and RPS help ensure the liturgical, private, and communal religious practices of those in their units. Religion takes onto it gendered, cultural, and political commitments which play out in the power structure of the military. Secondly, religion is the organized and communal practices that associate with an institutionalized religious group (that is, a coherent expression of beliefs, practices, identity, and belonging). Chaplains represent specific religious traditions and must be approved by nonmilitary religious endorsing agencies who credential chaplains for service in the Armed Forces on behalf of their respective religious organizations. Because of the separation of church and state in the United States, endorsing agencies are the point of contact between the Department of Defense and specific religious denominations and faith groups.[9]

Early in our training, we noticed that chaplains who were making a point about the tensions between military requirements and their religious practices would grasp the insignia on the collars of their uniforms. They did this when making a distinction between how different notions of religion were playing out in their ministries. This, we learned, was what they experienced as the Two-Collar Dilemma.[10] On the right collar of the chaplain's uniform is the insignia of their military rank. Rank signifies one's power and place in the military system (chain of command), who they may engage in the environment and how, and their role in the larger military mission. Navy chaplains (officers) and RPS (enlisted) know that rank is central to their identity in the military. Regularly we would hear enlisted people called by their rank and nothing else; "RP1 has a good contribution" or "Master Chief would like to make an announcement." Rank reifies the notion that one is a member of the military first and foremost, fulfilling a function in the system. Their identity as a person is less important than their role in the system.

On the left collar of a chaplain's uniform is the insignia of their faith—for example, a cross (Christian and Unitarian Universalism), a tablet (Jewish), a crescent (Muslim), or a Dharmachakra (Buddhist). The Two-Collar Dilemma is the very tension that the commanding officer was naming in this chapter's opening paragraph; he needs chaplains who attend to the moral and spiritual commitments of Sailors, Marines, and Coast Guardians[11] who also recognize that the military mission involves domination and violence. One chaplain, speaking more to the group than to us, reminded participants that he understands his role as "bringing humanity to the military." Chaplains told us that this was an ongoing dilemma that some handled better than others. One of the ways we saw the instrumentalization of religion in the chaplaincy was in the way the Navy Chaplain Corps frames their work into four core functional capabilities. Each chaplain is to (1) *provide* for their own faith group, (2) *facilitate* for other religious/spiritual traditions, (3) provide *care* for all, and (4) *advise* the commanders on ethical decisions.[12] Chaplains are called to be pastors to some and chaplains to all. For those chaplains whose profession of faith welcomed interfaith dialogue and operated with a cooperative pluralism,[13] these functional capabilities helped them navigate both sides of their collar. For those whose faith commitments and theologies are threatened by engaging other traditions, facilitating for other faith groups is a betrayal of their missional theological commitments. In the case of conservative Christian chaplains, they can feel that anything less than the implementation of the Great Commission—to make disciples of all people for Jesus Christ—is an untenable compromise to their own faith and as such prohibited by their religious endorsing bodies.

The present-day U.S. military Chaplain Corps is largely evangelical and Christian in nature. This gets its roots during the unrest of the Vietnam War era. With the buildup of the Vietnam War and the American public's increasing distrust of military involvement, mainline and progressive seminaries and rabbinical schools refused to train or support the training of military chaplains because most publicly defended the war or refused to engage the religious or moral questions it raised.[14] On the other hand, conservative Christian faith communities realized they could fill the gap as they intentionally stepped in as the dominant faith communities to equip and endorse military chaplains.

Today a large percentage of U.S. military chaplains have received their theological education from conservative Christian seminaries, most notably Liberty University. The faith communities likely to support military chaplains are the same ones whose denominational polity and cultural practices do not ordain women. The way conservative Christian theol-

ogies frame gender both shape and align with militarism. This is a significant factor in the very low number of women serving as military chaplains. With changing American notions of the U.S. military, informed by
long and repeated periods of U.S. military engagement abroad and the
repeal of both "Don't Ask, Don't Tell" (DADT) in 2011 and The Defense
of Marriage Act (DOMA) in 2013, mainline and progressive seminaries
and rabbinical schools only recently have begun to change their practices
of supporting their students interested in military chaplaincy.[15]

Our 2018 training contract—officially entitled "Strategy for the Deliv-
ery of Religious Ministry to Nones (unaffiliated from religion), Dones
(disaffiliated from religion), and Millennials"—raised questions precisely
at the intersection of militarism and religion. The growing number of U.S.
service members who do not identify with a religious tradition pushes
against the entanglement of U.S. militarism and religion. This is especially true in Christianity, the tradition we most directly explored. Having
feminist theologians as the instructors only added to the perceived notion
that the training was dismantling core values of militarism, theological
commitments, and gendered practices of authority.

CASE STUDY ON BECOMING OUTSIDER-INSIDERS

Unlike Navy chaplains who undoubtedly occupy a two-collar dual posi-
tionality as they serve in the military and also serve their denomination
or endorsing agent, our outsider-insider status was temporary and
granted by invitation. Our welcome came with a number of expectations,
the most important being a genuine good faith effort on our part to learn
about and understand the struggles and successes of being a Navy chaplain or RPS. Kristen had more experience with military chaplaincy than
Kate prior to this PDTC. However, the full immersion into RMT culture
and Marine or Navy base residence required that we learn to follow
applicable protocols, interpret new language, and respond with curiosity
rather than skepticism or cynicism. This good faith effort allowed us to
gain credibility and build relationships that provided ready space to uncover and challenge specific intersections of feminism, militarism, and
religion.

For the past fifteen years, both Kate and Kristen have been engaging
theological, ethical, and pastoral matters important to military environments. Kristen's work has concentrated on both military sexual trauma
and religious proselytizing in the military.[16] Kate's work has focused on
sexual ethics and professional formation. Kristen started her work in 2003
as a consultant to chaplains at the U.S. Air Force Academy when they
were in the midst of a congressionally mandated initiative to assess and
improve Academy protocols and care related to sexual assault. Kate began her work in 2010 at the Coast Guard Academy, offering programs

related to sexual health, dating, and ethics for cadets through the Command Religious Program.

For Kristen, the invitation to train Air Force chaplains was a surprise that created a conundrum. As a feminist committed to ending violence and building individual and communal healing practices of resilience, training chaplains felt like an invitation to enter the belly of the beast. She was raised in the 1960s and '70s, the child of a nurse and a college chaplain who worked for women's liberation and protested military involvement in Vietnam. Her faith development included standing in picket lines and protesting outside the gates of military bases. What Kristen knew of the military was from the outside, looking (and yelling) in. The phone call from a chaplain at the Air Force Academy was an invitation to come inside the gates. As a feminist formed by the lives and works of Letty Russell, Margaret Farley, Marie Fortune, and Emilie Townes, Kristen knew that hard work starts by finding and creating allies. She reached out to a number of colleagues. Kristen remembers a specific conversation with Marie Fortune, then director of The FaithTrust Institute (FTI), who had held a number of federal contracts, including one with the Department of Defense on domestic violence. In that conversation, Marie talked about how she had to translate her own skills and language so that those on the inside of the military gates could receive and be served by her work. Kristen knew she needed to develop new skills and new knowledge to engage her feminist and liberative commitments for work on the inside.

Through the relationships that Kristen had developed, she recommended Kate to the religious command program at the Coast Guard Academy. At that point, we were both working in outsider-insider positions we had not imagined possible in our academic careers. While Kate has a number of family members who have served in various armed forces and some who continue to work with veterans, her faith commitments align with anti-violence and anti-militarism activism. Over the next few years, our experiences provided training in how to resist from the inside out, something both of us are familiar with given other ethical commitments and our faith tradition affiliations. For example, we both advocate for full LGBTQ inclusion in the United Methodist and Roman Catholic traditions.

Kristen's early conversation with Marie Fortune at FTI provided wisdom, but also partnership. It was the example and leadership at FTI that set the stage for our most recent work serving as SMEs for the Navy Chaplain Corps training. In 2014, Kristen and Marie Fortune were awarded the contract that trained Navy and Marine Religious Ministry Teams in responding to military sexual trauma (MST). As outsiders working to be received as insiders, Kristen and Marie had to retool their work on sexualized violence to reflect the realities of the military environment. Because oppressive systems function in part by determining the terms of suffering, pastoral/spiritual care in a military context required a clear focus on how the military system itself perpetuates and even allows for sexualized and gender-based violence. The success of the trainings and the allies created with the Navy Chief of Chaplains Office in the Pentagon, the Naval Chaplaincy School and Center (NCS&C), and individual chaplains became formative for securing the contract for the PDTC in 2018.

In 2017, the Navy advertised the topic of the PDTC FY18: the Work of Military Chaplains with Millennials who are Religious, Nones (unaffiliated from religion), and Dones (disaffiliated from religion). When FTI approached Kristen as a possible SME, Kristen called Kate. Kristen and Kate had taught together on multiple occasions, most recently a bi-located synchronous course on the ethics and care of young adults. We agreed to work as SMEs with FTI as a subversive practice to support the mission of FTI (to end sexual and domestic violence). It was an unusual contract for FTI to engage because it was far afield from their mission, but like many feminist activist organizations, funding sources were limited and FTI was seeking new avenues for federal funding. While training military chaplains was an interesting draw, that in itself was not enough to compel us to commit. It was the subversive notion itself that drew us in: having the military-industrial complex support an organization that is working to end violence. This became an example of a subversive method that redistributed military spending and benefited nonviolent education. We, of course, are not the first to make this connection. In his work on "Money, Masculinities, and Militarism," Ray Acheson attended to a similar subversive method: "In our work at the UN and in campaigns, we believe that demonstrating the connections between money, masculinities, and militarism is one way to challenge the resistance to disarmament and the promotion of militarism."[17] This subversive monetary approach is not perfect or altruistic, rather it contends with the realities of funding and mission in a global capital economy.

During the course of the trainings, we had to negotiate repeated experiences of cognitive dissonance. Learning the military acronyms, ranks, language, and protocols was an essential reality of doing work as an outsider-insider. Immersion in a new and potentially feminist-hostile environment was tiring and required space to negotiate the differing realities of home, seminary, and military bases. For example, our second visit to the Navy Chaplaincy School and Center in 2017 included a base shutdown for an active shooter exercise. One of the officers remarked, "No big deal, it just means we need to stay inside and there will be more gun fire around the campus." To which Kate remarked, "You realize we have a very different relationship to guns than you do." Returning from a military base always meant readjusting to living out various feminist commitments with ease and comfort, not readily accepted on a military base. This code-switching regularly made us question what it meant to be a feminist and why (exactly!) we were doing this work.[18] Having each other as feminist allies helped us process the cognitive dissonance and negotiate the code-switching as both a source of humor and a location for feminist curiosity and growth.

As already noted, many of the Navy chaplains come from theologically conservative, non-denominational Christian traditions. While a few have studied and profess more progressive theological stances, most have not read or engaged feminist theology or been taught by feminist theologians. The PDTC topic, while ripe for theological engagement, was not a pedagogical opportunity to engage in theological conversation as directed by the Naval Chaplaincy School and Center. Chaplains and RPS serve in a pluralistic religious environment generally and an ecumenical community more specifically. However, unlike a seminary where we create classroom experiences for students to engage in confessional theological conversations across their differences, we were instructed to stay away from theological education and focus on sociological implications of religious identity and digital technological shifts related to religious practice and communication. From our perspective and from the comments of some participants, this was a missed opportunity. In reality, theological conversations did pop up, as one cannot talk sociologically about religious identity or formation without it having theological implications.

Even when not specifically teaching about feminist theology, we intentionally used feminist pedagogical approaches which attend to how social power relations are constructed within the teaching environment. We will discuss these in more detail in the next section related to feminist praxes. Our outsider-insider status required a negotiation of our feminist identity, commitments, and approaches. While not specifically teaching feminist content as we would in our seminary contexts, we regularly invited a feminist curiosity into our official training discussions and into many side conversations. This feminist curiosity kept us alert to embedded gendered notions of behaviors and ideas deemed normative, intuitive, and genetic.[19] Needless to say, our very presence as SMEs elicited questioning of the workings of masculinized and feminized assumptions related to the confluence of militarism and religion.

FEMINIST PRAXIS OF OUTSIDER-INSIDERS

Power differentials based on constructions of gender and sex are embedded in military and religious institutions. The training spaces of the PDTC for the Navy RMTs evidences many of the overlaps between these gender constructions. As the SMEs or "teachers," we negotiated these social relations at each new venue with participants ranging from twenty-five to one hundred chaplains and RPS. Over the course of the twelve months, we found that performance of authority, deployment of insiders's expertise, and internal network development were three feminist strategies that disrupted oppressive gender and sex constructions perpetuated both by militarism and complimentarity-based gender theologies.

Performance of Authority

Performance of authority is embedded within religious and military culture with regard to the bodies represented in high-ranking positions, titles, and dress. It is also present in unique ways with regard to specialized knowledge. For example, in the professional context of our seminaries, white feminine presentation (gender) for middle-aged women (sex) is usually short hair or long hair worn down. In the military context, all women must wear their hair short or in a short ponytail, tight braid or bun. These differences point to a number of assumptions about gender, sex, age, race, and profession that are constructed by context. Historically, there is no single, non-context specific, "correct," gendered way to wear one's hair. In the course of trainings, we often wore our hair in ponytails which helped us to fit in and take advantage of a military culture that values speed and uniformity over academic culture that values uniqueness and age. That is to say, in our experience, the military rules about women's hair do not see a ponytail as a "childhood" hairstyle, whereas academic culture does; in the context of women's hairstyles, a ponytail or bun also minimizes a number of beauty standards rooted in racialized gender differences in hair type. Hair is one example of how "the study of gender investigates the ways that societies and cultures have defined women's and men's expected roles and behaviors and thus, in turn, shape how women and men understand their experiences."[20] We include in this study of gender the ways in which gender intersects with race, class, sexuality, geographic context, education, and so on.

That was one way in which we used military gender construction to our benefit. There were a number of ways we chose to disrupt oppressive gender constructions that directly implicated our authority. Over and again, we were referred to as "ladies." This typically occurred when a senior ranking Navy officer introduced us at the beginning of the day or during participant feedback. In referring to each other during the training, we specifically used "Dr. Leslie" and "Dr. Ott." The lead officer from the Naval Chaplaincy School and Center routinely called us "Dr. Leslie" and "Dr. Ott." He would make a point to correct himself publicly if he used our first names or used the term "ladies." We insisted on the use of our academic titles to provide authority that was already compromised by our gender and theologically liberal background of which the participants were well aware. (Web searches on our public profiles were significantly higher prior to trainings). Unlike military custom where one's dress shows one's rank, our titles became present reminders of our authority.

Of course, titles do not erase gender or sex when the person is present. Body and dress also communicate the gender and sex of a person. We did not have the benefit of a single uniform that reduced gender and sex differences like the chaplains and RPS. Rather, our clothing choice signaled various constructions of gender that either fed into stereotypes or disrupted them, both of which have power and authority implications. Overwhelmingly, we chose to wear pants or longer skirts with flat shoes, which communicated professionalism without playing to the stereotypical feminine dress code of pencil skirts and high heels (which is the alternative dress female uniform choice in the Navy, Coast Guard, and Marines). We routinely received comments with regard to clothing. Some participants were curious how we made our choices because they were aware of the implications, others complimented us, one participant in particular noted with surprise that we had both worn skirts on the same day and asked it if was intentional. The awareness level of our clothing suggests this is a key aspect of the performance of authority related to gender in a military culture.

The last way in which we were keenly aware of issues of authority was with regard to knowledge. As the SMEs, we were given a "stamp of approval" by the Navy Chaplain Corps leadership and the NCS&C staff. Often in opening remarks, the "flag officers" (those with the rank of General or higher, signified by a flag on their uniform) would reinforce our level of knowledge via personal testimony related to the curriculum materials and past teaching experiences with us. Yet our level of knowledge was often challenged during the trainings as a way for a participant or two to check our authority, most often related to religious or theological issues. Selecting a primarily women-led teaching team for the PDTC already signals a disruption to male gender authority, in much the same way allowing women into different branches of the military or into ordained leadership in religious communities does. Women's presence in leadership roles is not sufficient to destabilize a normative male gender approach to knowledge creation. Mariz Tadros addresses this issue when considering women's leadership in transnational feminist movements. She writes, "Promoting women's representation in leadership roles in the religious establishment is one of the many ways through which religious feminists have sought to engage with the gendered and religious identifiers of women's agency. The adoption of a feminist lens in the reinterpretation of sacred texts is an example of another approach to women's agency."[21] By pointing to how a feminist lens changes interpretation of scripture, Tadros is noting that women's presence alone does not change gendered notions of authority. Rather, an analysis of how gender affects critical issues of authority like scriptural interpretation is important as well.

In the trainings, we routinely inserted specific examples that might pique the feminist curiosity of the participants to consider how social relations of power with regard to gender were constructed. For example, there was an exercise that asked participants to name sacred texts that provide insight related to transitions of young adulthood. These "sacred texts" could be religious or secular, past or present. The shared responses of secular texts were often diverse, related to race, gender, and genre. Yet the religious texts participants named referred to all male characters, with the exception of one training day. We adopted a practice of both pointing out this difference and naming Jewish and Christian texts that included women related to young adulthood transitions. This practice exemplified, on day one of each training, our awareness of participant gender-based religious bias, our knowledge of scripture, and inserted a feminist curiosity regarding scripture more generally. We often had follow-up conversations with individual participants with regard to various feminist interpretations of scripture after this exercise.

We utilized existing structures of how authority is established in military and religious contexts to maximize our authority with regard to title, dress, and knowledge. The repeated use of professional titles, attention to gender performativity in dress, and strategic use of religious and theological knowledge disrupted existing gender hierarchies present in militarism and religion that could minimize our authority as cisgender white women. Related to "outsider" knowledge, that is, information related to young adult development, religious formation, identity, belonging, practices, or digital technology, we asserted our knowledge and thus established our authority as SMEs. Of course, there were instances where participants sought to challenge our knowledge and we had back-and-forth debate and disagreement—a common occurrence in classroom teaching, more often experienced by women and instructors of color. In these instances, we collaboratively supported each other as co-facilitators, tag teaming responses. Yet with regard to military-specific information, we used a different pedagogical feminist praxis.

Deploying Insiders's Expertise

As outsider-insiders, we found it very important to gain facility with the terminology and various cultural aspects of the Navy more generally and RMTs specifically. Our effort in this area demonstrated our commitment to listen, observe, and learn as well as to teach. Of course, knowing more about our audience also made us better educators. However, there were limits to the breadth of insider knowledge and status we could authentically occupy as outsiders. We learned there was a continuum of insider knowledge. While it was to our benefit as educators to employ some insider knowledge, at other times it was more beneficial to create space for peer-to-peer interactions. We found that as outsider-insiders, our critiques and corrections of military-specific concerns did not carry the same authority as having another insider correct a participant by sharing an example that supported our point. This means we had to both strategically facilitate space for these conversations, intentionally invite co-learning, and be mindful of our limitations. All of these approaches have roots in feminist pedagogy.

The most basic area of insider knowledge related to language, especially acronyms and terms. We have laced a number of these throughout the article to give the reader an experience of learning the language. We used Navy-specific language within our presentation like CONUS and OCONUS, referring to participants's hats as covers and their uniform shirts as blouses, and using only military time or the twenty-four-hour clock cycle during the training.[22] On the other end of the language spectrum would be terms specific to the Navy, like boat boo—a hook-up partner for the duration of a service assignment while underway on a ship. We were educated about the term and practice of a boat boo, including the use of a written contract between sailors, from a female chaplain who does work related to sexual assault throughout the Navy. The training focused on the changing behaviors and values of current young adults related to religion and technology. Hook-up culture highlights shifts in religious values related to sexuality, and technology plays a key role in hook-up practices. We attributed our fluency with a term like boat boo to other chaplains and RPS educating us. This fluency allowed us to invite and engage an insider conversation during the training that went directly to issues of sexuality, relationship formation, health, safety, and morality. The use of peer-to-peer insider knowledge meant a topic directly confronting issues of gender, sex, and sexuality arose as a community issue rather than a feminist agenda of the instructors, opening the space for us to share our expertise.

Peer-to-peer learning happened between participants who were present at a training and by our use of stories or examples shared at previous sessions. In the latter, we could cite a participant's comment from examples we accumulated throughout the trainings, such as the boat boo example. Yet, it was most effective to have direct in-person examples. There were specific areas of the training where we intentionally created space for these conversations to model co-learning and deploy insider knowledge to support points we were trying to communicate. There are two specific instances—one related to technology and gender and the other to racial demographic shifts across the United States.

When developing a snapshot of young adult experiences with digital technology, we shared the research that boys tend to play video games at a higher rate and girls tend to use social networking sites. We were careful to note that these are trends, not truisms about every boy or girl.

However, what was most important about any gender difference represented by the data was hidden in details only avid video gamers understood. So, we would share the data and then ask, "What do you make of this information?" Often, older male chaplains would respond with a mix of pseudoscience and religious conviction that women are naturally more social and men are created to accomplish things. We would respond to these remarks by simply saying, "No, that's incorrect, the data does not support that." Rarely did participants who held this view believe "our facts." It was not until another, often younger male participant would report that he plays video games all the time and that is his social network that the conversation opened up to the cultural construction of play and the pretenses that gender requires. Playing a video game provides a pretense to "chat" or "network" that is not seen as socially acceptable masculine behavior. The same is true of in-person sports or kickball on the playground in elementary school. The younger men and the fathers with teenage boys understood the development of video games as both social networks and war-making training tools. Periodically, a woman would contribute to the conversation and remark that fewer women played video games because of the online harassment they receive and the depiction of women in most video games. The use of insider expertise bolstered a gender constructivist argument that confronted gender-complimentary theology and military ideology.

In another example, we shared a slide from Pew Research on shifting racial and ethnic demographics in the United States. The data is presented in U.S. census categories. We would display the slide and note that the United States is increasingly more racially and ethnically diverse; that racial and ethnic diversity is a common experience for today's young adults in comparison to previous generations. Then we would ask folks born after 1980 in the room to tell us how they reacted to the way the slide presents the data. Participants, often persons of color or white participants who were part of interracial families (they would include this information in their remarks), would respond in a few ways. They would comment: the slide mixes race and ethnicity in ways that collapse them; it seems like people had to pick a category when more often people fit a bunch of those categories; more people and families are interracial but that hasn't ended racism; or, some young people still live in communities that aren't racially diverse, but then you get to the military, and it's more racially diverse than any place you have been. While we could have pointed out all these facts about the slide and current young adult experience, insider expertise had a greater impact on the participants and opened the conversation for us to name the ways the United States has historically forced various racial and ethnic affiliation and that a decrease in the white population does not equate with an end to racism. Based on the age restriction of responders to the question, this often meant it was RPS (enlisted) who spoke. They were overwhelmingly a more racially and gender diverse group than the chaplains. We strategically provided space for those of lower rank and often of minoritized communities to be the first to respond to issues of race and ethnicity.

The use of insider expertise encourages co-learning and provided support for topics that could have been dismissed as part of our outsider, feminist agenda. It also provided opportunities to subvert ideologies and practices of gender, race, and rank hierarchy. We employed similar strategies with periodic activities that engaged multiple intelligences and kinesthetic learning upon which we do not have space to elaborate. These were explicit practices to deploy insider expertise to disrupt military and theological constructions of social power relations. In order for these practices to be successful, we often had to assume there were allies who would speak up or cultivate them prior to these various pedagogical moments.

Develop Internal Network (aka Unlikely Allies)

For an institutional structure rooted in hierarchy, we learned early on that this hierarchy (like most) was not sustained by the singular division of power (rank) it projected. That's not to say that rank did not matter. Gender, race, educational background, religious affiliation, and age created valences of power that layered over and in some cases superseded rank. Thus, we began to develop a network of allies in order to support our professional needs, pedagogical commitments, and to hold participants accountable in the few instances of behavior that bordered on sexual harassment.

The first and most important allies were the officers, all male chaplains, from the Navy Chaplaincy School and Center. At the beginning of the contract and curriculum development, there was skepticism between the FTI and the school house. It was not until we met in person to work through the curriculum that all sides realized we shared specific values: we respected each other's theology while being able to openly disagree, as contractors we demonstrated a willingness to listen and learn about Navy-specific culture, and school house staff affirmed our expertise and knowledge. Together there was a commitment to professionalism that transcended religious affiliation, civilian or military status, and gender.

The collegiality modeled in this relationship was on display during the trainings as well. We already noted the NCS&C representative's intentional practice of the use of our professional titles. Additionally, formally and informally, other staff from NCS&C as well as the Navy Chief of Chaplains Office would "vouch for us" as a way of sharing power and credibility in the space. In fact, our primary representative, who traveled to every PDTC training with us and with whom we share very little political or religious leanings, became our most significant advocate. The mutual respect we showed to each other modeled the impact individuals can have when serving in outsider-insider roles. None of us changed our political or religious views. However, we were able to have debate and dialogue in a fashion often missing in today's culture, including repeated conversations about gun rights, LGBTQ theology, and government spending, to name a few. As feminists, we were able to gain a deeper understanding of the histories, lives, and commitments that motivate many military service members. As a Navy chaplain, he was able to hear criticism of the internal system from an outsider viewpoint. Often missing in single-sided pro- or anti-military rhetoric is attention to the lives of those affected, the numerous allies within and without, and the everyday ways that these individuals disrupt militarism as we have defined it.

As we started the trainings, we assumed that our feminist commitments would alienate chaplains and some RPS coming from conservative religious traditions. While we did engage chaplains who were suspicious and highly critical of what they rightly assumed were our feminist commitments, across all of the bases we engaged a noteworthy minority of female and male chaplains who had studied feminist and womanist theology, postcolonial theologies, and post-structural notions of empire. Because the overall military environment was not committed to liberationist or feminist views, conversations about feminism/womanism, and interfaith collegiality most often happened when individual chaplains approached us during training breaks, at women-only arranged lunches, or in the women's restroom.

While some would assume that women chaplains and RPS would be automatic allies for us, this was not always the case. As Isabelle Geuskens notes in the introduction to *Gender & Militarism*, "The notion of 'just add women and stir' completely instrumentalizes women's lives."[23] It relies on a view of gender and sex as stable characteristics that will simply balance out the masculinity or maleness of any institution by adding more women. We found that relationships with women were often tenuous and constantly under scrutiny by male colleagues. Many of the women would find or create separate gender-specific spaces to discuss how to negotiate these power relationships. The women's restroom and women-only lunches were the two examples we experienced most often. It was in the women's restroom where other female participants would check in with us to ask how we were "surviving all the testosterone" or "adjusting to the boy's club." At almost every training, the senior-most female chaplain would invite the other female chaplains to a lunch. Some of the lunches were about sharing camaraderie; others were explicitly strategic and intended to share practices and resources for surviving and responding to the sexism that the female chaplains faced from male chaplains and other service members. We were invited to participate in these lunches, which recognized us as equal female religious leaders and signaled to the wider group an acceptance of feminist theological perspectives. There were both risks and benefits to the chaplains who participated in these gatherings.

Like many of the women chaplains and RPS, our gender made us targets for sexual harassment. There were a few senior white male chaplains who would challenge us during open response sessions; there were two who engaged in direct outbursts. Then there were others who shared their anonymous sexist comments on evaluations. Our knowledge and expertise embodied as female was a threat to normative gendered power relations, and some male chaplains felt the need to reassert their masculinity through sexist comments. In most cases, the basic hierarchy of teacher-student could be used to reestablish our power in the learning environment. In other cases, Navy staff or ranking officers (rank hierarchy and duty) would engage the individual and compel them to change their behavior during the PDTC or be removed. When the basic hierarchies of power established in the environment failed, we learned that insisting on public forms of accountability was our last resort. Military culture tends to rely on forms of closed-door accountability, taking someone aside or in private instructing someone to behave differently. As feminists, we noted that these practices did not sustain changed behavior because there was no community that knew about the problem and would hold the person accountable in the future. In one instance of particularly problematic sexist behavior, we refused to lead a training unless all direct staff, our contractor, and additional Chief of Chaplains staff were collectively made aware of the behavioral requirements for one male chaplain. This was unprecedented. Based on the network of allies we had already built, we were able to impact the system of accountability for the PDTC.

Cultivating allies and internal networks, deploying insider expertise, and engaging in performance of authority were various strategies we used to point out, survive, and disrupt social relations of power determined by oppressive gender constructions. These feminist praxes will not upend militarism on their own, though they point to ways that outsider-insiders can do the work of dismantling militarism from a distinct location that resources allies within the military and shares positions of privilege from outside the military. In some sense any person serving as a Navy chaplain or religious program specialist resides in a dual role within the military. It is not the same as the position of outsider-insider we have described. Yet many who serve in these roles are unlikely allies for feminists working against U.S. militarism as an ideology that is dependent on gender hierarchy, Christian hegemony, and violence as the only solution to conflict.

BIBLIOGRAPHY

Acheson, Ray. "Money, Masculinities, and Militarism: Reaching Critical Will's Work for Disarmament." In *Gender and Militarism: Analyzing the Links to Strategize for Peace,* edited by Isabelle Geuskens, Merle Gosewinkel, and Sophie Schellens, 14–17. Hague: Women Peacemakers Program, 2014.

Demby, Gene. "How Code-Switching Explains the World." National Public Radio. April 8, 2013. www.npr.org/sections/codeswitch/2013/04/08/176064688/how-code-switching-explains-the-world. Accessed July 21, 2018.

Enloein, Cynthia. "Understanding Militarism, Militarization, and the Linkages with Globalization: Using a Feminist Curiosity." In *Gender and Militarism: Analyzing the Links to Strategize for Peace,* edited by Isabelle Geuskens, Merle Gosewinkel, and Sophie Schellens, 7–9. Hague: Women Peacemakers Program, 2014.

French, Peter A. *War and Moral Dissonance.* Cambridge: Cambridge University Press, 2011.

Geuskens, Isabelle. "Introduction." In *Gender & Militarism: Analyzing the Links to Strategize for Peace,* edited by Isabelle Geuskens, Merle Gosewinkel, and Sophie Schellens, 3–6. Hague: Women Peacemakers Program, 2014.

Hutcheson, Richard G. *The Churches and the Chaplaincy.* Atlanta: John Knox Press, 1975.

Khalid, Maryam. "Feminist Perspectives on Militarism and War: Critiques, Contradictions, and Collusions." In *The Oxford Handbook of Transnational Feminist Movements,* edited by Rawwida Baksh and Wendy Harcourt, 632–638. Oxford: Oxford University Press Online, 2014. DOI:10.1093/oxfordhb/ 9780199943494.013.006.

Leslie, Kristen J. "'Ma'am, Can I Talk to You?' Pastoral Care with Survivors of Sexualized Violence at the United States Air Force Academy." *The Journal of Pastoral Theology* 15, no. 1 (Spring 2005): 78–92.

National College on Ministry to the Armed Forces, www.ncmaf.net/. Accessed July 19, 2018.

———. "Pastoral Care in a New Public: Lessons Learned in the Public Square." *The Journal of Pastoral Theology* 18, no. 2 (Winter 2008): 80–99.

Loveland, Anne C. "Military Chaplains in Cultural Transition, 1946 to the Present." Unpublished presentation for Yale University conference, "Faith and Arms in a Democratic Society: A Working Conference on Religion in the Military." November 13, 2009.

Rambo, Shelly. "Changing the Conversation: Theologizing War in the Twenty-First Century." *Theology Today* vol. 69, no. 4 (2013): 441–462.

Secretary of the Navy. "Religious Ministry within the Department of the Navy." SEC-NAVINST 1730.7D, 2008.

Tadros, Mariz. "From Secular Reductionism to Religious Essentialism: Implications for the Gender Agenda." In *The Oxford Handbook of Transnational Feminist Movements,* edited by Rawwida Baksh and Wendy Harcourt, 651–654. Oxford: Oxford University Press Online, 2014. DOI:10.1093/oxfordhb/ 9780199943494.013.017.

Vuic, Kara Dixon. "Gender, the Military, and War." In *At War: The Military and American Culture in the Twentieth Century and Beyond,* edited by David Kieran, Edwin A. Martini, Sahr Conway-Lanz, and Stefan Aune, 195–216. New Brunswick: Rutgers University Press, 2018.

NOTES

1. RPS–Religious Program Specialists–are enlisted women and women on a Religious Ministry Team (RMT) who serve as chaplain assistants and security detail for U.S. military chaplains in combat areas. Chaplains are by law non-combatants and may not carry weapons.

2. Like most faith communities, military environments are rich with insular acronyms. This shorthand practice serves to accentuate the outsider-insider reality. We have also chosen to capitalize almost all military terms (Army, Navy, Coast Guardian, Sailor, Marine, etc.) per current military practice. The Chicago Manual of style does not require capitalization. This is yet another way we are seeking to introduce the reader to an outsider-insider position.

3. Shelly Rambo, "Changing the Conversation: Theologizing War in the Twenty-First Century," *Theology Today* 69, no. 4 (2013): 444.

4. Maryam Khalid, "Feminist Perspectives on Militarism and War: Critiques, Contradictions, and Collusions," in *The Oxford Handbook of Transnational Feminist Movements*, ed. Rawwida Baksh and Wendy Harcourt (Oxford: Oxford University Press Online, 2014), 3.

5. Khalid, "Feminist Perspectives on Militarism and War," 2.

6. Khalid, "Feminist Perspectives on Militarism and War," 17.

7. Rambo, "Changing the Conversation," 443–445.

8. See Kara Dixon Vuic, "Gender, the Military, and War," in *At War: The Military and American Culture in the Twentieth Century and Beyond*, ed. David Kieran, Edwin A. Martini, Sahr Conway-Lanz, and Stefan Aune (New Brunswick: Rutgers University Press, 2018). She details the ways in which militarization has used gender, race, and class configurations from the Civil War to present to "enlist" all members in U.S. society into war-making roles.

9. For an example of a religious endorsing agency, see National College on Ministry to the Armed Forces, www.ncmaf.net/ (accessed July 19, 2018).

10. We draw on the work by Peter French who uses the phrase Two-Collar Conflict. See Peter A. French, *War and Moral Dissonance* (New York: Cambridge University Press, 2011).

11. "Coast Guardian" is a gender-neutral term offered by a Coast Guard chaplain when we asked for an inclusive term for "Coast Guardsmen." This gender-neutral alternative was regularly contested by chaplains who argued that the term "Coast Guardsmen" does include women.

12. "Religious Ministry within the Department of the Navy," SECNAVINST 1730.7D, 2008.

13. Richard Hutcheson uses the term "cooperative luralism" to describe the work of engaging other faith traditions without feeling that one's own theological commitments are endangered. For more on this, see Richard G. Hutcheson, *The Churches and the Chaplaincy* (Atlanta: John Knox Press, 1975).

14. Anne C. Loveland, "Military Chaplains in Cultural Transition, 1946 to the Present," unpublished presentation for Yale University conference, "Faith and Arms in a Democratic Society: A Working Conference on Religion in the Military," November 13, 2009.

15. The Defense of Marriage Act prohibited LGBT from legally marrying. DADT was a policy legislated by the Clinton administration in an attempt to protect LGBTQ military members. It claimed to support closeted LGBTQ, although it did not protect those who were out. In the end, it did neither.

16. For more on this, see Kristen J. Leslie, "'Ma'am, Can I Talk to You?' Pastoral Care with Survivors of Sexualized Violence at the United States Air Force Academy," *The Journal of Pastoral Theology* 15, no. 1 (Spring 2005): 78–92; Kristen J. Leslie, "Pastoral Care in a New Public: Lessons Learned in the Public Square," *The Journal of Pastoral Theology* 18, no. 2 (Winter 2008): 80–99.

17. Ray Acheson, "Money, Masculinities, and Militarism: Reaching Critical Will's Work for Disarmament," in *Gender & Militarism: Analyzing the Links to Strategize for Peace,* ed. Isabelle Geuskens, Merle Gosewinkel, and Sophie Schellens (Hague: Women Peacemakers Program, 2014), 14.

18. Code-switching was first defined by the field of linguistics to refer to the use of two different languages in the same conversations. We are using it in the popular sense of the term that refers to negotiating two different cultures. "Many of us subtly,

reflexively change the way we express ourselves all the time. We're hop-scotching between different cultural and linguistic spaces and different parts of our own identities—sometimes within a single interaction." See "How Code-Switching Explains the World," National Public Radio, www.npr.org/ sections/codeswitch/2013/04/08/176064688/how-code-switching-explains-the-world (accessed July 20, 2018).

19. For more on feminist curiosity and militarism, see Cynthia Enloein, "Understanding Militarism, Militarization, and the Linkages with Globalization: Using a Feminist Curiosity," in *Gender and Militarism: Analyzing the Links to Strategize for Peace*, ed. Isabelle Geuskens, Merle Gosewinkel, and Sophie Schellens (Hague: Women Peacemakers Program, 2014).

20. Vuic, "Gender, the Military, and War," 196.

21. Mariz Tadros, "From Secular Reductionism," in *The Oxford Handbook of Transnational Feminist Movements*, ed. Rawwida Bakshe and Wendy Harcourt (Oxford: Oxford University Press Online, 2014), 4.

22. CONUS (Continental United States) and OCONUS (Outside the Continental United States) refer to geographical locations inhabited by military bases. Yes, a uniform shirt is referred to as a blouse. This of course has a number of gender implications, as outside the Navy, a blouse would be a fancy women's shirt. There were times that we referred to this oddity, again to point out gender constructions related to masculinity and femininity. Participants often shared jokes related to these seemingly trivial gender differences. But it was an opportunity to engage feminist curiosity and evidence examples of the construction of gender norms.

23. Isabelle Geuskens, "Introduction," in *Gender & Militarism: Analyzing the Links to Strategize for Peace*, ed. Isabelle Geuskens, Merle Gosewinkel, and Sophie Schellens (Hague: Women Peacemakers Program, 2014), 4.

Index

About the Contributors

Lisa Dellinger (Chickasaw and Mexican American) received her Master of Divinity with high honors in 2008 from Phillips Theological Seminary in Tulsa, Oklahoma. She also served as a pastor with the Oklahoma Indian Missionary Conference of the United Methodist Church from 2015 to 2017. She successfully defended her dissertation, "Reclaiming Indigenous and Christian Narrative Epistemologies: Refusing U.S. Settler Colonialism's Theological Anthropology of Sin," at Garrett Theological Seminary in Evanston, IL. She will graduate in May of 2020. She is a contributor to the book, *Coming Full Circle: Constructing Native Christian Theology*, edited by Steven Charleston and Elaine A. Robinson, writing the chapter, "Sin-Ambiguity and Complexity and the Sin of Not Conforming." She is also the 2017 Forum for Theological Exploration's recipient of the James L. Waits Fellowship. Dr. Dellinger is also a United Methodist Woman of Color Fellowship Scholar.

Wonhee Anne Joh is professor of theology and culture at Garrett Theological Seminary, the faculty director of Asian American Ministry Center, faculty affiliate in the Departments of Religious Studies and Asian American Studies at Northwestern University, and member of the research faculty cohort on religion, race, and global politics of the Buffett Institute for Global Studies at Northwestern University. Her publications include, *Heart of the Cross: A Postcolonial Christology*, and she is co-editor of *Critical Theology against U.S. Militarism in Asia: Decolonization and Deimperialization*. Forthcoming from Fordham University Press is *Trauma, Affect, and Race*.

Nami Kim is associate professor of religious studies and chair of the Department of Philosophy and Religious Studies at Spelman College. She is the author of *The Gendered Politics of the Korean Protestant Right: Hegemonic Masculinity* and co-editor of *Critical Theology against U.S. Militarism in Asia: Decolonization and Deimperialization*.

Kristen J. Leslie, PhD is a feminist pastoral theologian who addresses issues of survivor resilience in the aftermath of sexualized violence on college campuses, in the United States military, and in post-genocide Rwanda. An ordained United Methodist minister, she is the professor of pastoral theology and care at Eden Theological Seminary in St. Louis,

Missouri. She is the author of *When Violence is No Stranger: Pastoral Counseling with Survivors of Acquaintance Rape* (Fortress Press, 2003) and numerous essays on topics related to sexualized violence and moral injury.

Mai-Anh Le Tran is vice president of academic affairs and academic dean at Garrett Theological Seminary. With research and teaching focused on critical pedagogy and transnational, intersectional, religious identity formation and practices, she is the author of *Reset the Heart: Unlearning Violence, Relearning Hope* (Abingdon Press, 2017).

Pamela Lightsey, PhD is the vice president for academic and student affairs at Meadville Lombard Theological School in Chicago. Among her most recent publications include, *Our Lives Matter: A Womanist Queer Theology* (Wipf and Stock).

Kate Ott is author of *Christian Ethics for a Digital Society* and *Sex + Faith: Talking with Your Child from Birth to Adolescence* in addition to numerous chapters and articles. She leads workshops across North America on sexuality and technology issues related to children, teens, young adults, and parents. She is associate professor of Christian social ethics at Drew Theological School and lecturer in practical theology at Yale Divinity School. To find out more about her work visit www.kateott.org.

K. Christine Pae is associate professor of religion/ethics and chair of the Department of Religion at Denison University. She has published numerous book chapters and journal articles on the topics of the ethics of peace and war, spiritual activism, transnational feminist ethics, U.S. overseas militarism, and Asian/Asian American religious ethics.

B. Yuki Schwartz is the associate pastor for justice formation at Keystone Congregational UCC and the Justice Leadership Program in Seattle, and is adjunct faculty at Phillips Theological Seminary in Tulsa. She has a PhD in theology and ethics from Garrett Theological Seminary.

Andrea Smith is professor of ethnic studies at University of California, Riverside. She is the author of *Unreconciled: From Racial Reconciliation to Racial Justice in Christian Evangelicalism, Native Americans and the Christian Right and Conquest: Sexual Violence and American Indian Genocide* (both Duke University Press).

Ingram Content Group UK Ltd.
Milton Keynes UK
UKHW021556030423
419573UK00003B/7